# Praise for *Other People's Money*

"*Other People's Money* is not merely another broadside content to denounce finance's dysfunction, but rather a masterly attempt to locate its various origins and connect them with analytical and theoretical rigor. [John] Kay provides by way of context a panoptic overview of the history, evolution and structure of the financial system in the United States and Britain, one that is impressive in its ability to weave together a comprehensive range of material, from the mechanics of banking to the Gaussian copula, in elegant, jargon-free prose."

*—New York Times Book Review*

"Mr. Kay is a brilliant writer with an ability to explain the role in the 2007–08 financial crisis of such concepts as credit default swaps, collateralized debt obligations and moral hazard. . . . [He] is at his best in reminding us that the financial system is still fragile and in explaining that more regulation is not the answer. . . . We can applaud his call for a cultural change that will enhance ethical standards and put the customer first."

*—Wall Street Journal*

"[*Other People's Money*] should be read by everyone concerned with preventing the next crisis. . . . [Kay] skewers the pretensions of the finance sector and questions whether its high rewards reflect its true economic contribution. Barely a page goes by without an acute observation or pithy aphorism. . . . Above all, the finance sector should be judged on the same basis as other industries; if an activity is unprofitable without taxpayer support, it should not occur. 'Our willingness to accept uncritically the proposition that finance has a unique status has done much damage,' the author wisely says. Let us hope those in authority will listen."

*—Economist*

"What makes Kay's analysis so probing is that he's no knee-jerk anti-market type. . . . Kay's insistence on stepping back, on judging finance by the humdrum standards of any other industry, with its self-serving mystique and aura of inevitability stripped away, makes *Other People's Money* one of the best two or three books I've read on the crash."

—Clive Crook, *Bloomberg View*

"This important book is simultaneously a clear primer on modern financial systems and a scathing indictment of them."

—*Foreign Affairs*

"An important new book."

—Robert Lenzner, TheAtlantic.com

"Thanks for writing this book. Only [John Kay] could have done it. This is going to be a classic."

—Frank Partnoy, professor of law and finance, University of San Diego School of Law, and bestselling author of *Fiasco* and *Wait*

"Kay is an admirable debunker of myths and false beliefs—he can see substantial things that others don't."

—Nassim Nicholas Taleb, author of *The Black Swan*

# OTHER PEOPLE'S MONEY

ALSO BY JOHN KAY

*Obliquity*
*The Long and the Short of It*
*The Truth about Markets*

# OTHER
# PEOPLE'S
# MONEY

## The Real Business
## *of* Finance

———

## JOHN KAY

**PUBLIC**AFFAIRS
*New York*

Originally published in Great Britain by Profile Books Ltd.
Published in the United States by PublicAffairs™,
An imprint of Perseus Books, a division of PBG Publishing, LLC,
a subsidiary of Hachette Book Group, Inc.

PublicAffairs books are available at special discounts for bulk purchases in the US by
corporations, institutions, and other organizations. For more information, please contact the Special Markets Department at the Perseus Books Group, 2300 Chestnut Street,
Suite 200, Philadelphia, PA 19103, call (800) 810-4145, ext. 5000, or e-mail special.markets
@perseusbooks.com.

A catalog record for this book is available from the Library of Congress.
LCCN: 2015944758
ISBN 978-1-61039-603-5 (HC)
ISBN 978-1-61039-604-2 (EB)
ISBN 978-1-61039-715-5 (PB)

First US trade paper Edition

10 9 8 7 6 5 4 3 2 1

# Contents

The directors of such companies, however, being the managers rather of other people's money than of their own, it cannot well be expected, that they should watch over it with the same anxious vigilance with which the partners in a private copartnery frequently watch over their own . . . Negligence and profusion, therefore, must always prevail, more or less, in the management of the affairs of such a company.

ADAM SMITH, *The Wealth of Nations*, 1776

When I speak of high finance as a harmful factor in recent years, I am speaking about a minority which includes the type of individual who speculates with other people's money—and you in Chicago know the kind I refer to.

FRANKLIN D. ROOSEVELT, presidential campaign address, Chicago, 14 October 1936

# The Parable of the Ox[1]

In 1906 the great statistician Francis Galton observed a competition to guess the weight of an ox at a country fair. Eight hundred people entered. Galton, being the kind of man he was, ran statistical tests on the numbers. He discovered that the average guess was extremely close to the weight of the ox. This story was told by James Surowiecki, in his entertaining book *The Wisdom of Crowds*.[2]

Not many people know the events that followed. A few years later, the scales seemed to become less and less reliable. Repairs would be expensive, but the fair organiser had a brilliant idea. Since attendees were so good at guessing the weight of an ox, it was unnecessary to repair the scales. The organiser would simply ask everyone to guess the weight, and take the average of their estimates.

A new problem emerged, however. Once weight-guessing competitions became the rage, some participants tried to cheat. They even tried to get privileged information from the farmer who had bred the ox. But there was fear that, if some people had an edge, others would be reluctant to enter the weight-guessing competition. With few entrants, you could not rely on the wisdom of crowds. The process of weight discovery would be damaged.

So strict regulatory rules were introduced. The farmer was asked to prepare three monthly bulletins on the development of his ox. These bulletins were posted on the door of the market for everyone to read. If the farmer gave his friends any other information about the beast, that information was also to be posted on the market door. And anyone who entered the competition who had knowledge about the ox that was not available to the world at large would be expelled from the market. In this way the integrity of the weight-guessing process would be maintained.

Professional analysts scrutinised the contents of these regulatory announcements and advised their clients on their implications. They wined and dined farmers; but once the farmers were required to be careful about the information they disclosed, these lunches became less useful. Some smarter analysts realised that understanding the nutrition and health of the ox wasn't that useful anyway. Since the ox was no longer being weighed—what mattered was the guesses of the bystanders—the key to success lay not in correctly assessing the weight of the ox but in correctly assessing what others would guess. Or what other people would guess others would guess. And so on.

Some people—such as old Farmer Buffett—claimed that the results of this process were more and more divorced from the realities of ox-rearing. But he was ignored. True, Farmer Buffett's beasts did appear healthy and well fed, and his finances ever more prosperous; but he was a countryman who didn't really understand how markets work.

International bodies were established to define the rules for assessing the weight of the ox. There were two competing standards—generally accepted ox-weighing principles, and international ox-weighing standards. But both agreed on one fundamental principle, which followed from the need to eliminate the role of subjective assessment by any individual. The weight of the ox was officially defined as the average of everyone's guesses.

One difficulty was that sometimes there were few, or even no, guesses of the weight of the ox. But that problem was soon overcome. Mathematicians from the University of Chicago developed models from which it was possible to estimate what, if there had actually been many guesses as to the weight of the ox, the average of these guesses would have been. No knowledge of animal husbandry was required, only a powerful computer.

By this time, there was a large industry of professional weight-guessers, organisers of weight-guessing competitions and advisers helping people to refine their guesses. Some people suggested that it might be cheaper to repair the scales, but they were derided: why go back to relying on the judgement of a single auctioneer when you could benefit from the aggregated wisdom of so many clever people?

And then the ox died. Amid all this activity, no one had remembered to feed it.

# Far Too Much of a Good Thing

In the City, they sell and buy. And nobody ever asks them why. But since it contents them to buy and sell, God forgive them, they might as well.

HUMBERT WOLFE, *The Uncelestial City*, 1930

Anyone passing the skyscrapers of Wall Street or the City of London will be impressed by the scale and scope of modern finance. Logos display familiar names such as Citigroup and HSBC. More discreet brass plates identify organisations that do not deal with the general public. The most important headquarters building in the industry, the head office of Goldman Sachs, at 200 West Street in Manhattan, remains anonymous. The premises are lavish, the limousines ubiquitous. Individuals with offices in the executive suites earn more in a month than most people will expect in a lifetime. But what do these people do? To an extent that staggers the imagination, they deal with each other.

In most Western economies today, the assets and liabilities of banks exceed the assets and liabilities of the government and the aggregate annual income of everyone in the country. But these assets and liabilities are mainly obligations from and to other financial institutions. Lending to firms and individuals engaged in the production of goods and services—which most people would imagine was the principal business of a bank—amounts to less than 10 per cent of that total (see Chapter 6). In Britain, with a particularly active financial sector, that figure is less than 3 per cent.

Modern banks—and most other financial institutions—trade in securities, and the growth of such trade is the main explanation of the growth of the finance sector. The finance sector establishes claims against assets—the operating assets and future profits of a company, or the physical property and prospective earnings of an individual—and almost any such claim can be turned into a tradable security. 'High-frequency trading' is undertaken by computers which are constantly offering to buy and sell securities. The interval for which these securities are held by their owner may—literally—be shorter than the blink of an eye. Spread Networks, a telecoms provider, has recently built a link through the Appalachian Mountains to reduce the time taken to transmit data between New York and Chicago by a little less than one millisecond.

World trade has expanded, but trading in foreign exchange has grown much faster. The value of daily foreign exchange transactions is almost a hundred times the value of daily international trade in goods and services. Fedwire, the payments mechanism operated by the US Federal Reserve System, processes more than $2 trillion of transfers every day, about fifty times the US national income.

Trade in securities has grown rapidly, but the explosion in the volume of financial activity is largely attributable to the development of markets in derivatives, so called because their value is derived from the value of other securities. If securities are claims on assets, derivative securities are claims on other securities, and their value depends on the price, and ultimately on the value, of these underlying securities. Once you have created derivative securities, you can create further layers of derivative securities whose values are dependent on the values of other derivative securities and so on. The value of the assets underlying current derivative contracts outstanding is three times the value of all the physical assets in the world.

What is it all for? What is the purpose of this activity? And why is it so profitable? Common sense suggests that if a closed circle of people continuously exchange bits of paper with each other, the total value of these bits of paper will not change much, if at all. If some members of that closed circle make extraordinary profits, these profits can only be made at the expense of other members of the same circle. Common sense suggests that this activity leaves the value of the traded assets little changed, and cannot, taken as a whole, make money. What, exactly, is wrong with this common-sense perspective?

Not much, I will conclude. But to justify that conclusion, it will be necessary to examine the activities of the finance sector and the ways in which it does, or might, make our lives better and our businesses more efficient. Assessing the economic contribution of the industry is complex, because there are many difficulties in interpreting reported information about the output and profitability of financial sector activities. But I will show that its profitability is overstated, that the value of its output is poorly reported in economic statistics, and that much of what it does contributes little, if anything, to the betterment of lives and the efficiency of business. And yet many things that finance could do to advance these social and economic goals are not done well—or in some cases at all.

Modern societies need finance. The evidence for this is wide-ranging and conclusive, and the relationship is clear and causal. The first stages of industrialisation and the growth of global trade coincided with the development of finance in countries such as Britain and the Netherlands. If we look across the world today, statistical evidence associates levels and growth of income per head with the development of finance.[1] Even modest initiatives in facilitating payments and providing small credits in poor countries can have substantial effects on economic dynamism.

And we have experienced a controlled experiment of sorts, in which Communist states suppressed finance. The development of financial institutions in Russia and China was arrested by their revolutions of 1917 and 1949. Czechoslovakia and East Germany had developed more sophisticated financial systems before the Second World War, but Communist governments closed markets in credit and securities in favour of the centrally planned allocation of funds to enterprises. The ineffectiveness and inefficiency of this process contributed directly to the dismal economic performance of these states.

A country can be prosperous only if it has a well-functioning financial system, but that does not imply that the larger the financial system a country has, the more prosperous it is likely to be. It is possible to have too much of a good thing. Financial innovation was critical to the creation of an industrial society; it does not follow that every modern financial innovation contributes to economic growth. Many good ideas become bad ideas when pursued to excess.

And so it is with finance. The finance sector today plays a major role in politics: it is the most powerful industrial lobby and a major provider of campaign finance. News bulletins report daily on what is happening in 'the markets'—by which they mean securities markets. Business policy is dominated by finance: the promotion of 'shareholder value' has been a mantra for two decades. Economic policy is conducted with a view to what 'the markets' think, and households are increasingly forced to rely on 'the markets' for their retirement security. Finance is the career of choice for a high proportion of the top graduates of the top schools and universities.

I will describe the process by which the finance sector has gained such a dominant economic role over the last thirty to forty years as 'financialisation'. This ugly word[2] provides a useful shorthand description for a historical process that has had profound implications for our politics, our economy and our society. I shall also use the term 'global financial crisis' to describe the events of 2007–9 and their consequences.[3]

However, this is not another book about the global financial crisis: it is a book about the nature of finance and the origins of financialisation. Major changes in social and economic organisation are generally the combined product of a rise in the political influence of particular social groups, the promotion of a supportive framework of ideas and a favourable overall conjuncture. That is how the modern market economy came into being, how democracy took root and how over the twentieth century socialism rose—and declined. That process explains the other major economic development of my lifetime: the expansion of the scope of the market economy from a population of fewer than a billion people to one that, for better and worse, embraced half the people of the globe. In the first part of this book I will describe the political changes, the intellectual framework and the wider technological and economic shifts that brought about financialisation.

A remarkable feature of the global financial crisis is that most people in finance seemed to regard it as self-evident that government and taxpayers had an obligation to ensure that the sector—its institutions, its activities and even the exceptional remuneration of the people who work in it—continued to operate in broadly its existing form. What is more remarkable still is that this proposition won broad acceptance among politicians and the public. The notion that finance was special was uncontroversial, and the inability of many intelligent people outside finance to understand quite what financiers did only reinforced that perception.

But finance is not special, and our willingness to accept uncritically the proposition that finance has a unique status has done much damage. All activities have their own practices, and those who engage in them have their own language. Every industry I have ever dealt with believes its characteristics are unique, and there is something in this, although never as much as those who work in them think. But the financial sector stands out for the strength of this conviction. The industry mostly trades with itself, talks to itself and judges itself by reference to performance criteria that it has itself generated. Two branches of economics—finance theory and monetary economics—are devoted to it, a phenomenon that Larry Summers mocked as 'ketchup economics'—the exercise of comparing the price of quart and pint bottles of ketchup without regard to the underlying value of the ketchup.[4] Summers—variously brilliant academic, US Treasury secretary under Bill Clinton, dethroned President of Harvard, director of Barack Obama's National Economic Council and rejected candidate for chairman of the Federal Reserve Board—is a figure who will appear several times in this book.

Summers' derogatory references to 'ketchup economics' deny the unique character of finance and reject the view that a different and specialist intellectual apparatus is required to understand the nature of financial activity and the operation of financial markets. This book reiterates Summers' challenge. Finance is a business like any other, and should be judged by reference to the same principles—the same tools of analysis, the same metrics of value—that we apply to other industries, such as railroads, or retailing or electricity supply. I will not hesitate to draw lessons from these industries.

The perspective that views finance as just another business invites us to ask 'What is finance for?'—the question that dominates the second part of this book. What needs does the industry serve, viewed from the perspective of market users, rather than market participants? Financialisation has led to a substantial increase in the scale of resources devoted to finance. More people have been paid more. But what has happened to the *quality* of financial activity?

Finance can contribute to society and the economy in four principal ways. First, the payments system is the means by which we receive wages and salaries and buy the goods and services we need; the same payments system enables business to contribute to these purposes. Second, finance matches lenders with borrowers, helping to direct savings to their most effective uses. Third, finance enables us to manage our personal finances across our lifetimes and between generations. Fourth, finance helps both individuals and businesses to manage the risks inevitably associated with everyday life and economic activity.

These four functions—the payments system, the matching of borrowers and lenders, the management of our household financial affairs and the control of risk—are the services that finance does, or at least can, provide. The utility of financial innovation is measured by the degree to which it advances the goals of making payments, allocating capital, managing personal finances and handling risk.

The economic significance of the finance industry is often described in other ways: by the number of jobs it provides, the incomes that are earned from it, even the tax revenue derived from it. There is a good deal of confusion here, discussed in Chapter 9. But the true value of the finance sector to the community is the value of the services it provides, not the returns recouped by those who work in it. These returns have recently seemed very large. In all the thousands of pages that have been written about the finance industry in recent years, very little space has been devoted to one fundamental question. Why is the industry so profitable?

Or perhaps the relevant question is 'Why does it *appear* so profitable?' The common sense that suggests that the activity of exchanging bits of paper cannot make profits for everyone may be a clue that much of this profit is illusory: much of the growth of the finance sector represents not the creation of new wealth but the sector's appropriation of wealth created elsewhere in the economy, mostly for the benefit of some of the people who work in the financial sector.

And yet, although the finance industry today displays many examples of egregious excess, the majority of those engaged in it are not guilty or representative of that excess. They are engaged in operating the payments system, facilitating financial intermediation, enabling individuals to control their personal finances and helping them to manage risks. Most people who work in finance are not aspiring Masters of the Universe. They are employed in relatively mundane processing activities in banking and insurance, for which they are rewarded with relatively modest salaries. We need them, and we need what they do.

So the third part of this book will be concerned with reform. Structural reform, not regulation. I will explain how the regulation which has been applied with more and more intensity and less and less effect through the era of financialisation is part of the problem—a major part—not part of the solution. There has not been too little regulation, but far too much. What is needed is an entirely different regulatory philosophy. We need to give attention to the structure of the industry, and the incentives of the individuals who work in it, and to address the political forces that have prevented the application of regulatory and legal sanctions that have existed for decades, even centuries. We should put an end to the seemingly endless proliferation of complex rulebooks which are even now beyond the comprehension of the far too numerous regulatory professionals.

The objective of reforming the finance industry should be to restore priority and respect for financial services that meet the needs of the real economy. There is something pejorative about the phrase 'the real'—meaning the non-financial—economy, and yet it captures a genuine insight: there is something unreal about the way in which finance has evolved, dematerialised and detached itself from ordinary business and everyday life.

If buying and selling in the finance sector not only absorbs a significant amount of our national wealth but also occupies the time of a high proportion of the ablest people in society, Humbert Wolfe's complacency—'since it contents them, they might as well'—can no longer be easily justified. In the final chapters of this book I shall describe how we might focus attention on a more limited finance sector more effectively directed to real economic needs: making payments, matching borrowers with lenders, managing our money and reducing the costs of risk. We need finance. But today we have far too much of a good thing.

# PART I

# FINANCIALISATION

*From the 1970s until the global financial crisis of 2007–8, the financial sector grew in size, revenues and sophistication. The effects were felt by all businesses and households, and there were major consequences for economic policy and the political system. How did these changes come about (Chapter 1)? What claims were made for the benefits of this process (Chapters 2 and 3)? And what were the sources of the extraordinary levels of profit and remuneration that financialisation generated for financial businesses and their senior employees (Chapter 4)?*

# CHAPTER 1

# History

## The Road to Pottersville

A British bank is run with precision
A British home requires nothing less
Tradition, discipline and rules must be the tools.
Without them: disorder, catastrophe, anarchy
In short, you have a ghastly mess.

*MARY POPPINS*, Walt Disney, 1964

I was a schoolboy in Edinburgh in the 1960s. The capital of Scotland is Britain's second financial centre and was the headquarters of two major banks, the Bank of Scotland and the Royal Bank of Scotland. Banking was then a career for boys whose grades were not good enough to win them admission to a good university.

The aspiration of many of my contemporaries was to join either 'the Bank' or 'the Royal Bank'. With appropriate diligence, they might, after twenty years or so, become branch managers. The branch manager was a respected figure in the local community, and social interaction at the golf club or Rotary lunch was part of his job. He would know personally the local professionals—the accountant, the lawyer, the doctor, the minister and the more prosperous tradesmen. The bank manager would receive their savings and occasionally make loans. The regional office might review his figures, but would rely heavily on the manager's assessment of character. He—there were no female managers—expected to spend his career with the bank, and to retire with a pension. It never crossed his mind, or the minds of his customers, that the institution he had joined at the age of seventeen would not continue for ever, in broadly its existing form.

A little later, I began my career teaching in an institution that still believes it will continue for ever in broadly its existing form: Oxford University. Few of my students then contemplated careers in the City of London, and those who did were generally less academic but socially well connected. If you had told me that within twenty years many of the best and brightest of Oxford students would spend more time preparing applications and seeking internships and interviews at City firms than they did in the library, I would have reacted with disbelief.

When my friends were joining 'the Bank' or 'the Royal Bank,' and I was beginning the study of economics, it was possible to believe that the historic problems of financial instability had largely been solved. There had been no major financial crisis since the Great Depression, and the failure of a major financial institution seemed inconceivable. My school-mates were the last generation to aspire to fill the shoes of George Banks, the bank manager in *Mary Poppins*, who returned home at 6.01 each evening and expected his pipe and slippers at 6.02.

It is probably not a coincidence that the cinema celebrated the tra-ditional bank manager—who was simultaneously a figure of fun and a pillar of the community—at precisely the moment such characters were being ushered from the stage. *Mary Poppins* was released in 1964. In the UK the television series *Dad's Army*, a comedy about the wartime Home Guard, was a popular hit between 1967 and 1974; its lead character was the pompous, unimaginative, honest bank manager Captain Main-waring. Frank Capra's film *It's a Wonderful Life*, though much admired when first released in 1946, was nevertheless a box office flop; but in the 1970s it became a Christmas favourite with US television audiences, and has remained so ever since. The hero was Jimmy Stewart as George Bailey, manager of the Bedford Falls savings and loan institution. Banks, Mainwaring and Bailey epitomised the role my classmates expected to assume.

That was about to change. In a scene at once comic and shocking, Bailey is shown by his guardian angel how the world might have been without him. Bedford Falls has been renamed Pottersville, after Mr Potter, the grasping member of the board who is single-minded in his pursuit of money. Pottersville is riven by self-interest and characterised by tawdry commercialism, and the housing project that was George Bailey's great achievement is unbuilt.

Capra could never have imagined that Pottersville might actually come into being. But by the time my contemporaries accepted early retirement, the world they joined had altered beyond recognition. The causes of this transformation include globalisation, deregulation, technological and product innovation, new ideologies and narratives as well as a shift in social and cultural norms. These factors were not independent: each was bound up with the others.

Finance has always been global. The City of London became a pre-eminent financial centre as a result of Britain's imperial role. The Fidelity Fiduciary Bank in which Mr Banks was manager financed 'railways through Africa, dams across the Nile'. Wall Street rivalled London in scale and importance because of the size of the US domestic market and the voracious need for finance implied by the scale of its landmass. But the expansion of global trade and finance was set back by departure from the gold standard, protectionism in the years between the First and Second World Wars, and the decline of empire. The modern phase of globalisation of finance began with the development of the Eurodollar market in London in the 1960s.

In the USA, 'Regulation Q' meant that American banks were subject to restrictions on interest rates they could pay on deposits, and were required to hold funds with the Federal Reserve System, the US central bank, to demonstrate the security of these deposits. Restrictions could be avoided if the funds were placed with European institutions and then lent on to US banks; there were no controls on transactions between banks. Routing deposits through London therefore enabled dollar depositors to earn higher interest rates on their balances. This manoeuvre lowered funding costs for American banks while enabling European banks to earn a profit for renting out their services.

The structure of the global financial system was changing in other ways. In the immediate post-war era it was expected that America would remain the world's dominant creditor nation. The post-war institutions of global finance, such as the International Monetary Fund (IMF) and

World Bank, were designed around this assumption. But as Germany and Japan rapidly recovered from wartime destruction, and the American economy weakened in the 1960s, US economic hegemony declined, and in 1971 the dollar was devalued.

The oil shock of 1973–4 gave oil-producing countries, particularly Saudi Arabia and other states in the Persian Gulf, windfalls beyond their capacity to spend. 'Petrodollars' were recycled as loans to Europe and the US. Meanwhile, Japan, followed by other Asian countries such as South Korea, Taiwan and Hong Kong, first imitated and then improved modern production methods, and began to export manufactured goods to Europe and North America. After 1980 mainland China followed these countries into the world trading system. Asian export success created trade surpluses, with corresponding trade deficits in the West. As the oil producers had done a decade earlier, the surplus countries lent the funds back to those economies with trade deficits.

The scene was set for the bizarre developments of the early years of the twenty-first century, in which the forced savings of Chinese peasants (who had little choice about the economic decisions of their authoritarian government) would fund the excess spending of American consumers. The mechanism by which this was achieved was the growing dependence of Western banks on wholesale funding derived from global capital markets. These persistent global financial imbalances upset the traditional model of local depositors finding local lenders: the mainstay of traditional banking. The undermining of Regulation Q was a harbinger of the ways in which globalisation put pressure on existing—nationally based—regulatory structures.

The new financial markets were no longer a business for nice boys who had few academic pretensions but were agreeable golfing companions. By the time 'the Bank' and 'the Royal Bank' failed in 2008, most of their senior executives had good degrees from fine institutions of higher education. Andy Hornby, CEO of 'the Bank', had won an MBA from Harvard after graduating from Oxford; his counterpart at 'the Royal Bank', Fred Goodwin, had acquired qualifications in both law and accountancy after graduating from the University of Glasgow. The two dominant figures on Wall Street—Lloyd Blankfein of Goldman Sachs and Jamie Dimon of J.P. Morgan—were Harvard alumni, from its Law School and

Business School respectively. The best students from Oxbridge and the Ivy League clamoured for jobs in the City and on Wall Street.

Larry Summers (of ketchup economics) described the transformation in this way: 'In the last 30 years the field of investment banking had been transformed from a field that was dominated by people who were good at meeting clients at the 19th hole, to people who were good at solving very difficult mathematical problems that were involved in pricing derivative securities.'[1] Summers (whose friends and enemies both know he is better at solving mathematical problems than schmoozing clients) reported this shift with evident approval.

Yet these cleverer people managed things less well—much less well—than their less intellectually distinguished predecessors. Although clever, they were rarely as clever as they thought, or sufficiently clever to handle the complexity of the environment they had created. Perhaps the ability to meet clients at the nineteenth hole is more relevant to making good investments than the ability to solve very difficult mathematical problems.

There may be less need today for the networker, the individual who knows whom rather than what; technology helps make connections, although personal relationships remain important. But there remains a need for individuals with the skills necessary to assess the quality of the underlying assets and the abilities of those who manage them. People with good understanding of the residential property market and experience in judging the capacity of prospective purchasers to meet their debts. People with knowledge of shops and offices and the finances of their tenants. People familiar with the financial operations of government, and with the management of large infrastructure projects. Above all, people with insight into the changing nature of business.

But the skills that were valued in the finance sector that had developed in the first decade of the twenty-first century were very different. The exercise of these skills by people with an exaggerated idea of their relevance and of their own competence in managing them plunged the global economy into the worst financial crisis since the Great Depression.

How did these changes come about? In the remainder of this chapter I will begin by explaining the two main components of financialisation: the substitution of trading and transactions for relationships, and the restructuring of finance businesses. I shall then move on to the broader economic effects of financialisation on economic stability, on the performance of business and on economic inequality.

## The Rise of the Trader

No sooner did you pass the fake fireplace than you heard an ungodly roar, like the roar of a mob . . . It was the sound of well-educated young white men baying for money on the bond market.

TOM WOLFE, *The Bonfire of the Vanities*, 1987

We are Wall Street. It's our job to make money. Whether it's a commodity, stock, bond, or some hypothetical piece of fake paper, it doesn't matter. We would trade baseball cards if it were profitable. . . .
We get up at 5am & work till 10pm or later. We're used to not getting up to pee when we have a position. We don't take an hour or more for a lunch break. We don't demand a union. We don't retire at 50 with a pension. We eat what we kill, and when the only thing left to eat is on your dinner plates, we'll eat that. . . .
We aren't dinosaurs. We are smarter and more vicious than that, and we are going to survive.

Reported by STACY-MARIE ISHMAEL, FT Alphaville, 30 April 2010[2]

A shift from agency to trading, from relationships to transactions, is a central aspect of the financialisation of Western economies in the past four decades. The world of George Bailey was one of relationships with customers, borrowers and depositors. This was true of most areas of finance. Like the bank manager, the stockbroker would befriend his clients. He would be personally familiar with the companies he recommended to them. Investment banks maintained long-term relationships with large companies. They would have similar connections with institutions such as the insurance companies that channelled the capital of small savers.

The world of finance today is dominated by trading, and trading is a principal source of revenue and remuneration. Fifty years ago there was one large speculative financial market: the stock exchange. The volume of trading in it was, by modern standards, modest: the average holding period for a share was seven years.[3] The stock exchange was also the place where government bonds were traded, but the bond market was sleepy in the extreme. Nick Carraway, the colourless narrator of F. Scott Fitzgerald's 1925 novel *The Great Gatsby*, was a bond trader. The London Metal Exchange was the global centre for trade in copper, tin and other 'hard' commodities. 'Soft' commodities had their own exchanges. The Chicago Board of Trade (and its spin-off the Chicago Butter and Egg Board) was the centre of American trade in agricultural products. Shipping contracts were concluded on the Baltic Exchange. Twenty-five years ago the key location was shifting to the trading floor of investment banks. Today the screen is the source of information and the basis of trading: an increasing proportion of trade is conducted by computers silently trading with each other.

Anonymous markets have thus replaced personal relationships. A century ago the German sociologists Ferdinand Tonnies and Max Weber articulated this change by describing the difference between *Gemeinschaft* and *Gesellschaft*, words that lack precise equivalents in English but which broadly distinguish the personal and the informal from the formal and the regulated.[4] The transition from *Gemeinschaft* to *Gesellschaft* is fundamental to understanding the processes of financialisation, and global differences in the methods of finance and the management of risk.

The rise of the trading culture has no single explanation but is the product of a series of developments, interrelated in origin and cumulative in impact. The globalisation of financial markets was part of the story, and so was the breakdown of the global financial architecture devised by the Allied Powers in 1944 in a conference at Bretton Woods (a beautiful location in remote New Hampshire intended to be difficult to access from New York or Washington). The creation of new markets in derivative securities, and the development of the mathematics of financial markets needed to analyse them, was another factor. Regulation and deregulation played a large, but partly accidental, role: few of the consequences of regulatory policy changes were intended. Institutional reorganisation played a part; traditional forms of business organisation, such as the partnership and the mutual, were folded into public limited companies. The support for free markets that followed the elections of Margaret Thatcher and Ronald Reagan influenced public and business policy in many ways.

The list of factors contributing to the change is long, and has one striking feature: the change in the nature of finance had little to do with any change in the needs of the real economy. Those needs remain much the same: we need financial institutions to process our payments, to extend credit, to provide capital for business. We want financial institutions to manage our savings and help with the risks we face in our economic lives. Some aspects of these services are better; many are not. Information technology has changed the ways in which financial services are delivered. But there has been no transformation in the services provided to customers comparable to the transformation in the nature and political and economic role of the industry that provides them. The process of financialisation had its own internal dynamic.

The USA's abandonment of the gold standard in 1971 ushered in a new era of flexible exchange rates, which fluctuated far more than most economists had anticipated. There had always been speculative activity in foreign exchange markets, but as the post-war system of fixed rates established at Bretton Woods came under more and more pressure, the typical speculator was no longer an individual dealing on his own account but a trader employed by a large financial institution. The traditional business of converting foreign exchange for customers (and making an appropriate margin on the conversion) became linked with taking positions in currencies to benefit from anticipated changes in their value.

The Chicago Mercantile Exchange (CME) is the successor to the Chicago Butter and Egg Board. Futures contracts, which enabled a farmer to agree today a price for the produce he would bring to market in three months' time, had been traded on the CME for many years. An innovative chairman of the CME, Leo Melamed, launched a financial futures contract in 1972. The idea was to apply the same type of contract to foreign exchange and subsequently to other financial instruments. Butter and eggs would soon be left behind.

This was the beginning of the development of markets in derivative securities. It is not a coincidence that the University of Chicago was then and is today a leading centre of the study of financial economics. In the following year two members of its faculty—Fisher Black and Myron Scholes—would publish a seminal paper on the valuation of derivatives.[5] Much of the growth of the financial sector in the three decades that followed would be the direct and indirect consequence of the growth of derivative markets. Futures were not the only kind of derivative. An option gave you the right, but not the obligation, to buy or sell—you could use an option to insure yourself against a rise, or a fall, in price.

But you didn't have to own a pig to sell pork belly futures: you might simply want to bet on the price of ham. And you didn't have to plan to travel abroad, or buy foreign goods, to trade currency. As derivative markets grew, people used them to back their judgement on more or less anything—not just foreign exchange, or interest rates, but the possibility that a business might fail, a mortgage would default or a hurricane would strike the East Coast of the USA.

This revolution in the technology of finance was matched—indeed was only possible because of—the parallel revolution in information technology. When trading in financial futures began, the Chicago Mercantile Exchange still centred on 'the pit', in which aggressive traders shouted offers as they elbowed deals away from their colleagues. Today every trader has a screen. The Black–Scholes model, and the many techniques of quantitative finance that came out of Chicago and elsewhere, could not have been widely applied without the power of modern computers.

Regulation also promoted the growth of a trading culture. The growth of the Eurodollar market demonstrated that regulatory anomalies could be used by banks to attract business. And by countries. Governments that promoted the interests of these banks could make regulatory arbitrage easier. The Bank of England, which in the 1960s saw advocacy of City of London interests as one of its principal functions, actively encouraged the growth of the Eurodollar market. Regulatory measures intended to make the financial system safer may, as Regulation Q had done, have had the opposite of the intended effect: the consequence of the rule was to increase system complexity and to take transactions out of the regulatory net altogether. Inability, or unwillingness, to learn that broader lesson about regulation would have severe, and continuing, consequences.

Regulation Q was one of the many reforms introduced as a result of the Wall Street Crash. But the most important was the establishment of a Securities and Exchange Commission (SEC) with broad regulatory oversight of the activities of financial institutions and listed companies. The agency's title is revealing. The focus of regulation was on securities and exchange. The new commission would be performing its task well if it facilitated the issue of securities and promoted exchange. As the agency increased the scope of its activity, if not necessarily its effectiveness or authority, that philosophy permeated the regulation of finance. And not just in the USA: the SEC would become a model for the regulation of financial markets around the world.

In the 1980s fixed-income trading was added to the list of active markets. Bond trading had previously been a backwater for the likes of Nick Carraway: in London it was an activity in which success depended largely on being born into the right family. Lew Ranieri had been born in Brooklyn, and not to the right family—he had begun his Wall Street career in the mailroom of Salomon Bros. But his invention of the mortgage-backed security would transform the bond market. The growth of securitisation, not just of mortgages but of all kinds of financial claim, changed the nature of banking for ever. Such securitisations eventually extended to the future royalties of pop stars (David Bowie raised $55 million in this way) and the revenues of film studios (Dream-Works) and entire football teams (Leeds United).

The mortgage-backed security consisted of a tradable package of mortgages. This idea could be applied not just to mortgages but also to other consumer loans—credit card balances, for example—and to small business loans. Credit and interest rate exposures, traditionally managed within banks, could be reduced or eliminated through markets. Swap markets enabled banks to manage interest rate risk: a loan whose rate was variable annually might be exchanged for a loan fixed for ten years.

These markets received a boost later in the 1980s, when the Basel rules on bank lending tended to treat asset-backed securities more favourably than the assets that went into them. Rating agencies—businesses such as Moody's and Standard & Poor's (S&P)—had diversified from their original business of commercial credit assessment into assessment of the credit quality of bonds. In the 1970s two changes occurred that gave rating agencies a central place in the financialisation process. The agencies began to charge issuers of securities for their services as well as—or, increasingly, instead of—investors, and they achieved regulatory recognition as 'Nationally Recognised Statistical Rating Organisations'.[6] Many financial institutions and regulatory bodies restricted investments to securities that met standards laid down by a rating agency. Ratings determined the regulatory risk-weighting of securities. The banks that created asset-backed securities paid the rating agencies—which appreciated that there was a competitive business in supplying such accreditation—and the banks 'reverse-engineered' their products to fit the agencies' models. Many investors and traders did not care much what was in the package so long as it achieved the required credit rating. The collapse of the asset-backed securities market would be at the centre of the global financial crisis.

The elements of the new trading culture—based around fixed income, currency and commodities, and turbo-charged by derivatives—were now in place. Markets in shares were no longer the centre of speculative activity. Fixed interest, currency and, later, commodities (FICC) were central to the new trading culture. Sherman McCoy, the vainglorious anti-hero of Wolfe's 1987 novel *The Bonfire of the Vanities*, was, like Nick Carraway, a bond trader.

But the environment in which McCoy worked was very different from that experienced by Nick Carraway. The changes that occurred in the structure of financial services firms are described in more detail below, but within these firms the dominant ethos changed radically. Wolfe's fictional account satirises the new culture of financialisation, but the contemporaneous account of Michael Lewis' time at Salomon Bros, where Lew Ranieri had made the firm a market leader in bond market innovation, demonstrates how little exaggeration was contained in Wolfe's caricature.

The world Wolfe and Lewis described was aggressively male (there would in due course be a few women traders, but the links between testosterone and trading would become the subject of serious academic research).[7] That world is full of obscenity, fuelled by drugs—notably cocaine—and given to sexual and alcoholic excess. Young men—some with high educational qualifications, some with none—suddenly found themselves in possession of amounts of money far in excess of those they were capable of handling.

Alongside the traders, though with very different personalities, were the 'rocket scientists' or 'quants', research analysts with quantitative skills and advanced degrees—often from the former Soviet Union. 'Mortgages are math', Ranieri had announced.[8] His innovations, like the CME's development of options markets, opened doors for the PhDs, whom

Summers had described as 'good at solving very difficult mathematical problems'. The 'Gaussian copula'—a formula for calculating the expected losses on a package of loans which had different but related chances of default—was a piece of actuarial mathematics that found application in the evaluation of securitised packages. With some hyperbole, this esoteric algebra would achieve notoriety in the global financial crisis as 'the formula that killed Wall Street'.[9]

Most traders and quants were employed by investment banks (including those who worked for investment banks within commercial banks). But there had always been a few traders who operated independently, raising funds from sophisticated investors. Alfred Winslow Jones, a journalist who had reviewed stock market forecasts for *Fortune* magazine in 1949 and concluded he could do better, was the first person to be described as manager of a hedge fund: George Soros would become the best-known hedge fund manager when he 'broke the Bank of England' in 1991 with a massive and successful bet against Britain's attempt to align its currency with those of France and Germany.[10]

In the 1980s and 1990s rising stock prices had enabled almost all investment funds to earn good returns. The bursting of the 'new economy' bubble in 2000 ushered in a decade of mediocre performance in equity markets and led many institutional investors to turn to hedge funds in search of higher returns. The outcome was profitable for hedge fund promoters although not, in general, for their investors.[11] Groups of traders with a successful record in investment banks established their own operations. Some hedge fund managers made extraordinary sums. George Soros has reported wealth of $26.5 billion: Jim Simons, a former mathematics professor, $15.5 billion.[12] The reward for traders within banks increased, substantially if not commensurately, as these companies tried to keep hold of what they called 'the talent'.

The rise of the trader and the development of a trading culture cannot be dissociated from the political climate of the times: the power of a market fundamentalist ideology, the election of Thatcher and Reagan, the collapse of the Soviet Union and the discrediting of central planning as an economic system. The dominant ideology of the times legitimised the more aggressive pursuit of self-interest and encouraged a different and more limited view of the social responsibility of the large business organisation. Markets were deemed to be good, and more markets were better. It was not possible to have too much of a good thing.

But the economic philosophy of politicians such as Thatcher and Reagan was the product of moral conviction rather than technical economic argument. And their moral convictions found little to applaud in the culture of the trader. The Thatcherite emphasis on hard work and self-reliance sat alongside a belief that compassion should be a private virtue rather than a social practice. These are attitudes very different from the greedy individualism and sense of personal entitlement characteristic of much of the finance sector today.


## New Markets, New Businesses

> I would like to pay tribute to the contribution you and your company make to the prosperity of Britain. During its one-hundred-and-fifty-year history, Lehman Brothers has always been an innovator, financing new ideas and inventions before many others even begin to realise their potential.
>
> GORDON BROWN, Chancellor of the Exchequer, with DICK FULD,
> opening Lehman Brothers' new London headquarters, 5 April 2004

The great names of the banking world have a long history. Modern finance begins, like so much else, in the Renaissance, with the merchants of the Italian city-states. The oldest surviving bank of all is Monte dei Paschi Bank of Siena, founded in 1472, though its future has recently been in question. The Bank of Scotland was founded in 1695, and the Royal Bank in 1727. The long history of all these institutions has been threatened by a generation of financiers who mistakenly thought they knew much better than their predecessors. The Bank of New York (now incorporated into BNY Mellon) is America's oldest bank, dating from 1764; it survived better than the others by changing its character and effectively ceasing to be a bank. But the business of all of these firms has changed as economies have developed.

Yet that evolution has followed very different trajectories. Through the nineteenth and twentieth centuries the financial services sectors of Britain, the USA and continental Europe developed in distinctive ways.

In Britain commercial banking became steadily more concentrated in the nineteenth century as a result of acquisitions. By 1900 the dominant players in England were Lloyds, Barclays, Midland (which would eventually become the UK arm of HSBC) and the National Provincial and Westminster Banks. In 1970 the two last of these merged to become National Westminster Bank. Thus the broad structure of UK retail banking changed very little in the course of the twentieth century.

In the USA Wall Street banks—epitomised by the name and personality of J.P. Morgan—played a major role in financing large US businesses in steel, railways and oil. But populist suspicion of finance, and the wide US attachment to the life of small communities, limited the development of interstate banking. As a result, the USA's retail banking sector was fragmented. Britain's concentrated banking system, dominated by a few national banks, sailed through the Depression without serious mishap. But in the USA many small banks with concentrated loan portfolios failed in the Depression that followed the Wall Street Crash. Depositors feared for the security of other, similar banks, which suffered runs even if their underlying finances were sound. Amid growing panic, Franklin Roosevelt's first act as president in March 1933 was to require all banks in the USA to shut their doors.

The events of 1929–33, in which a financial crisis became an industrial depression, threatened not just economic prosperity but political stability. A Senate inquiry into these events was led by a brilliant chief counsel, Ferdinand Pecora, who single-handedly destroyed the reputations of many Wall Street institutions and Wall Street figures. The Glass–Steagall Act of 1933 imposed the separation of commercial and investment banking. The House of Morgan was divided into J.P. Morgan, the commercial banking arm, and Morgan Stanley, an investment bank. The Federal Deposit Insurance Corporation (FDIC) would in future insure depositors against losses from bank runs or bank failures.

In both Britain and the USA different functions within the financial system were provided by different institutions. Commercial banks operated the payments system and met the short-term lending needs of their customers. Investment banks (then called 'merchant banks' in the UK) handled larger transactions involving the issue of securities. If the buyer wanted to sell these securities, he or she would contact a stockbroker, who would negotiate the trade with a specialist (also called a jobber or market-maker). While banks undertook some mortgage lending, most such loans were made by specialist non-profit businesses—thrifts in the USA, building societies in the UK.

Banks specialised in what I will call the deposit channel, diverting short-term savings into relatively low-risk activities. There has always been a need for a parallel investment channel, to facilitate the deployment of longer-term savings. In 1812, with Britain at war with both Napoleon and the USA, some public-spirited Edinburgh gentlemen founded the Scottish Widows' Fund to make provision for their dependants. Scotland has played a disproportionately large role in the history of financial innovation for a small country on Europe's periphery. The Bank and the Royal Bank of Scotland are among the oldest surviving institutions in the deposit channel (even if their survival was a close call). The Bank of England, which saved them, was also founded by a Scot.

My parents and teachers, believing my destiny was to be an actuary, sent me to work at Scottish Widows in the school holidays. I reported to a building in St Andrew's Square that faced the imposing headquarters of the Royal Bank. Just round the corner were the offices of Standard Life, Scottish Widows' worldwide rival. At the other end of George Street lies Charlotte Square, the two squares the showpieces of James Craig's inspired eighteenth-century design for Edinburgh's New Town. After America's Civil War yet another group of Edinburgh dignitaries established investment companies to exploit opportunities overseas, especially in the USA. Charlotte Square was then the centre for Scotland's investment trusts.

While the Royal Bank of Scotland facilitated the deposit channel, the investment channel was operated by the life insurers of St Andrew's Square and the investment trusts of Charlotte Square. These bastions of finance developed the two principal mechanisms—pension funds and life insurance on the one hand, and pooled investment funds on the other—by which investment is still intermediated today.

The distinction between deposit and investment channels has been less marked in continental Europe, which has a long tradition of universal banks. These institutions provided a full range of financial services to both industrial and personal customers, and themselves held significant shareholdings in major companies. However, Paris, Berlin and Frankfurt were never global financial centres in the manner of London and New York, and stock markets in these countries never achieved the scale of the London and New York exchanges. Europe's universal banks were conservative institutions, focused on the needs of their domestic industry.

Insurance companies (and, to a lesser degree, banks) have remained the principal vehicles for intermediating long-term investment in these countries. Germany's Allianz, France's AXA and Italy's Generali continue to dominate their respective markets. The investment trust was exported to Britain and the USA but proved to be a vehicle for many Wall Street excesses in the years up to the 1929 crash. As a result of US regulation and saver scepticism, investment trusts (closed-end funds) have been supplanted by mutual funds (open-ended investment companies). I will describe these different kinds of investment vehicle more fully in Chapter 7.

George Bailey's attachment to the community of Bedford Falls exemplified the notion—then shared in Britain, the USA and continental Europe—that a bank served public as well as private purposes. Bankers have never been shy of making profits, but the local bank was seen as a community institution, along with the church and the hospital, and the bank manager was a community figure, alongside the doctor and the lawyer. At state or national level, banks enjoyed a special relationship with government, entailing both privileges and responsibilities. Scottish Widows (like Standard Life) was a mutual, owned by its policyholders, and this was true of many European (and some American) insurance businesses.

The banks that failed in 2008 were very different organisations from the institutions that they had been for many years—even centuries. The innovations pioneered by Salomon Bros, which created markets in loans, potentially undermined the traditional conception, and role, of a bank in channelling savings from depositors to borrowers. Some thoughtful commentators believed that the financial institutions of the future would be narrow specialists.[13] And indeed most functions of banks are now also performed by specialist institutions, such as credit card companies and mortgage banks. Supermarkets diversified into simple financial services, such as deposit accounts. Private equity houses (venture capital firms) specialise in the provision of finance for business. Specialist hedge funds—tightly run speculative trading ventures such as those of George Soros and Jim Simons—attracted funds in the years after 2000.

But, apparently paradoxically, the trend to specialisation was accompanied by a trend to diversification. Regulation Q, which restricted interest rates, was successively relaxed and finally scrapped. The American finance sector, which had been publicly humiliated in 1933, became a more and more powerful lobby. That lobby secured steady relaxation of the restrictions that had been imposed on the industry fifty years earlier. The separation of investment from commercial banking—the principle that had become synonymous in the public mind with the Glass–Steagall Act—was steadily weakened, although not finally repealed until 1999.

In Britain, the trigger for change was the 'Big Bang'—the deregulation of finance in 1986—which swept away a mass of restrictions, including most obstacles to the creation of financial conglomerates. The large British commercial banks, with the enormous capital strength derived from their retail deposit base, were immediate diversifiers.

These changes in the structure of banking were related to changes in the organisation of stock markets. Traditionally, buyers and sellers of securities traded through agents, and the London and New York stock exchanges enjoyed a monopoly on trading in stocks. A buyer or seller approached a broker, who would then contact the specialist who dealt in these stocks or fixed interest securities. The broker acted for the client, and was responsible for securing the best price. The market-maker tried to match buyers and sellers: specialists had very little capital of their own. They attempted to locate an investor willing to take the other side of a trade and made money from the 'spread'—the difference between the prices charged to the buyer and paid to the seller.

This was no golden age. Brokers cultivated relationships with corporate clients as well as private and institutional investors, and would promote the shares of companies with which they had such relationships. These brokers would favour selected clients with inside information. The practice of 'front running'—in which the broker trades for his own benefit ahead of filling his client's order—has been a means of abuse since the earliest days of securities trading. But venality was mostly held in check by widely accepted social norms. Commissions were fixed by the exchange, generally as a percentage of the value of the transaction.

In the 1960s most stocks and shares were held by private individuals. But pension funds grew in size, and these funds and insurance companies which collected individual savings diversified from bonds to shares. These institutional vehicles would provide savers with benefits from liquidity and diversification. They would also provide professional management. And professional managers would buy and sell much more frequently than private individuals—how else could they justify their fees? These managers were unwilling to accept the fixed—and high—commissions demanded by the cartel of traditional stockbrokers.

In order to circumvent these rules, they received kickbacks from brokers, not just in the form of 'free' research on companies but also through the provision of services—such as trading screens—which investment institutions might reasonably have been expected to purchase themselves. This practice of 'soft commission' continued even after fixed commissions were abolished—as they were in New York in 1975 and in London in 1986. Asset managers could charge commission to the account of their clients, while office expenses would have to be met from their own pockets.

From the 1970s the structure of exchanges changed radically. The change had multiple strands, and causes. The monopoly of the New York Stock Exchange (NYSE) was challenged, first by NASDAQ, an electronic exchange established in 1971 by broker–dealers, led by Bernard Madoff. A broker is an agent; a dealer is a trader. The rise of the broker–dealer blurred the distinction between two types of transaction. The conflict of interest inherent in the broker–dealer concept, and the name of Bernard Madoff, will recur in this book.

Some hot new companies, such as Intel and Microsoft, chose to list on NASDAQ rather than the NYSE. The technological shift was paralleled by regulatory changes that encouraged competition between exchanges. Today there are multiple exchanges on which shares can be traded—the London and New York stock exchanges both own electronic exchanges which compete with their main markets. The major investment banks have established 'dark pools' which dispense with many of the transparency and disclosure requirements associated with trading on exchanges. In the twenty-first century the distinction between brokers—who acted for clients—and specialists—who made the market by matching buyers and sellers—has effectively disappeared.

These new trading activities required more capital. The finance industry was historically characterised by several different types of business organisation. Commercial banks were generally structured as public companies, their shares quoted on the national stock exchange. Investment and merchant banks, and other financial institutions such as stockbrokers and market-makers, were mostly legal partnerships (some were closely owned companies with a handful of shareholders who would take an active part in management). In a traditional partnership each partner is liable for all the debts of the organisation.[14] In some cases regulation prohibited incorporation and the limitation of liability that went with it, but mostly the partnership form was chosen by the businesses themselves.

Partnerships and owner-managed businesses differed from public companies with dispersed shareholding in significant ways. Ownership and control of the business were combined in the hands of senior employees. The risks of the business—upside and downside—were absorbed by a few individuals, whose personal finances were ultimately on the line. Partners would monitor each other closely, and limit the risks the business incurred. They preferred activities that they understood well, and would review carefully the extent to which the business held speculative positions on its own account. The capital of the business was more or less limited to its accumulated profits and the resources of its partners.

Mutuals once played a significant role in retail financial services in every country. Most such businesses originated in the nineteenth century, when mutual organisation provided a basis for the trust relationships central to financial services. Scottish Widows remained a mutual until 2000, Standard Life until 2006. Small savers and investors feared they would be exploited by unscrupulous financiers, and there was often good reason for this fear. While many mutual organisations began as self-help societies, as they grew the members hired professional managers to run the businesses on their behalf. In more recent times some of these mutual societies became very large businesses. Management structures became self-perpetuating, and the membership voice was effectively silent.

Between 1980 and 2000 most financial businesses that were not already public companies listed on stock exchanges became so, or were absorbed into companies that were listed. One motive for conversion was the need for capital, as market-makers became increasingly likely to take positions on their own account. But many businesses that became public companies did not need, or raise, new capital. The primary motive for conversion was to enable a current generation of partners or members to realise the goodwill of the business for their own profit. This realisation of goodwill happened to businesses as different as Goldman Sachs—whose partnership became a limited company in 1999, making some partners millionaires several hundred times over—and Halifax Building Society, the largest mortgage lender in Britain (and the world), which converted from a mutual to a listed company in 1997, distributing shares with a total value of almost £20 billion to some 8 million people.

Exchanges such as the Chicago Mercantile Exchange and the New York and London stock exchanges transformed themselves from membership organisations into listed companies. They became business organisations with revenue and profit objectives of their own, rather than utilities providing services to their members. They sought to attract business by facilitating and promoting trading, and found themselves in competition with the new trading mechanisms facilitated by new information technology and by deregulation, which removed exchange monopolies.

Sceptics had always feared that limited liability companies would be vulnerable to negligent management, speculation and excessive risk-taking. That concern was the essence of Adam Smith's warning of the problems associated with the management of other people's money, and was why limitation of liability was tightly restricted until the second half of the nineteenth century. But with financialisation the risk-averse culture of mutual and partnership was replaced by competitive machismo in the public company. Although formal risk controls would increase greatly in complexity and sophistication, the practical effectiveness of risk control was diminished; the incentives of senior management to ensure such controls were implemented had been greatly reduced. The scale and scope of trading increased rapidly when decision-makers gained more from good decisions than they lost from bad ones. Readier access to capital led to misconceived diversification: most of the companies that failed in the global financial crisis were brought down by activities that were not their mainstream business.

Long-term commitment to institutions would be replaced by short-term opportunism in the pursuit of individual gain. But these consequences were not to be understood for twenty years, and not sufficiently well or widely understood even then.

The first major investment bank to take the route of conversion to public company was—of course—Lehman, which made the switch in 1982, and ran into its first financial crisis only two years later.[15] Members of the Halifax Building Society who retained the shares they received on flotation in 1997 lost practically all their windfall when the business, merged into HBoS, collapsed in 2008. The institutions that failed in 2008 were limited-liability companies, not partnerships, so that Dick Fuld, the chief executive who had presided over the bankruptcy of Lehman, continued to be a very rich man indeed. Many of the leaders of the numerous US financial institutions bailed out by the US government did not even lose their jobs.

Within every diversified financial conglomerate there was evidence of the fundamental tension between the cultures of trading and deal-making—buccaneering, entrepreneurial, grasping—and the conservative bureaucratic approach appropriate for retail banking. In the short run, the retail and commercial bankers ran the show: their control of the vast funds raised from retail deposits gave them a dominant role. But their acquisitions were almost all failures. The more senior figures in the firms that had been purchased, enriched by the transactions, retired: the more junior, deprived of the chance of the rich pickings of partnership and ill at ease in the new environment, left.

The most important development in the structure of the industry, however, was the global expansion of American investment banks. These institutions developed activities in London as well as New York, and would become dominant players in London in the 1990s. British merchant banks—once princes of the City—disappeared or were absorbed into large—and mostly foreign—retail banks. Continental European banks had been universal banks, providing the services of both retail and investment banks, but conservative in approach. But as the finance sectors of Britain and the USA changed in the 1980s and 1990s, the men who ran these institutions in France, Germany and Switzerland acquired global ambitions. Today banks such as Deutsche Bank, BNP Paribas and UBS have re-invented themselves along Anglo-American lines. They operate internationally, although their global activities are based in London and New York and were largely created by the acquisition of businesses already located there.

But these mergers were handled very differently from those that had failed in the 1980s. Now the investment bankers—and in due course the traders—were on top. Greedier and smarter, they took control, damaging first the retail banking activities and then the whole bank. Neither retail nor investment bankers had the capacity to manage financial conglomerates that combined the two activities. Probably no one does.

Some of this expansion was rapidly disastrous. In Michael Lewis' account of the events before the 2008 crash, the patsy who can be relied on to take the losing side of a trade is a banker from a small town in Germany.[16] Germany's regional *Landesbanken* have, as I shall describe in Chapter 5, played a positive role in Germany's domestic financial system; but they have repeatedly failed in their international diversification. Crédit Lyonnais, bailed out in 1993 by the French state (which already owned a majority of the shares), was the first global diversified bank to fail in the modern era, after a farcical expansion in which the bank actually became owner of the Hollywood film studio MGM.

In the USA the archetypal deal-maker was Sandy Weill, architect of Citigroup. The Glass–Steagall Act was repealed for the more or less explicit purpose of allowing Weill's Travelers Group to merge with Citicorp, after which Weill rapidly moved to eject his co-CEO, the urbane retail banker John Reed. Citicorp became Citigroup, the world's largest financial institution, absorbing investment bank Salomon, broker Smith Barney, and insurer Travelers, providing virtually every financial product available.

The first great unravelling would occur at Citigroup. The company, and Weill himself, came under fire for abuses during the 'new economy' bubble of 1999. As reputational problems mounted, Weill's achievement in creating the world's largest, most complex, financial institution looked less remarkable. Weill announced his retirement; his hapless successor, Chuck Prince, would be for ever remembered for the remark that encapsulated the mood preceding the global financial crisis: 'as long as the music is playing, you've got to get up and dance.'[17] Soon after, Prince was forced from office and Citigroup was bailed out by the US taxpayer.

Fred Goodwin of Royal Bank of Scotland (RBS) helped turn an Edinburgh-based retail bank into a global financial conglomerate, but as the global financial crisis developed RBS tottered, then hurtled towards bankruptcy. After recapitalisation, the British government owned 84 per cent of RBS's shares. Goodwin was sacked and stripped of his knighthood.

Bob Diamond, an American investment banker, was determined to create a global investment bank under the umbrella of the Barclays retail bank. He had the good fortune to be blocked by the UK government in his attempt to acquire the collapsing Lehman Brothers in September 2008. Barclays nevertheless bought most of Lehman's US assets and operations in the liquidation that followed. In 2010 Diamond gained control of the whole Barclays group.

Not all of the conglomerates formed around retail banks failed. HSBC, perhaps the most successful example of a global retail bank, lost billions on sub-prime lending in the USA, having in 2003 unwisely purchased Household International, which lent to customers whose poor credit ratings made them ineligible for conventional bank loans. But the strength of its Asian franchise enabled HSBC to emerge largely unscathed from the global financial crisis. The hero of the new financial world, however, was Jamie Dimon, Weill's former lieutenant. The great deal-maker, fearing that his protégé would seize the crown, had fired him from Citigroup. But six years after his dismissal Dimon returned to Wall Street as CEO of J.P. Morgan and inherited the strongest brand name in financial services. The house of Morgan, broken up by Congress in 1935, was once again a business spanning retail, commercial and investment banking activities. Dimon successfully steered his organisation away from the worst excesses of the years to 2007 and emerged with a reputation unparalleled in the industry.

But in 2012 Dimon's image would be tarnished when his bank was forced to disclose large losses on so-called hedging activities. Bruno Iksil, the 'London whale', had made huge and unsuccessful bets in derivative markets. Barclays' Diamond would be engulfed by a scandal invoking false disclosure of his bank's cost of funds—the LIBOR scandal—and the Bank of England forced his resignation. HSBC would be excoriated by regulators in Europe and the USA for its facilitation of money laundering and tax evasion. Politicians and the public began to suspect that the recurrent crises of the finance sector were not simply the result of unexpected and unpredictable events, but symptomatic of deep-seated problems with the culture of the financial services industry. They were right.

## From Crisis to Crisis

> I can predict the motion of heavenly bodies but not the madness of crowds.
>
> ISAAC NEWTON[18]

Speculative booms and busts have recurred throughout financial history. In the 1630s Dutch merchants pushed the price of tulips to levels at which a prize bulb was as valuable as a house. A century later, the cream of English society participated in the South Sea Bubble. In the 1840s railway mania seized the public imagination. The 1920s saw boom and bust in stock and land values and ended in the Wall Street Crash and the Great Depression. The immediate consequences of the Crash and Depression were political as well as economic: the rise of political extremism led to the Second World War.

But the post-war settlement established regulated capitalism in most of the developed world, while the Soviet empire maintained financial stability, of a sort, in eastern Europe. The regulatory structures implemented in response to the Wall Street Crash, and the global financial architecture created at the Bretton Woods conference, served the world well for several decades. It was an age of prosperity and calm, although incipient inflation would become apparent as the era came to a close. While the USA was the dominant economic power, Germany's recovery would earn the description of 'economic miracle', and in Japan a pace of economic growth never previously experienced anywhere would turn the country into a major industrial power. France enjoyed the '*trente glorieuses*', Britain had 'never had it so good'.[19]

Financial crises are not natural disasters like hurricanes or earthquakes, which we cannot avoid and must simply learn to manage. Financial crises have their origins in human behaviour. Economic policies can

Figure 1: **The incidence of banking crises**

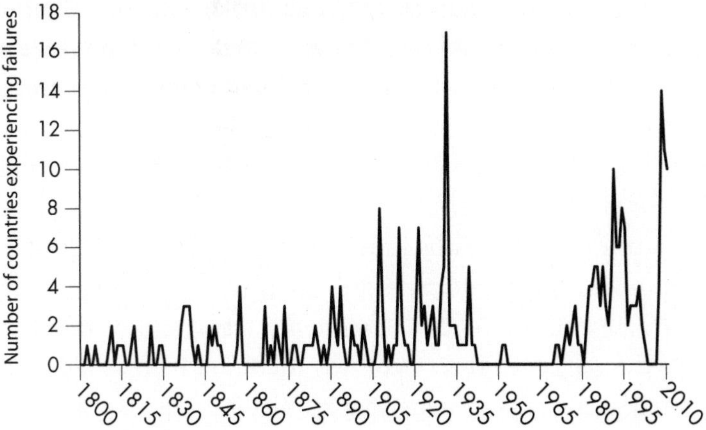

Source: Own calculations, based on the reported numbers of major bank failures in OECD economies, from Reinhart and Rogoff (2010)

increase or reduce their frequency and size. And they have. The pattern shown in Figure 1 is striking. The nineteenth century displays a recurrent pattern of boom and bust. In the early part of the twentieth century the amplitude of crisis increases, culminating in the Wall Street Crash and Great Depression. The period that follows is one of historically unprecedented stability followed by a steady rise in volatility as financialisation gathered pace, through to the global financial crisis of 2008. What went wrong?

By the early 1970s the fixed exchange rate system was disintegrating, American economic hegemony was receding, and as these factors came into question the conservatism of financial institutions was abandoned. In 1971 President Nixon announced the abandonment of the gold standard—the US Treasury had fixed the price of gold at $35 per ounce for four decades. This amounted to a devaluation of the dollar against other currencies. America's economic power was further challenged when the political crisis that began with the Yom Kippur War of 1973 led Arab states to impose drastic increases in the price of oil.

Since many oil-producing countries could not easily spend their new revenues, and many oil-consuming countries did not wish to reduce what they spent, banks established a seemingly profitable business lending the petrodollars earned by oil exporters back to the governments of oil importers. Countries can't go broke, Citicorp chief executive, Walter Wriston famously proclaimed.[20] Technically he was correct: but the consequence—the absence of any orderly judicial or administrative process for handling debt default by nation-states—has proved to be an enduring problem rather than a source of stability for the banking system or for global finance.

Many countries that became indebted in this period had little capacity or intention to repay. African states often borrowed further funds to meet the interest on these loans, frequently using aid or development money for the purpose. Their debt was therefore increasingly owed to international agencies—an issue that rumbled on as the 'Third World debt problem' into the twenty-first century. Countries could not go broke, but need not pay.

Several Latin American states defaulted in the early 1980s, when interest rates on US dollars—in which they had borrowed—rose sharply. The resolution of the crisis set a clear precedent for the future: the US government and the IMF would intervene as needed to protect the balance sheets of large American banks. The scale of the losses banks had incurred was disguised by a combination of central bank support and accounting devices. Bankers, regulators and governments held the hope—often justified—that the banks concerned would be able to trade their way back to solvent and even well-capitalised positions. Lloyds and Citicorp did just that. These zombie banks, neither dead nor alive, came back to life. But the zombie bank, insolvent but still trading, would be a recurrent motif in the aftermath of the recurrent financial crises.

Stock markets rose steadily in the 1980s and 1990s. But the new world of concentrated shareholding and active trading displayed a new fragility. On 19 October 1987 the US market experienced a fall of 20 per cent in a single day—an unprecedented, and still unrepeated, event. No compelling explanation of how and why this happened has ever been provided, although some blame was ascribed to 'portfolio insurance', a scheme by which institutions sought to limit their downside exposure by trade in derivatives. Parallel, though slightly smaller, falls were experienced in the stock markets of other countries. But a few days later markets resumed their upward trend.

On 6 May 2010 an even more bizarre incident occurred when US market indexes fell by over 5 per cent in twenty minutes. Some shares were quoted at nonsensical prices—Accenture at 1 cent, Apple at $150,000. The causes of the 'flash crash' are alleged to have been a genuine but mishandled stock order which triggered responses from computer-trading algorithms that dealt insanely with each other until stabilised by human intervention. As this book went to press, the British police swooped at the instigation of the FBI on a semi-detached house in Hounslow, an unprepossessing suburb in southwest London, and arrested a man who, they implausibly suggested, had caused the incident by trading from his front room. The frightening truth is that no one really knows the cause of the crash. Although no particularly serious consequences followed on that occasion, the vision of technology out of control was a disturbing portent of the future.[21] On 15 October 2014 an equally inexplicable 'flash crash' was experienced in the market for US Treasury securities.

The first great speculative bubble of the modern era was seen in the late 1980s in Japanese shares and Japanese property. At the peak of the boom it was claimed that the grounds of the emperor's palace were worth more than the state of California. Whether this had been true or not, it would not remain so: the bubble burst. Japanese and foreign investors incurred large losses: the principal Japanese stock market indexes are even today less than half the level they reached at the peak. Japanese banks, which had expanded massively on the security of inflated asset values, were effectively but not formally bankrupted. These zombie banks would haunt the Japanese economy for two decades.

The fund manager Antoine van Agtmael claimed to have coined the term 'emerging markets'.[22] The inclusion of new countries in the global trading system would be the most important economic development of the three decades after 1980. The first countries to embrace change were those of East Asia. Hong Kong and Singapore became trading hubs. Japan's post-war growth was imitated in Korea and Taiwan and then in Thailand, Indonesia and the Philippines. At the end of the 1980s the Communist regimes of eastern Europe collapsed, and many of these countries embraced capitalism and its financial institutions. Transformational economic changes occurred in China and India. Brazil, Turkey and Mexico became places to do business: there were even signs that some African states were shaking off their dismal post-colonial economic legacies.

So emerging markets became an investment theme. But financial markets can always have too much of a good thing. Enthusiasm to place funds in emerging markets—especially in Asia—left the countries concerned with unsupportable foreign debt levels and overvalued domestic assets. In 1997 the Thai exchange rate collapsed as foreign investors rushed to salvage their positions while some value remained. Contagion spread through Asia. The following year Russia defaulted on its debts.

The emerging market crises were partly defused by interventions from the International Monetary Fund, which provided support through loans for countries, and, implicitly, the banks that had foolishly provided finance. The IMF imposed much-resented austerity programmes on Asian economies. The phrase 'Washington consensus' was widely used to describe the common set of neo-liberal economic policies that were conditions of their support. Privatisation and capital market liberalisation contributed to both national and international financialisation.

The internet came to the educated public, and the financial community, in the 1990s. The dot-com boom began in 1995 with the publication of a research note pointing out the commercial opportunities of the internet from Mary Meeker of Morgan Stanley (who would become known as 'the internet goddess') and the flotation of Netscape (which devised the first accessible internet browser).[23] By 1999 journalists, consultants and business people talked of a 'New Economy'. Businesses that had never made a penny of profit, and never would, were floated on world stock exchanges at fantastic valuations. The demand for 'New Economy' stocks spilled over into every business that promoters could associate, however tenuously, with high technology.

The last phase of the New Economy bubble in early 2000 was aided by the liquidity pumped into the US economy by the Federal Reserve to avert the threat supposedly posed by the 'millennium bug': errors in computer programmes in handling the date 2000. In the spring of 2000 the New Economy boom came to its predictable, if not widely predicted, end. The Fed then cut interest rates and gave a further monetary stimulus. While the collapse in the value of internet stocks was initially mirrored in the wider stock market, the effect of cheap money encouraged share prices to rise again from the autumn of 2001.

The events of the new economy bubble excited media attention. But the next—and still the largest—boom and bust took place mostly out of public sight. Although there were many signs of future instability for those who cared to look, it is hard to overstate the complacency that characterised the period from the bursting of the internet bubble to the global financial crisis. The Nobel Prize-winning economist Robert Lucas told the annual meeting of the American Economic Association that the 'central problem of depression prevention has essentially been solved'.[24] Another academic economist, Ben Bernanke, who had been appointed to the Board of the Federal Reserve System, popularised the phrase 'the Great Moderation'[25] to describe a supposed new era of economic stability.

In retrospect, the critical development during this period was the growth in trade in asset-backed securities, especially mortgage-backed securities, and subsequently collateralised debt obligations, between financial institutions. A false belief in the credit strength provided by such packaging stimulated demand for these assets. Further reassurance appeared to be provided by the development of a market in credit default swaps—derivative securities that would pay out if there was default on the underlying security. Little thought was given at the time to the capacity of the institutions that wrote these contracts to pay in the event of widespread defaults. Thus a downgrading of the credit rating of AIG in 2008—which had insured over $500 billion of securities through credit default swaps—was devastating in its consequences for the perceived safety of bond portfolios.

The insatiable demand for asset-backed securities led to the pursuit of assets of lower and lower quality. In many US cities mortgage salesmen promoted loans to people who had no realistic prospect of being able to repay. But rating agencies—and the Federal Reserve Board—continued to base their expectations on databases from an era in which house prices always rose gently and borrowers were people of good standing. Even a pause in the upward progression of US house prices would be sufficient to collapse this house of cards. In 2008 concerns about the value of securities on the balance sheets of banks had reached a level that cast doubt on the value of the liabilities of the banks themselves. A complete meltdown of the global financial system was averted only by public intervention on an unprecedented scale. Government funds were used to provide liquidity support for the banking system and directly recapitalise failed or failing institutions. This event was the most severe financial crisis since 1929–33—perhaps the most severe financial crisis ever.

The global financial crisis began in the USA but immediately crossed the Atlantic, in large part because European banks were large purchasers of doubtful paper that had originated in the USA. But the next crisis was made in Europe. The Eurozone—an ambitious scheme to link the currencies of France with Germany and the countries closely bound into the German economy—had grown into a political project that included Spain, Italy, Portugal and even Greece.

The adoption of a common currency by these countries in 1999 (Greece followed in 2001) led to convergence of interest rates across the continent. Traders no longer discriminated between the euro liabilities of different Eurozone governments, believing that not only currency risks but also the credit risks that had once distinguished well-managed European economies from those with unstable public finances had been eliminated. Banks in Germany and France borrowed euros in the north of the continent to lend to southern Europe. By 2007 yields on Greek government bonds were barely higher than those on equivalent German bonds. Several states, including Greece, took advantage of what appeared to be inexhaustible supplies of credit at low rates to grow public and private debt.

As European banks struggled with the global financial crisis, the quality of their assets was viewed more sceptically. Credit risks were appraised much more carefully, and interest rate differentials across the Eurozone widened again. Greek bonds appeared less attractive, as interest rates rose and the refinancing of Greek credit became more difficult. The country effectively defaulted on its debts in 2011.

But Greece was not the Eurozone's only problem. Ireland's entire banking system had collapsed in 2008. A property bubble of extreme magnitude had burst in Spain. Other Eurozone members—Portugal, Italy and Cyprus—faced their own distinctive economic and political difficulties. All experienced spiralling debt service costs. With each mini-crisis, the scale and scope of European Central Bank intervention increased. In 2012 the new Governor of the European Central Bank, Mario Draghi, promised to do 'whatever it takes' to preserve the Eurozone.[26] Given the potential resource available to an institution empowered to print Europe's money, that commitment stabilised the Eurozone crisis. For the time being.

The proximate causes of these successive crises are very different— emerging market debt problems, the new economy bubble, defaults on asset-backed securities, the political strains within the Eurozone—yet their basic mechanism is the same. They originate in some genuine change in the economic environment: the success of emerging econo- mies, the development of the internet, innovation in financial instru- ments, the adoption of a common currency across Europe. Early spotters of these trends make profits. A herd mentality among traders attracts more and more people and money into the asset class concerned. As- set mispricing becomes acute, but prices are going up and traders are mostly making money.

Although seemingly sophisticated rationalisations are provided for these revaluations, the underlying reality is an emotional process, de- scribed by the psychologist David Tuckett in the course of many inter- views with traders.

> Once some euphoric momentum is reached, the emotional develop- ment underlying the belief tends to indicate only a one-way path. . . . There is the excitement propelling the move forward and the pain that would have to be undergone if it were to be reversed. The latter would entail loss of the euphoric dream and giving up expectations. Sceptics are felt as spoilers and it is to stave off frustration that they are special- ly maligned during this phase. The doubts they raise about the new story need to be refuted and so are mocked and maligned through dismissal.[27]

Yet reality cannot be deferred for ever. The mispricing is corrected, leaving investors and institutions with large losses. Central banks and governments intervene, to protect the financial sector and to minimise the damage done to the non-financial economy. That cash and liquidity then provide the fuel for the next crisis in some different area of activity. Successive crises have tended to be of increasing severity.

The booms are generally triggered by events external to the financial system. The busts may also appear to have extraneous causes: Russian default, a set-back to US house prices, the collapse of Lehman. But these are triggers rather than explanations. The mechanisms of crisis are an intrinsic part of the modern financial system. It is not just that the modern financial system is prone to instability. Without the mechanics that produce recurrent crises the financial system would not exist in the form it does today. This point will emerge more clearly in Chapters 2 and 4.

## The Robber Barons

> The determination of the government (in which, gentlemen, it will not waver) to punish certain malefactors of great wealth, has been responsible for something of the trouble . . . I regard this contest as one to determine who shall rule this free country—the people through their governmental agents, or a few ruthless and domineering men whose wealth makes them peculiarly formidable because they hide behind the breastworks of corporate organization.
>
> THEODORE ROOSEVELT, address at the Pilgrim Memorial Monument, Provincetown, Massachussets, 20 August 1907

The late nineteenth century is described as 'the gilded age' of American capitalism. The dominant figures of that era—men such as Henry Clay Frick, Jay Gould, J.P. Morgan, John D. Rockefeller and Cornelius Vanderbilt—are often called 'the robber barons'.[28] They were both industrialists and financiers, in varying degrees. They built, or helped build, the railroads, oil supply systems and steel mills that made the USA an industrial powerhouse. But their immense personal wealth was as much the product of financial manipulation as of productive activity.

At the beginning of the twentieth century the power of the robber barons was abruptly checked. The 'muckrakers'—hostile journalists—exposed some of the excesses of financial capitalism directed towards industrial monopoly. Ida Tarbell engaged in a sustained campaign against Rockefeller's Standard Oil.[29] Upton Sinclair's novel *The Jungle* (1906), which described Midwest meat-packing plants, is still a literary classic.[30]

The term 'muckraker' was coined—not disapprovingly—by Theodore Roosevelt, a Republican who had unexpectedly become president following the assassination in 1901 of the benignly pro-business William McKinley. Roosevelt was an unashamed publicist and populist.

Ten years earlier, a suspicious Congress had passed the Sherman Act, anti-trust legislation aimed at the financial consolidations of the robber barons: but it was only under Roosevelt's administration that enforcement action began.

Standard Oil and American Tobacco were broken up. The great new American industries of the twentieth century, such as automobile manufacture, developed in a competitive market. The largest trust of all, US Steel, withstood the anti-trust movement but began a process of inexorable decline. The links between finance and business were not broken but were loosened. While the 'robber barons' were both financiers and businessmen, the leading industrialists of the first half of the twentieth century—men such as Alfred Sloan and Pierre du Pont—were primarily businessmen. Their skill was in developing the systems and cadre of professional managers needed to run a modern corporation.

The rise of the large manufacturing company—diversified into related business, vertically integrated through control of supply and distribution, increasingly self-financing—was a key economic development of the first half of the twentieth century. The industrialists who ran these businesses had little time for the stock market—or for finance generally; Henry Ford bought out the external shareholders in his company, which did not regain a listing until 1956. None of these figures could have imagined the time that senior executives of large corporations now spend on 'investor relations'.

Still, investment bankers were rarely short of work. Financiers urged companies to do deals. The rationale they offered for large transactions, from which they would derive correspondingly large fees, varied along with fashions in business strategy. The urge to consolidate—a polite term for the attempt to create monopolies—is always strong in the business community, and had not died with the introduction of anti-trust policies in the USA. A new wave of mergers in the 1920s established companies such as General Motors and Imperial Chemical Industries (ICI). In the 1960s domestic consolidation was widely seen, for no obvious reason, as an appropriate response to growing international competition. The conceit that great managers and their teams had skills relevant to almost any business led to a fad for conglomerates: companies such as ITT and Litton Industries were market favourites, able to use their overvalued shares to make cheap acquisitions.

Financialisation drew the attention of corporate managers back to stock markets. Not, in general, because they needed to raise capital for their businesses, but because the times dictated fresh priorities. Companies were encouraged to pursue 'shareholder value'.[31] Many chief executives came to see themselves as meta-fund managers, buying and selling a portfolio of companies rather as asset traders might buy and sell portfolios of securities. Jack Welch became CEO of America's largest industrial company, General Electric, in 1981. In a speech he gave that year at New York's Pierre Hotel he announced that the corporation would sell or close any business in which it was not number one or number two. This occasion is widely described as the beginning of the application of shareholder value principles in American business: and as he implemented this strategy over the following two decades, Welch became America's most admired business leader.[32]

In 1965 an American economist, Henry Manne, had coined the phrase 'the market for corporate control'.[33] The right to manage a corporation was an asset that could be bought and sold. Neglect of 'shareholder value' exposed managers to the threat of hostile takeovers. In the 1980s this threat intensified when Michael Milken of Drexel Burnham Lambert invented 'junk bonds', and found institutional investors to subscribe for them. These securities, which offered high yields and acknowledged high risks, enabled raiders to threaten even the largest company. The contested takeover in 1988 of RJR Nabisco, the tobacco and food conglomerate, is described by Bryan Burrough and John Helyar in their book *Barbarians at the Gate: The Fall of RJR Nabisco*, perhaps the best business book of that decade.[34] Burrough and Helyar end their book with the plaintive question 'But what did it have to do with business?' The question was pertinent.

The era of Milken and junk bonds ended in farce. In 1990 the Campeau Corporation, which had used junk bonds to acquire many of the USA's leading department stores—Macy's, Bloomingdale's, Jordan Marsh—defaulted on its debt mountain. Robert Campeau, a Canadian property speculator, had no qualifications to run these businesses, only access to the funds of Milken's clients. Appetite for junk bonds disappeared along with the hopes of the Campeau Corporation: Drexel Burnham Lambert, unable to refinance the bonds, went bankrupt: Milken went to prison.

But the metaphor of 'the market for corporate control' fitted with the process of financialisation and the rise of the trading culture. Managers who gave insufficient attention to the goal of 'shareholder value' were under threat from financial markets. No company illustrated the transition more clearly than Britain's largest industrial company, ICI, a business that had declared in its annual report in 1987 that:

ICI aims to be the world's leading chemical company, serving customers internationally through the innovative and responsible application of chemistry and related science. . . .

Through achievement of our aim, we will enhance the wealth and well-being of our shareholders, our employees, our customers and the communities which we serve and in which we operate.

In ICI's 1994 annual report the company had a very different statement of corporate objective:

Our objective is to maximise value for our shareholders by focusing on businesses where we have market leadership, a technological edge and a world competitive cost base.

We now benefit from hindsight and can describe what happened before—and after. The older ICI was a world leader in its industry from its formation in the 1920s.[35] The origins of the company were in explosives and dyestuffs, but in the inter-war period the emphasis of the business shifted to petrochemicals and agricultural fertilisers. After the Second World War the ICI board recognised, presciently, that the most important 'responsible application of chemistry' in future would be the nascent pharmaceutical business. But ICI's pharmaceutical division lost money for almost two decades. In the 1960s, however, the company discovered one of the first blockbuster drugs, under the direction of James Black, the father of Britain's strong pharmaceutical industry. Beta-blockers were the first effective anti-hypertensives. In the quarter-century that followed, drugs would be the principal driver of ICI's growth and source of its profit.

The experience of the newer ICI was not such a happy one. The stock market reacted favourably to the announcement of its changed objectives, but less favourably to the subsequent reality. ICI's share price peaked in early 1997, and the decline thereafter was relentless. In 2007 what remained of the once great business was acquired by a Dutch company. The company whose objective was 'to maximise value for shareholders' was not successful even in achieving that. Bear Stearns, which famously proclaimed 'we make nothing but money', was an early casualty of the global financial crisis. The paradox that the most profit-oriented companies are not necessarily the most profitable is the subject of my book *Obliquity*.[36]

After Sandy Weill's Travelers acquired Citicorp in 1999, Weill briefly shared the position of CEO with the veteran banker John Reed. The two men provided contrasting views of the future of the company for an American journalist from a conference room overlooking the East River.

> 'The model I have is of a global consumer company that really helps the middle class with something they haven't been served well by historically. That's my vision. That's my dream', said Reed. 'My goal is increasing shareholder value', Sandy (Weill) interjected, glancing frequently at a nearby computer monitor displaying Citigroup's changing stock price.[37]

Weill ousted Reed, but within eight years Citigroup's share price would have lost almost all its value and the business would be rescued by the US government. In an illuminating comment on the financialisation of business, Jack Welch—now long retired from General Electric—would in 2009 proclaim shareholder value 'the dumbest idea in the world'.[38]

## We Are the 1 Per Cent

> Ill fares the land, to hastening ills a prey
> Where wealth accumulates, and men decay.
>
> OLIVER GOLDSMITH, *The Deserted Village*, 1770

John Reed had spent his entire business career at Citigroup, where he had pioneered the roll-out of ATMs, before becoming CEO in 1984. Reed was a corporation man, in the model created by Alfred Sloan, one of a breed that was often mocked in the decades that followed. Like other corporation men, he expected—and received—a substantial salary, but did not expect to become very rich through his ascent of the corporate ladder, and did not in fact do so. (Sloan was wealthy—the Sloan Foundation is his legacy—but his wealth was derived from the amounts General Motors had paid to acquire his ball-bearing company, not his remuneration as CEO.) Even Reed's pay-off when removed by Weill seems modest by current standards, at $5.5 million.

In retirement, Reed stood in as chief executive of the New York Stock Exchange: the previous incumbent, Dick Grasso, had been fired after the press revealed that the board of the NYSE had agreed to commute his retirement benefits for an immediate cash payment of $140 million. Today Reed, a gentlemanly figure redolent of another era, is an advocate of radical banking reform. If Reed was among the last of an old guard, Weill was the archetype of the new. Weill is a billionaire, his wealth acquired through shares, options and bonuses in the course of his inveterate deal-making.

The partnership model had dominated high-risk activities within the financial sector, such as market-making and corporate advice in mergers and acquisitions. Senior people in these organisations would share widely volatile but often very large rewards among themselves at the end of the year. The conversion of these structures to public companies in the 1980s had the effect, in principle, of transferring both these risks and these rewards from the partners (who realised lump sums from the transactions) to the shareholders. In reality, it had little effect on the financial expectations of those who worked in the firms. Thus the practice of allocating a substantial share of profits to senior staff—now employees—continued: indeed, as activities once undertaken in partnerships were absorbed into wider conglomerates the principle that employees should receive a substantial share of the profits of the businesses that employed them was widely applied across the financial sector through the bonus system. The miserable outcome for the shareholders in financial conglomerates will be described in Chapter 4.

At the same time, the growth of the trading culture led businesses to report profits that were widely variable, but often very high, for reasons that will be explained in Chapter 5. The individuals who had planned or facilitated the relevant trades naturally felt entitled not just to credit but to a share in the rewards. This expectation operated in one direction only: they did not plan to share losses and indeed generally had no capacity to do so. The award by a French court of €4.9 billion damages against 'rogue trader' Jérôme Kerviel—compensation for the losses his inept trading had supposedly inflicted on Société Générale—had symbolic significance only.

The bonus culture spread throughout financial conglomerates. Even very junior employees in retail banks found themselves chasing aggressive targets to earn bonuses—which would in due course give rise to well-founded claims that products such as mortgages and payment protection insurance had been mis-sold. The bonus culture, and a much-increased level of expectations about pay, spilled over into the rest of the corporate sector. Senior executives of large businesses—often, like Sandy Weill, themselves engaged in deal-making in the new market for corporate control—observed the levels of remuneration being earned in the financial sector, and raised their sights (so did people employed in activities close to the financial sector, such as accountants and corporate lawyers).

Linking executive bonuses to share prices through options was legitimised by the need to pursue 'shareholder value'. As share prices rose steadily in the 1980s and 1990s, these options transformed the personal finances of many of these executives. Jack Welch of General Electric, who, like Reed, joined his company straight from university in 1960, was an icon of the new incentive-based approach to corporate management. His personal fortune today is estimated at $720 million,[39] and such wealth is not exceptional among modern business executives in the USA. That outcome was simply unimaginable for a previous generation of corporation men such as John Reed.[40]

But the linkage between executive pay and performance provided by share options was weak. Based on market expectations rather than business realities, rewards linked to share prices were the product of fickle opinion and, like the bonuses of traders, asymmetric. The option allowed beneficiaries to participate in the upside but did not require them to share in the downside, a structure that encouraged the risky transformational change that proved so destructive of ICI and Citigroup: the link to share prices—Weill's 'nearby computer monitor displaying Citigroup's changing share price'—created an intensely short-term focus. What useful business information could a chief executive glean from minute-by-minute fluctuations in the value of the company he ran?

The bonus culture in both financial and non-financial sectors, far from aligning the interests of managers and traders with those of shareholders, produced an outcome in which the objectives of managers and traders were materially different from those of the organisations for which they worked. This agency problem—companies being run for the benefit of a group of senior employees—was most acute in the financial sector but also infected the corporate sector more widely. The very large fees paid to investment bankers for their role in facilitating deals and financial engineering were another aspect of this agency problem. Managers were spending other people's money, with the profusion and negligence that Adam Smith had anticipated. The extension of Smith's agency problem throughout modern business and finance—the divorce of ownership and control—was identified by Adolf Berle and Gardiner Means eighty years ago.[41] The attempt to tackle this issue by designing complex incentive schemes did not, in fact, align managerial interests with those of shareholders, still less align them with the long-term success of the company: today it has become the principal source of friction between companies and their shareholders.

Little imagination is needed to see parallels between the 'robber barons' of the USA's late nineteenth century, such as John D. Rockefeller and Andrew Carnegie, and the influential industrialist–financiers of the emerging markets of the late twentieth century, such as Mexico's Carlos Slim and India's Dhirubhai Ambani, or the men who have made fortunes from the appropriation of formerly state-owned properties in eastern Europe. But the arrival of corporation men such as Welch among the super-rich is a new phenomenon. The ability of the senior employees of large corporations to appropriate significant fractions of corporate revenues for their own purposes mirrors, perhaps, the lavish lifestyle opportunities once exploited by prelates and courtiers.

And so the combination of the bonus culture in the financial sector and its associated activities, a new generation of robber baron, and the multi-millionaire CEO, has produced a reversal of the egalitarian trends of most of the twentieth century. 'We are the 99 per cent' was the slogan of the 'Occupy' protesters, drawing attention to the degree to which a small minority have benefited disproportionately during the era of financialisation.

Figure 2: **Share of top 1 per cent and 0.1 per cent in total gross income in four countries, 1919–2005**

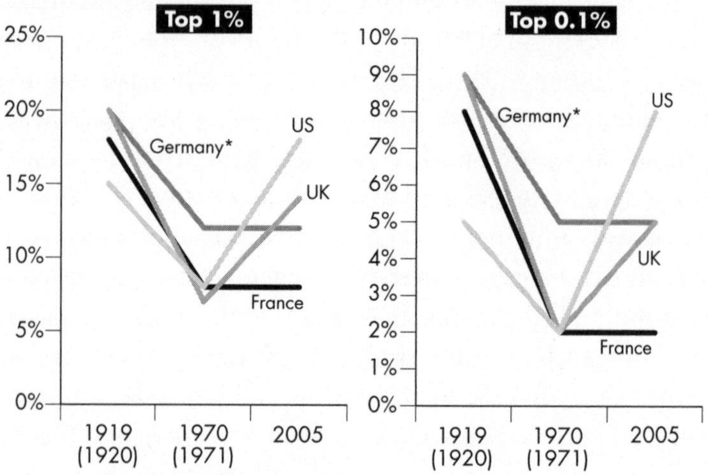

Incomes are those of tax reported units.
*Prussia 1919, West Germany 1970, Germany 2005.
Source: A.B. Atkinson and S. Morelli, *Chartbook of Economic Inequality*, ECINEQ Working Paper, 2014

At the end of the First World War 'the 1 per cent'—the highest-earning percentile of the income distribution—received between 15 and 20 per cent of gross income. The USA, land of immigration and opportunity, was more equal than the countries of old Europe. But the rise of democracy, and the growth of social security and the modern state, led to sharp reductions in income inequality across the developed world in the fifty years that followed. As Figure 2 shows, by 1970 the share of the top 1 per cent had fallen by around half, and the share of the top 0.1 per cent had diminished even more sharply. Since these figures relate to gross income, and benefits and top rates of taxation increased everywhere, the equalising effect was even greater than these figures suggest.

Many people may be surprised that Germany in 1970 was significantly less equal than Britain, France or the United States. The main explanation is the success of that country's largely family-owned *Mittelstand*, or medium-size business sector, which I will discuss further in Chapter 5.

The egalitarian trends did not continue. In France and Germany they simply came to an end; these measures of income inequality have not changed since 1970. In Britain and the USA incomes of the top 1 per cent and 0.1 per cent have increased sharply. The reversal is particularly marked in the USA. The share of 'the 1 per cent' there is now greater than it was a century ago, and US income distribution is now by some margin the most unequal of the four countries. What has happened to capital is much less clear. As I shall describe in Chapters 5–7, the growth of the owner-occupied housing stock and of pension rights has broadened the distribution of personal wealth.

Many factors have contributed to these shifts in income distribution. The liberal political trends that dominated most of the twentieth century were stalled or reversed in its final decades. Globalisation has had dramatic effects on world income inequality: economic growth in China and India has lifted more people out of poverty in the last two decades than in any previous era of world history. But globalisation has tended to increase income inequality within already rich countries. While it enabled people with unique or distinctive skills—whether musical or sporting celebrities or consulting engineers—to deploy these skills in a wider market, it also intensified competition and depressed earnings for unskilled labour as low-tech manufacturing was able to relocate to low-wage countries.

Still, the divergence of experience between Britain and the USA on the one hand, and France and Germany on the other, is striking. Britain and the USA were the countries of Thatcher and Reagan, but the rising share of the 1 per cent continued under Labour and Democratic administrations. The direct and indirect effects of financialisation are key—the extraordinary levels of remuneration generated for the highest-paid individuals in the finance sector itself, and the knock-on impact on the pay of top corporate executives outside the financial sector. In the USA in 2005, 45 per cent of the top 1 per cent and 60 per cent of the top 0.1 per cent of income-earners were either corporate executives or employed in finance. (Doctors and lawyers make up 22 per cent of the top 1 per cent, but only 10 per cent of the top 0.1 per cent.[42])

The cumulative effect of all these factors in the USA was that reported economic growth in the era of financialisation had little effect on the experience of the typical individual. Median household income has increased by less than 5 per cent in real (inflation-adjusted) terms since 1973.[43] But the era of financialisation was also one of wide expansion of the availability of consumer credit in these countries. Fuelled by securitisation, credit card debt and other consumer lending increased rapidly. Home-owners were able to obtain 'equity release' (i.e., to borrow against the increased value of their property), while mortgages were extended to people who had never previously been eligible for housing finance. This credit expansion allowed consumption to continue growing even if incomes did not.

Credit expansion could not continue indefinitely: it would inevitably go into reverse when the low quality of much of the induced lending was revealed. And that was what happened in the global financial crisis. The social tensions that had been suppressed when consumption was growing faster than incomes were no longer contained. Public opinion turned against banking and finance, reflected in the Occupy movement and the surge in popularity of fringe political movements.

A century after Upton Sinclair and Ida Tarbell the tradition of the muckraker was revived. A new generation of journalists sought to expose corporate and—especially—financial malpractice. When the internet journalist Matt Taibbi described Goldman Sachs as 'a giant vampire squid, sucking money from wherever it finds it',[44] the description quickly went viral. The firm which did not even advertise its presence at 200 West Street was pilloried in Congress and the press. The power of Taibbi's metaphor comes from its implication that Goldman was not creating wealth itself but benefiting from wealth that had been created by other people and businesses. And this suspicion is at the centre of many people's concerns about the role of the financial sector. Later chapters will consider how far these concerns are justified.

One of the many factors that distinguished Sandy Weill and the subscribers to 'We are Wall Street' from Mr Banks and George Bailey was their attitude to risk. Risk had been anathema to Banks and Bailey; if a bank loan was perceived to be risky, it was not made. Of course, these traditional bankers sometimes made mistakes, and their borrowers failed to repay; but there was no such thing as a calculated risk, and no accounting provision for expected losses, because none were expected. In the era of financialisation, bankers embraced risk. Risk was a source of return, and—with the aid of Larry Summers' mathematicians—could be calculated and managed. Perhaps.

CHAPTER 2

# Risk

## Cows, Coffee and Credit Default Swaps

> Whenever material gain follows exchange, for every plus there is a pre-
> cisely equal minus.
>
> JOHN RUSKIN, Unto this Last, 1860

> The key insight of Adam Smith's *Wealth of Nations* is misleadingly sim-
> ple: if an exchange between two parties is voluntary, it will not take place
> unless both believe they will benefit from it.
>
> MILTON FRIEDMAN, Free to Choose, 1980

In 2005 the Federal Reserve Bank of Kansas held a symposium at the
agreeable Wyoming resort of Jackson Hole. The purpose was to honour
Alan Greenspan, who would soon retire from his position as chairman
of the Federal Reserve Board. Raghuram Rajan, then chief economist at
the IMF, queried the value of recent innovation in financial markets and
warned of troubles ahead.[1]

Rajan's paper was not well received. The principal discussant was the
vice-chairman of the Federal Reserve Board, Don Kohn. Kohn treated
the speech as an attack on what he called 'the Greenspan doctrine',
which proclaimed the virtues of the financial innovations that Rajan
had queried. Kohn made a robust defence of these innovations. 'By allowing institutions to diversify risk, to choose their risk profiles more

precisely, and to improve the management of the risks they take on, they have made institutions more robust.'[2] He went on to explain that 'these developments have also made the financial system more resilient and flexible—better able to absorb shocks without increasing the effects of such shocks on the real economy'.

This was indeed Chairman Greenspan's view. Had he not explained that 'these instruments enhance the ability to differentiate risk and allocate it to those investors most able and willing to take it'?[3] If Kohn was critical, he was at least polite: Larry Summers described Rajan's views as 'Luddite' and likened his thinking to those who would substitute runners and horses for cars and aeroplanes. Complexity, Summers argued, was inseparable from progress.[4]

The keynote address at Jackson Hole was delivered by Robert Rubin, who had served as President Clinton's Treasury secretary from 1995 to 1999. Rubin had previously been a Goldman Sachs executive, and after leaving government would receive more than $100 million for his work in non-executive roles at Citigroup between 2000 and 2009. Rubin was a key figure in the change of Summers' position from the denigration of 'ketchup economics' to enthusiastic support for financialisation, and had groomed the Harvard academic to be his successor. When Brooksley Born, chair of the Commodity Futures Trading Commission, had sought to extend the regulation of derivative markets, Rubin, Summers and Greenspan had led the opposition and supported legislation that excluded financial contracts from the remit of the agency.

The following year, another Federal Reserve Board governor, Ben Bernanke, reiterated Kohn's claim: 'Banking organisations of all sizes have made substantial strides over the past two decades in their ability to measure and manage risks.' Such advances resulted, he said, in 'greater resilience of the banking system'.[5] Bernanke was the Princeton professor and student of the Great Depression who had earlier proclaimed 'the Great Moderation'.

The chairman of the Federal Reserve Bank of New York similarly applauded the work of risk managers when he addressed their annual conference. Timothy Geithner told his audience:

> Financial institutions are able to measure and manage risk much
> more effectively. Risks are spread more widely, across a more diverse

group of financial intermediaries, within and across countries. These changes have contributed to a substantial improvement in the financial strength of the core financial intermediaries and in the overall flexibility and resilience of the financial system in the United States.[6]

The breathtaking scale of these misapprehensions proved no obstacle to the subsequent advancement of those who held them. When the global financial crisis broke, George W. Bush had already appointed Bernanke to succeed Greenspan as chairman of the Federal Reserve Board. Kohn became his vice-chairman.[7] President Obama formed his economic team by appointing Geithner as Treasury secretary and Summers as chairman of the National Economic Council. (Rajan left the IMF at the end of 2006 and returned to India, where in 2013 he became governor of the Reserve Bank.)

Bernanke, Geithner, Kohn and Summers had ready access to the best possible advice from both scholars and practitioners in financial markets. Bernanke and Summers had themselves been academic economists of considerable distinction. How could they have got it so wrong? The opinions expressed by the economic policymakers who congregated at Jackson Hole represented the views of a community of scholars (who advanced a mistaken, or at least inappropriate, theory) and practitioners (who seized enthusiastically on a description of the world that proclaimed that the activities they found so privately and personally profitable made that world a better place).

Economic theory did not cause the changes in the character of the financial system that the book describes, nor were economists responsible for the global financial crisis. But the influence of economic theory on these changes and these events was extensive and profound. In a broad sense, the development of a trading-oriented financial sector was closely associated with the free-market ideology that swept across public policy with the rise of Thatcher and Reagan. The roar of the trading floor was the apotheosis of the free market.

The commitment of leaders of the financial community to the values of the free market was a pragmatic alliance of convenience, not the product of deep intellectual conviction. If that had been in doubt, the global financial crisis dispelled it. The titans of finance were able to persuade themselves and others that arguments for letting the market take its course might be compelling as matters of general principle; but these arguments did not apply in the case of systemically important financial institutions such as Citigroup and Goldman Sachs and, in particular, did not apply to the businesses of which they had the good fortune to be senior executives. Finance is special. Once these exceptions to the general rule were recognised, however, the flow of free-market rhetoric from the financial community could continue unabated, and it did.

The provision of an intellectual rationale for free-market ideology is one part of the contribution of economics to policy for the financial sector. Another was more technical: the development from the 1960s of a comprehensive set of models in financial economics.

Popular legend recounts that Native Americans sold the site of the future Wall Street for trinkets worth $24. The two parties had different ideas about the value of the location. In this instance the purchaser (the Dutch governor-general of New Netherland, Peter Minuit) tricked the sellers: the Natives simply made a mistake. Or perhaps not. Another version of the legend has the Natives getting the better of the deal, since they never owned Manhattan Island in the first place.[8] In either case the trade was based on misinformation and disinformation. The notion that the market-place was a venue in which unscrupulous merchants robbed unwitting customers, and foreign trade a means of extracting wealth from foreigners, dominated economic thought from the days of Aristotle until the mid-eighteenth century. We might honour the seventeenth-century French economist and politician Jean-Baptiste Colbert as the champion of this doctrine, since many of his compatriots—along with Ruskin, whose grasp of economics was never strong, and more recent critics of commercial activity—adhere to it still.

Yet a central insight of modern economics—one that Friedman attributed, not unfairly, to Adam Smith—is that exchange can benefit both parties, if they have different preferences or different specialisms. Perhaps I have a dairy herd and you have a coffee plantation, and we both like milky coffee. Or perhaps we both practice mixed agriculture, but you drink only coffee and I drink only milk. In either case, trade will make us both better off.

Modern financial economics treats risk as a commodity like milk or coffee. People have different preferences and capabilities in their approach to risk and their ability to manage it, just as they have different tastes in food, or farm different kinds of land, or hold different agricultural skills. Trade between them benefits both parties. In this way markets in risk enable the inescapable risks of modern life to be handled more efficiently.

If this analogy between risk and other commodities were valid, the standard tools of economics could be applied to the trading of risk. This approach has been the basis of financial economics for half a century. The metaphor has many attractions for those who work in financial markets, implying that the claims of market efficiency that are made for trade in milk and coffee are equally applicable to trade in foreign currency and credit default swaps. The larger the volume of trade, the wider the scope of markets, the greater the benefits from free exchange in securities markets.

But you can have too much of a good thing. The fact that trade can benefit both parties does not imply that all trade does so: and if not all trade is tricky, some is. Both Ruskin and Friedman are sometimes right and sometimes wrong. The 'Greenspan doctrine' regards the exchange of risk as similar to the exchange of milk and coffee: the effect of the trade is to 'allocate (risk) to those investors most able and willing to take it'.[9] But three centuries after Colbert, a different strand of thought in modern economics revives the notion that trade is tricky by stressing 'information asymmetry'—people trade because they have different knowledge, or different perceptions of the same knowledge.

These two approaches to thinking about trade in risk have a long history. Michel Albert, a French economist turned insurance company boss, offered an entertaining account of the development of the global insurance market in the eighteenth century. He explained how, in Edward Lloyd's coffee house in London, leisured English gentlemen gathered to gamble on the fate of ships at sea. The value of these positions ebbed and flowed with the tides; their fortunes were buffeted by the weather. A thousand miles away, Swiss villagers came together to agree that, if a cow died, they would take collective responsibility for replacing it. The English traded risks; the Swiss mutualised them.[10] The Swiss practiced *Gemeinschaft*; the English, not knowing the meaning of *Gesellschaft*, equated it with wagering. The elision would have profound consequences.

In 1997 Robin Potts QC, a leading English barrister, was asked by the International Swaps and Derivatives Association (ISDA) to review the new market in credit default swaps. Were participants in this market the modern counterparts of the gentlemen of Lloyd's—engaged in a wager? Or were the buyers and sellers of credit default swaps more akin to the Swiss villagers, sharing the risks of disease and disasters?

Mr Potts expressed Michel Albert's distinction in legal terms. He drew attention to the famous case of Carlill *v.* Carbolic Smoke Ball Company. In 1892 a race-going judge, Sir Henry Hawkins, defined the meaning of a wager in English law as 'a contract by which two persons, professing to hold opposite views touching the issue of a future uncertain event, mutually agree that dependent on the determination of that event one shall win from the other'.[11] Insurance is different. The essence of insurance is (in Mr Potts' less felicitous words) 'a contract to indemnify the insured in respect of some interest which he has against the perils which he contemplates he will be liable to'.[12]

Having defined these terms, Mr Potts delivered the answer the ISDA hoped for and expected: these instruments were neither insurance (in which case they would have been taxed and regulated as insurance policies) nor wagers (in which case they would have been taxed and regulated as bets). Under English law as it was until 2005, these betting contracts would not have been legally enforceable. Counsel's opinion does not have the legal status of a court ruling, but neither regulatory nor fiscal authorities sought to challenge Mr Potts' view. Most credit default swap contracts were subsequently made under English law, providing a profitable activity for London lawyers. Some doubt remained as to the legality of such transactions for US residents, but this was settled by the Commodity Futures Modernization Act of 2000, promoted by Fed Chairman Alan Greenspan and by now Treasury Secretary Larry Summers.[13] Mr Potts deftly avoided the question of the motive for trading a credit default swap, a question to which I shall return in Chapter 4.

These two strands in the historic development of risk markets—laying bets on the interpretation of incomplete information, and the socialisation of individual risks—are still at the centre of how risk and insurance markets operate today. And, astonishingly, London and Switzerland remain key centres of the global insurance market. The villagers have descended from alpine meadows to the impressively prosperous urban centres of Zurich and Munich. The iconic Lloyd's building—designed by

Richard Rogers and perhaps the most striking of all City of London office buildings—is barely a hundred yards from the place where Edward
Lloyd's customers first smelt the coffee. And Lloyd's is still the principal
global location for marine insurance.

In the twentieth century both Lloyd's and the Swiss/German industry were primarily re-insurance markets. A policyholder's insurer will
normally handle the routine administration of premiums and claims,
but large losses are ceded, at an appropriate price, to re-insurers with
specialist risk evaluation skills. Even in the late twentieth century the
organisational form reflected the historic origins. Lloyd's was supported
by its 'names': (mostly) English individuals of means and social standing
who hoped to derive a regular income from profitable underwriting but
put their personal wealth on the line to meet any losses. Munich Re and
Swiss Re were financial behemoths, pooling risks globally and maintaining large capital reserves to meet future losses.

At Lloyd's the coffee-house tradition continued with business conducted in 'the Room'. The *Lutine* Bell at its centre reflected the maritime
history. (The bell had been salvaged from a bullion ship, the *Lutine*, that
had sunk in 1799 and was rung once to signify a wreck and twice to record
a safe return.) A broker placing a risk would attempt to find a lead underwriter willing to accept a substantial portion of it: if the lead underwriter
was well regarded, others would follow on behalf of their own 'names'.
This mixture of co-operation and competition encouraged individual
underwriters to develop specialist skills and to share the responsibility
for detailed diligence of individual risks. This practice of syndication was
equally common in the sharing of large loans among major banks.

By the 1980s, however, 'the Room' was becoming a trading floor
like those of other exchanges. If you can earn profit by selling re-
insurance contracts, you can also earn profit by selling contracts for the
re-insurance of re-insurance. You could even create contracts for the
re-insurance of re-insurance of re-insurance. And so on. The outcome was
a nexus of contracts known as the LMX spiral, so elaborate and complex
that it was simply impossible to ascertain the underlying risks to which
the holder was exposed. When the Piper Alpha oil rig went on fire in the
North Sea in 1987, killing 200 people and triggering what was then the
world's largest marine insurance claim, underwriting names who had
never heard of Piper Alpha discovered they had re-insured it over and

over again. The total value of claims at Lloyd's turned out to be ten times the value of the underlying loss.

The trade in risk that had occurred was not the spreading of risk on more and broader shoulders. The operator of the rig, Occidental Petroleum, was better placed to assess, monitor and accept the risk than those people who ultimately had to pay for the costs of the accident. Some 'names' suffered losses on a scale that forced the sale of their homes and ruined their lives. There were reports of suicides. The trade in risk that had occurred was between people who had some understanding of what they were doing—and of the nature of the risk—and people who did not. It was the world of Colbert and Ruskin, not that of Friedman and Greenspan. Far from spreading risk and placing it in the hands of people well placed to manage it, the LMX spiral concentrated it in the hands of people who had no capacity to manage it at all.[14]

A Lloyd's underwriter denounced to me in extravagant language the ignorance and incompetence of the agents who had promoted these structures and brought Lloyd's close to collapse. Why, I asked, had he not blown the whistle on the individuals concerned? He looked at me with a pitying gaze and simply said: because they were willing to buy risks at a price at which I was delighted to sell them. The Native Americans who sold Manhattan to Peter Minuit no doubt had the same self-satisfied look on their face.

And so did 'Fabulous Fab' Tourre. A decade after Mr Potts had given his opinion on those newly established collateralised debt obligations, Fabrice Tourre was selling synthetic CDOs (you don't really want to know) based on sub-prime mortgages to the clients of Goldman Sachs. He described the securities—called Abacus—to a girlfriend:

> I had some input into the creation of this product (which by the way is a product of pure intellectual masturbation, the type of thing which you invent telling yourself 'Well, what if we created a "thing," which has no purpose, which is absolutely conceptual and highly theoretical and which nobody knows how to price?').[15]

The Securities and Exchange Commission took a rather less colourful view of the trade. 'Mr Tourre put together a complex financial product that was secretly designed to maximise the likelihood that it would fail', it concluded.[16] Collateralised debt obligations were bought, and credit default swaps sold, by people who made mistakes in their assessment of the underlying value of these securities. That is why they bought or sold them. In most cases they did not really know what the securities were or how the payments would be determined. The growth of the market for credit default swaps followed closely the pattern set by the LMX spiral. Risky loans were bundled into packages, which were then split and re-arranged into new packages, to a point at which no one could know the underlying nature of the security that had been offered or the revenues on which the returns were based.

By the time 'Fabulous Fab' Tourre was promoting the Abacus transaction, it was perfectly clear what a hedge fund manager like John Paulson was doing (the product had been designed to his requirements, and he made billions from this and related trades). He was engaged in what Sir Henry Hawkins had identified a century earlier as a wager. Those who bought Fab's products, and took the losing side of Paulson's transaction, were also wagering. Paulson and the buyers of the Abacus securities held opposite views on the issue of a future uncertain event, the ability and willingness of mortgagors to meet their obligations, and agreed that one should win from the other on the determination of that event.

There is a paradox here. 'Ketchup economists', like others in the financial sector, emphasise the essentially unique characteristics of the field they study. But their analysis of risk aligns markets for risk with markets for other commodities. By doing this, they fail to acknowledge the fundamental difference that does exist between financial markets and markets for other commodities. Markets for securities are, in large part, based on differences in information, or perceptions of information, between the two parties to the transaction, rather than on differences in preferences and capabilities. This observation helps to explain both why finance can be, or can appear to be, inordinately profitable, and why that profitability need bear no relation to the value added from financial activities.

## Chasing the Dream

> When the capital development of a country becomes a by-product of the activities of a casino, the job is likely to be ill-done.
>
> J.M. KEYNES, *The General Theory of Employment, Interest and Money*, 1936

A lottery ticket, which millions of people buy each week, is a wager. Cynics have advised that you would do well to buy your ticket at the last minute, because otherwise the probability that you will die before the draw is greater than the probability that you will win the headline prize.

But that calculation misunderstands the nature of the activity. Lottery ticket-holders are buying a dream, and the longer they can hold the dream the more they benefit. A famously silly experiment showed that students would pay substantially more to receive a kiss from their favourite film star in three days' time than in three hours, or one year.[17] And when the lottery patrons lose, as they mostly do, they can sustain the dream by promising themselves that they will buy a ticket again next week. 'It could be you' was the well-judged slogan with which Britain's national lottery was launched.

Promoters have learned through experience how to design an attractive lottery product. A few very large prizes establish the dream. A large number of very small prizes encourage customers to maintain the belief that 'It could be you'. Even games of pure chance are more popular if you create an impression that the player can influence the outcome by choosing the numbers, placing the card or pulling the lever of the one-armed bandit. Flying in a commercial aircraft is much safer than driving one's own car: but we do not see it this way. We feel less vulnerable to risk if we have some element of control.

Most people think they are better drivers than average, better lovers than average, better most things than average. The shares we own are likely to go up, the fund managers we employ are the best, the advisers we use are shrewd. It would be surprising if many people did not think their partners were more attractive than average. Of course they are. That is why we hire our favoured fund managers, own these stocks and marry our spouses.

Many financial promotions exploit the control illusion and the excessive confidence people have in their own judgement. The most common means of chasing the dream is to believe that savers can successfully identify market highs or lows, or select stocks or managers that will out-perform the market. The overwhelming evidence is that they can't. Few investors or managers have any sustained capacity for out-performance.[18] Actively managed funds, taken as a whole, do worse than market averages by the amount of the fees charged. Retail investors do even worse than the average of investment funds by mistiming their purchases and sales. As with games involving mixtures of skill and chance, such as poker, there are a few people with genuinely outstanding abilities who profit at the expense of the general run of players, and many more who persuade themselves, and perhaps others, that recent runs of good fortune are the result of their exceptional skill.

These characteristics—chasing the dream, liking for control, bias towards optimism—have been repeatedly identified in experiments in what has become the popular subject of behavioural finance since the psychologist Daniel Kahneman was awarded the Nobel Prize for economics in 2002. Much of this literature, in a patronising tone, describes such behaviour as irrational.[19] But there is nothing irrational, in any ordinary sense of the word, about dreams, optimism or liking for control: few of us would make it through life if we did not imagine the future, take an optimistic view and try to take control of our fate. The lottery takes advantage of these behavioural characteristics for both public benefit and private profit. People who buy lottery tickets enjoy the thought that they might win. They mostly do not, except in a trivial sense, regret their purchase even when they lose. They are not making a mistake in chasing the dream.

In a considerable feat of persuasive marketing, economists have claimed ownership of the term 'rationality'. Rationality is defined as conforming to the axioms of economic models—and in the context of uncertainty such 'rationality' has a particularly strict—and complex—interpretation. 'Rational' people judge uncertain situations by attaching probabilities to the various outcomes, and they revise these probabilities in the light of the new information they constantly receive. They don't 'chase the dream', because they weigh outcomes by the likelihood they will actually occur. Rational people are able to assess all possible outcomes and attach probabilities to them. Rational people are free of bias towards optimism or control illusion. If they hold 'rational expectations', the outcomes of their risky choices will be validated by the relative frequency of events.

Not much introspection is required to see that most people don't behave that way. But the assumption that this way of thinking predominates is the basis of 'the Greenspan doctrine'. Robert Rubin, a deeper thinker than Greenspan, had emphasised the need for probabilistic thinking in his memoir of his time as Treasury secretary, *In an Uncertain World*.[20] And yet the very title of Rubin's book elides the critical distinction between risk—the known unknowns which we can describe with the aid of probabilities—and the 'unknown unknowns' or 'black swans'[21]—events to which we cannot assign probabilities because we may not even know what the events in question are. You cannot judge the probability of the invention of the wheel because in visualising the possibility you have already invented it.

In the 1920s John Maynard Keynes (whose Fellowship dissertation at Cambridge concerned probability) and Frank Knight had stressed the pervasive nature of the radical uncertainty of unknown unknowns. But Keynes and Knight effectively lost an intellectual battle with those— led by a Cambridge philosopher Frank Ramsey and another Chicago academic, L.J. Savage—who contended that the scope of probabilistic reasoning could be expanded more or less indefinitely. In Greenspan's famously apologetic testimony to Congress in October 2008, the former chairman seemed to acknowledge the limitations of the approach developed by Ramsey and Savage, which had by then become the basis of financial economics:

> In recent decades, a vast risk management and pricing system has evolved, combining the best insights of mathematicians and finance experts, supported by major advances in computer and communications technology. A Nobel Prize was awarded for discovery of the pricing model that underpins much of the advance in derivative markets. The modern risk management paradigm held sway for decades. The whole intellectual edifice, however, collapsed in the summer of last year.[22]

Yet, rather oddly, Greenspan went on to say that the reason for this collapse of this intellectual edifice was not its conceptual flaws but the numbers used. The problem was simply that 'the data inputted into the risk management models generally covered only the past two decades'.[23] Five years later, he was ready to recognise that the issue was more fundamental. In an interview with the *Financial Times*, he acknowledged that he had lost faith in 'the presumption of neoclassical economics that

people act in rational self-interest . . . the whole structure of risk evaluation—what they call the "Harry Markowitz approach"—failed'.[24]

Greenspan may have moved on, but most financial economists have
not. One reason why the model behind the Greenspan doctrine has a
powerful hold had been put forward most clearly by Frank Ramsey[25]
in that 1920s debate. If you don't behave 'rationally', you can be 'Dutch-
booked'—an offensive phrase (to the Dutch—the origins of the expression seem lost in the mists of time) which means that others can devise
strategies that will make money at your expense. Many economists use
this argument to insist that people *do* behave 'rationally'—behaviour
which does not conform to the model will be abandoned because those
who engage in it lose money. I used this reasoning myself with students. But I now see it differently. People do buy lottery tickets, week
after week, and they do so for reasons that seem entirely valid to them.
People don't behave—for both good and bad reasons—in line with the
economic model of rationality. In consequence others *do* devise strategies that make money at their expense. That consequence is critical to an
understanding of how financial markets operate today.

The models that have been developed in financial economics are
wide-ranging, and often technically ingenious. They include the Markowitz model of portfolio allocation (to which Greenspan referred) and
the Black–Scholes model (the derivative pricing model to which he al-
luded). The key components of academic financial theory, however, are
the 'efficient market hypothesis' (EMH), for which Eugene Fama won
the Nobel Prize in 2013, and the Capital Asset Pricing Model (CAPM),
for which William Sharpe won the Nobel Prize in 1990. Sharpe shared
that prize with Markowitz, and Myron Scholes received a Nobel Prize
in 1997, just before the famous blow-up of Long-Term Capital Management, in which Scholes was a partner; Black had died in 1995. All of
these financial economists have affiliations to the University of Chicago.

EMH asserts that all available information about securities is 'in the
price'. Interest rates are expected to rise, Procter & Gamble owns many
powerful brands, the Chinese economy is growing rapidly: these factors
are fully reflected in the current level of long-term interest rates, the
Procter & Gamble stock price and the exchange rate between the dollar
and the renminbi. Since everything that is already known is 'in the price',

only things that are *not* already known can influence the price. In an efficient market prices will therefore follow what is picturesquely described as a 'random walk'—the next move is as likely to be up as down. And since everything that is known is in the price, that price will represent the best available estimate of the underlying value of a security.

A small further step of analogous reasoning leads to the 'no arbitrage' condition: each security is appropriately priced in relation to all other securities, so that it is never possible to make money by selling one and buying another. The Black–Scholes model, and the whole subsequent development of quantitative models in derivative markets, relies on that assumption. The 'no arbitrage' condition was what Summers had in mind when he derided financial economists as people who ask whether two-quart bottles of ketchup sell for twice the price of one-quart bottles without taking an interest in how the price of ketchup is itself determined.

The legendary investor Warren Buffett presented the best summary critique of the efficient market hypothesis: 'Observing correctly that the market was frequently efficient, they (academics, investment professionals and corporate managers) went on to conclude that it was always efficient. The difference between these propositions is night and day.'[26] Or, in Buffett's case, a $50 billion fortune. EMH is based on an assumption—widely used in economic analysis—that all available profit opportunities, in securities markets and in business, have been taken.

In finance and business, most available profit opportunities *have* been taken. But trading in financial markets, and innovation in business, are directed to the search for profit opportunities that *have not* been taken. The efficient market hypothesis at once captures an important aspect of reality—the absence of easy profits—and neglects an equally fundamental one: that the search for profits that are not easy is the dynamic of a capitalist system. Henry Ford, Walt Disney and Steve Jobs were not attempting to exploit arbitrage opportunities but trying to change the world (as were many less successful entrepreneurs).

The wise investor will think twice before rejecting the efficient market hypothesis. Yet the volume of trading we observe in securities markets today would be wholly inexplicable if the hypothesis that all information relevant to security valuation is already in the price were true. There is a logical contradiction at the heart of EMH. If all information were already in the price, what incentive would there be to gather such information in the first place?

The capital asset pricing model takes the logic of EMH a stage further. The CAPM describes the equilibrium of an efficient market populated by rational agents each holding similar expectations. The financial journalist Justin Fox recounts the birth of the CAPM: its originator, Bill Sharpe, recognised the implausibility of the scenario he postulated, and his article was initially rejected for publication on precisely those grounds—the model assumptions were unduly fanciful.[27] Yet within a short time the CAPM was treated as descriptive of real markets. One evening, in discussion with a former student, now himself a professor of finance, I was asked: 'If you no longer believe in the CAPM, what do you believe in?' The attraction of the CAPM is that it provides clear answers to the question 'How are securities prices determined?'—and the availability of an answer, which is perceived to give financial economics claim to scientific objectivity, overrides the observation that the answer is not correct.

More realistic alternatives to the CAPM are necessarily messy, *ad hoc*, pragmatic. They need to accommodate disequilibrium, inefficiency that leaves profit opportunities on the table, and imperfect information which different people will interpret in different ways. They need to allow for control illusion and recognise that people chase their dreams.

Probabilistic reasoning does not play a large part in our lives because the situations in which it can usefully be applied are limited. We deal with radical uncertainty through storytelling, by constructing narratives. Steve Jobs' biographer, Walter Isaacson, wrote of his subject's 'reality distortion field', and the same phrase might equally have been applied to Ford or Disney.[28]

This, not the Panglossian world of 'the Greenspan doctrine', is the world in which business is conducted and securities are traded. The reality of market behaviour, as the psychologist David Tuckett recorded in his interviews, makes little use of probabilistic thinking but relies on conviction narratives—stories that traders tell themselves, and reinforce in conversation with each other. Such narratives are the means by which we cope with radical uncertainty—the unknown unknowns—that characterise not just business and securities markets but every aspect of our lives.

We all chase the dream, but when taken to excess by individuals or in crowds, the chasing of dreams becomes madness. And chasing the dream with other people's money is at best irresponsible and often fraudulent. Gambling is everywhere closely regulated because the organisation of gambling is an activity attractive to fraudsters and crooks; because gambling leads people to make bad decisions which can destroy their finances and their lives and damage their friends and families; because uncontrolled gambling will increase society's exposure to risk. And so it is with wagering in financial markets.

The occupants of Lloyd's coffee house did not just gamble on tides and ships. In a manner that anticipated the future extension of the scope of derivatives securities they would gamble on anything—on the longevity of King George, or the fate of Admiral Byng, the hapless commander who was supposedly executed 'pour encourager les autres'. The obvious undesirability of such wagering led in 1774 to a prohibition of bets on a person's life—unless it could be shown that the individual would have an 'insurable interest', to which Mr Potts referred, in the life of the individual concerned. A similar prohibition on wagering without insurable interest might have restricted the growth of credit default swaps before they became too much of a good thing.

Some jurisdictions have attempted comprehensive prohibitions on wagering. Mostly this is unsuccessful. The human propensity to gamble is too strong: prohibition of gambling has turned the industry into a magnet for organised crime—as prohibition did with other industries, such as prostitution and trade in alcohol. The most successful strategies to regulate gambling have involved rigorous appraisal of the character of individuals and organisations involved, the exclusion of criminals by intolerance of any hint of impropriety, and consumer protection rules aimed principally at proscribing misleading description.

But a better strategy still has been to channel gambling into harmless, even irrelevant, activities—such as horse-racing and lotteries—and limit the opportunities for addicted gamblers, or even those who enjoy a mild flutter, to indulge their habits in ways that have consequences for economic efficiency. And most importantly of all, to proscribe gambling with other people's money. These key insights were discarded as financialisation exalted the role of the trader and the overseers of the financial world assured each other that activities which in reality represented irresponsible gambling constituted a new era of sophisticated risk management.

## Adverse Selection and Moral Hazard

Regrets, I've had a few
But then again, too few to mention. . . .

FRANK SINATRA, 'My Way', lyrics by Paul Anka, 1968

I wake up every single night thinking what could I have done differently. And this has been going on, what could I have done differently, certain conversations, what could I have said, what should I have done? I have searched myself every single night. I come back to at the time—and that's why I said this in the beginning—at the time I made those decisions, I made those decisions with the information I had.

DICK FULD, former CEO, Lehman Bros, testifying to the<br>House of Representatives Oversight Committee, 6 October 2008

Bernanke, Geithner, Kohn and Summers had variously applauded at Jackson Hole what they perceived as the increased ability of the financial system to reduce and spread risk. Then the jets and limos sped them back to their Washington and New York offices. If they had stopped on the way in Main Street to ask 'Do you think that financial innovation in the last twenty years has made the world less risky?', the respondents would have thought the financial superstars had taken leave of their senses.

Greenspan claimed, with the support of his colleagues, that the effect of such innovation was to allocate risk to those investors most able and willing to take it. This proposition was wrong on two levels. The immediate mistake was to believe that the risk transfer he saw represented insurance rather than wagering. Its purpose and effect was not to spread risk more effectively by passing it to those better equipped to handle it, but to dump it on those who understood less about it. Risks were not more, but less, effectively managed as a result of the transfer.

But the larger mistake was to suppose that the risks under discussion at Jackson Hole were the risks that mattered in the first place. The error emerges immediately on parsing Summers' analogy between modern financial innovation and advances in transport. Successive waves of innovation in transport have brought us railways, cars and planes. These innovations have transformed the daily lives of ordinary people. No one could say the same of forward exchange rates, credit default swaps or collateralised debt obligations. The risks that engaged the Jackson Hole symposium—securities default, changing share values, fluctuating exchange rates—do not impinge significantly on Main Street. All of them are risks generated within the financial system itself.

The risks that do concern Main Street are different. They are risks associated with redundancy and unemployment. The pedestrians on Main Street fear accident, illness and mortality, and worry about provision for old age. Relationship breakdown is costly financially as well as personally. These risks are not dealt with through securities markets: they are mostly handled outside the financial system altogether. Such risks are dealt with—to the extent that they are dealt with at all—by social institutions: by friends and family, and by government and its agencies.

Market institutions cannot manage these risks, except at the margin. The reasons come under the headings of asymmetric information, adverse selection and moral hazard. You cannot insure against divorce because couples know more about the state of their relationship than any insurer. Happily married couples will not seek divorce insurance: the unhappily married will. The premiums will reflect this dichotomy, with the result that such insurance will seem attractive only to those whose marriage is already on the rocks. Asymmetry of information and adverse selection are so pervasive that no divorce insurance market can exist.

And since fear of the financial consequences of separation is one of the factors that keep unhappy couples together, the incidence of divorce would rise if such insurance existed. If you insure people against unemployment, the insurer will find that customers are mostly those who know that they are at risk of being fired, or who fear that their employer might go under, and when they make a claim they will be less anxious to secure new employment.

Moral hazard is the tendency of people to take more risk when they are protected against it. When single mothers were harshly treated, there were fewer of them, because people adapt to the social and economic conditions in which they find themselves. The patchy evidence we have suggests that the risk of violent or accidental death in England has remained roughly constant since the thirteenth century: 'The axe of the drinking companion and the neighbour's open well were regulated, to be replaced by unruly horses and unbridged streams; when these were brought under control it was the turn of unfenced industrial machinery and unsignalled locomotives; today we battle with the drunken driver.'[29]

Given the changes in the economic and natural environment over the period, this constancy is extraordinary. The geographer John Adams has coined the metaphor of the 'risk thermostat': we have a certain tolerance for risk and adjust our behaviour accordingly.[30] Fewer children are killed in road accidents today than eighty years ago: although traffic has increased very substantially, precautions taken by children and their parents have fully offset this.

The issue of moral hazard takes on particular importance in the financial sector in the context of 'too big to fail' banks. Critics of bail-outs complain that public indemnity of the liabilities of risk-taking financial institutions encourages these institutions to take more risk. This is a complex issue. It is unlikely that the chief executives of failed banks thought, 'I needn't worry about running my institution into the ground because the government will see the creditors right.' Still, the sense that Central Banks and Treasuries act as backstop has influence on the behaviour of a firm: Dick Fuld of Lehman was delusional both about the risks in his business and in his belief that Lehman both should and would receive support if it ran into financial difficulties. If Fuld had not made these errors, he would have made greater efforts to sell Lehman's business before it collapsed.

But the more serious problem of moral hazard is its impact on those who deal with banks. If potential creditors know that they will be made whole, then they have little incentive to undertake careful credit assessment. In the sub-prime mortgage fiasco such moral hazard arose at every level. Fannie Mae and Freddie Mac, the failed US mortgage agencies, could not conceivably have built their enormous, and severely under-capitalised, balance sheets had their lenders not believed (correctly, as it turned out) that their liabilities were guaranteed by the US government. 'Too big to fail' takes responsibility for the supervision of credit risks away from market participants and places it more or less exclusively in the hands of regulators: a duty that in this instance (and many others) they were not capable of discharging.

The term 'moral hazard' is perhaps unfortunate, because moral hazard is about incentives, not about ethics: about deterrence rather than punishment. Tim Geithner appeared to have missed this point—his memoir makes frequent dismissive reference to concern for moral hazard, almost invariably accompanied by a disparaging reference to 'Old Testament fundamentalists'.[31] Presumably this is with the intention of contrasting the retributive ethos of the Old Testament with the forgiveness found in the New. Many might feel retribution rather than forgiveness appropriate for those responsible for the global financial crisis. But those who worry about moral hazard are not motivated by revenge. Moral hazard in its application to the banking system is the well-founded concern that, if there is an expectation of government assistance for troubled financial businesses, the people who run and trade with these businesses will behave in ways that make the need for such assistance more likely.

In Michel Albert's Swiss village, community pressures handled the problems of information asymmetry, adverse selection and moral hazard. Information asymmetry was reduced, though not necessarily eliminated, by geographical proximity and personal ties. The obligation to participate was informed by the link between economic and social life, and for most it was no obligation at all. Some people were better guardians of their herds than others, some shirked their responsibilities, and others discharged them more than conscientiously, but these differences were ignored in the interests of maintaining a harmonious community.

Insurance markets exist for risks that involve a substantial degree of randomness—which reduces the problem of information asymmetry, and where the insured has limited influence over the incidence of risk—which reduces the effect of moral hazard. We can insure against car accidents, against our house burning down, against dying prematurely or against living too long. But these perils represent only a fraction of the risks that we face every day—and our ability to insure against even these is jeopardised by the ever-increasing capacity to assemble and analyse large data sets which may enable us to predict illness and death from genetic and environmental information. Wholly private insurance is possible only when knowledge is sufficiently imperfect to allow the pooling of random, independent events.

Since these conditions are rarely satisfied, risk in modern societies is managed by a mix of private and social institutions. Group

insurance—typically provided by employers—largely solves the problem of adverse selection by the insured. Some degree of compulsion—
enforced by law, group membership or social solidarity—is necessary to
establish pools of risk sufficiently broad for risk to be shared effectively.
Public intervention in the insurance market limits the ability of insurers to underwrite by reference to the specific characteristics of individual
risks. These interventions will need to increase in scope if private markets
in insurance, especially for health and life-expectancy, are to continue.

But the reasons why everyday risks are managed by risk pools with
common interests go deeper than the deficiencies of economic markets.
The Swiss villagers were not simply looking for a way to reduce the
individual costs of risk. They were expressing shared social concern: a
sense that a misfortune suffered by one individual or household was, to
some extent, a misfortune suffered by the village as a whole. 'No man
is an island . . . therefore never send to know for whom the bell tolls; it
tolls for thee.'[32] Decent societies do not give people the option of being
unable to afford necessary medical treatment, or of finding themselves
destitute in old age, even if these options have in some sense been chosen by the individuals themselves. Or at least enough people feel that
way to make it impossible, even if it were practicable, to implement
solutions to the challenges of everyday risk based exclusively on personal choices and market solutions.

The impassioned dispute over 'Obamacare' is perhaps the last skir-
mish in the battle to provide universal healthcare throughout the developed world. In other countries this issue is no longer contested, although
the precise mechanisms and the levels of provision vary. Private health
insurers, where they exist, are generally either social agencies or organisations that pool risks on behalf of employers. In many countries there
is some top-up provision through a genuinely private insurance market,
mostly aimed at providing extra amenities and convenience rather than
necessary medical treatment. The expectation that modern advanced
societies will assure everyone a minimum standard of living makes social provision and regulation inevitable. What that level should be, and
what conditions should be imposed on those who receive that state support, are matters that will reflect the different values prevailing at different times in different places. These expectations change from time to
time and from generation to generation.

The extended family has become a less powerful source of social support in personal misfortune, although it is still the principal mechanism for dealing with the most important 'new' risk of personal life: the risk of requiring lengthy periods of care in our extended lifespan. This seems in principle the kind of risk to which a private market solution is suited, but financial institutions have as yet made little effort to cater for this need.

Large employers used to provide substantial protection against risk for their employees. My contemporaries who joined 'the Bank' or 'the Royal Bank' expected to spend their career in these institutions. They did not think there was much risk that their job would disappear, and if it did, they expected that the company would find another role for them. They would enjoy a comfortable retirement, with a decent pension. If they became ill, they would be treated generously: if they died, there would be a pension for their spouse. Most big companies provided these benefits, and so did almost all public sector employers.

Few of these perks remain, at least in the financialised societies of Britain and the USA. There are no jobs for life in the private sector. Private-sector final salary pension schemes have closed, and employees must rely on their own contributions (still usually supplemented by employers) and the vagaries of the stock market for their retirement pension. Employers have greater statutory obligations to the sick and disabled, but are less inclined to do more than is legally required of them. In the public sector the retreat has been less dramatic, but the direction of travel is the same. Privatisation has over time reduced or removed many of the protections that public-sector workers once enjoyed. I will return in Chapter 9 to the most important of these changes in the risk environment facing individuals: the changes in pension provision.

These shifts are primarily the result of the effect of financialisation on corporate behaviour. The ICI of 1987, with its dedication to 'the responsible application of chemistry and related sciences' and its commitment to the welfare of its employees and the communities it served, naturally embraced these wider responsibilities to its employees. The modern ICI, focused on creating value for its shareholders, did not. And even if it had continued to acknowledge such commitments, it does not matter anymore. ICI no longer exists.

The main protections against everyday risks come from family support and state-sponsored mutualisation. Public tax and benefit systems assume most of the obligations that were once handled semi-voluntarily in Swiss villages. Social security provides support in the event of unemployment, disability, old age and long-term care. Governments underwrite the provision of low-cost housing. By these means, and through direct family support, the state helps to deal with the costs of relationship breakdown. Public agencies respond to fires, floods and other national catastrophes. Such arrangements are typically public/private partnerships, with governments offering emergency response and private insurers having a larger role in long-term clean-up.

As the symposium proceeded at Jackson Hole, Hurricane Katrina was about to sweep into New Orleans. It would kill 2,000 people and inflict $100 billion of property damage. But that was not the kind of risk that the participants had in mind when they reassured themselves that risk management had reached new levels of sophistication. They were concerned with the risks associated with volatile securities prices. Three years later Hurricane Lehman would sweep through Wall Street, demonstrating that the buffers of regulation were no more secure than the levees of the Mississippi delta.

Paradoxically, the Jackson Hole attendees who were seduced by the explanatory power of probabilistic models of rational behaviour were themselves in the grip of a conviction narrative—none more so than Chairman Greenspan, a one-time associate of Ayn Rand. David Tuckett the psychologist had anticipated their response to Rajan's challenge: 'The doubts they (sceptics) raise about the new story need to be refuted and so are mocked and maligned through dismissal.'[33] The great muckraker Upton Sinclair had expressed a deep insight into the relationship between the world of ideas and the world of practical men: 'It is difficult to get a man to understand something, when his salary depends on his not understanding it.'[34]

Chapter 3 will describe another idea central to financialisation: the perceived need for liquidity. The Jackson Hole participants discussed risk with the aid of a well-worked-out framework of analysis with impressive intellectual coherence (if little empirical relevance). But when they—and others—discussed liquidity, they did so in a context with all the clarity of Mississippi mud.

# Intermediation

## The Role of the Middleman

> There are some men whose only mission among others is to act as inter-
> mediaries; one crosses them like bridges and keeps going.
>
> GUSTAVE FLAUBERT, *Sentimental Education*, 1869

Commercial activity is based on exchange. But most exchange benefits from the services of intermediaries. Consumers are fragmented, dispersed and often ill-informed about the properties of the goods and services they buy. They need supermarkets and doctors, car salesmen and travel agents, Google and Amazon, if they are to trade with confidence.

These intermediaries perform a variety of functions. They provide logistics—delivering goods and services from producer to consumer. They identify the goods and services consumers are likely to want, and seek out the best and lowest-cost producers. They manage the supply chain, helping to avoid surpluses and shortages. They may provide information and advice to help us make good purchasing decisions.

Finance presents itself as a uniquely complex mechanism of intermediation. The arcane mysteries of finance are tantalisingly and partially revealed by business channels such as CNBC. Financial law, financial regulation and financial (ketchup) economics are distinctive areas of specialism and study. And, not coincidentally, remuneration in finance is dramatically higher than in any other business. But the services we want from financial intermediaries are very similar to the services we want from other intermediaries. Financial intermediaries need to provide logistics—to deliver services from the producer to the consumer. Financial intermediaries should identify the goods and services consumers want, and seek out the best and lowest-cost producers. Financial intermediaries need to ensure a reliable supply chain, free of surpluses and shortages. Financial intermediaries need to provide information and advice to enable users to make good purchasing decisions. Financial intermediaries need to do well the things that Walmart does well.

The internet has changed the nature of intermediation. Making connections is far simpler: a distributor in Connecticut can contact a supplier in remote China. Advice is plentiful, though its quality is variable and uncertain. And financial services (like music and travel tickets, but few other commodities) can be delivered electronically as well as ordered electronically.

Some enthusiasts have claimed that new technologies will eliminate intermediary functions. But connectedness, which the internet delivers so effectively, is only one of the functions of the intermediary. The greater ease of making connections increases the need to monitor these connections. Facebook illustrates how a broader range of relationships diminishes their average quality. Recent financial innovations, such as crowd-funding and peer-to-peer lending, cannot eliminate financial intermediation. If savers are to obtain returns that match the risks they take, they need to be able to judge how their money is used and how the assets purchased with that money are managed. Few have the time, knowledge or experience to do this. Cynicism born of experience is required to find the few viable opportunities among many optimistic business plans. Or to identify those who are likely to repay their debts, among compelling promises and persuasive hard luck stories. It helps a lot to meet people face to face.

Not all intermediation is useful: the tourist guide who directs us to his uncle's carpet shop; the fixer who provides no valuable service but can frustrate a transaction if he does not receive a cut; the doctor who recommends a battery of tests we do not know we do not need. Bad intermediaries exaggerate their own skill and our need for their services by imposing complexity on us—lawyers who baffle their clients with jargon, art dealers who talk a language we do not understand. The factors that make intermediation necessary leave consumers of intermediary services vulnerable. If we knew whether a lawyer's advice was good, we would probably not need the services of a lawyer.

Intermediation at its best hides a complex mechanism with a simple interface—like the face of a watch. Google is based on complex algorithms, but we do not need to understand them in order to search. The Walmart shopper has no conception of the elaborate supply chain behind the delivery and placement of every item in the store. The first personal computers required extensive programming skills to use and the ensuing personal computer revolution only became possible because highly skilled programmers created interfaces that allowed those with no knowledge of computers to use them. You can take a machine out of the box and connect to the internet or begin word-processing immediately.

Most everyday purchases are trades. When we shop for groceries, the supermarket owns its stock (which it has in turn bought from its suppliers), and when we pay at the till ownership of the goods is transferred to us. Other transactions are made through an agent. Most people sell houses through an estate agent, and buy insurance via a broker. The agent does not own the goods and services concerned, but earns a fee or commission for facilitating the transaction between buyer and seller. The agency model is more common for high-value, idiosyncratic transactions. The estate agent would need extensive capital resources to hold in stock the houses that he or she is instructed to sell, while buyers or sellers or both may value the services of the agent who ascertains their particular needs and seeks out the most appropriate means of meeting them. The trading model works well—and is used—for standardised, low-value products, especially where there are repeat purchases. Competition between sellers benefits consumers, and the costly services of an agent are unnecessary. Where information is imperfect, and the value of the goods is large, agency comes into its own.

The art market illustrates the full variety of commercial relationships. Auction houses act as agents for the seller. Galleries often act as agents for the artist, on commission. Or they may be selling pictures the gallery itself has bought. Sophisticated collectors usually employ agents to buy on their behalf.

Trading activities tend to be transparent: the gallery encourages you to wander and will answer questions, but you must yourself obtain the information you need to select the item you want. Agency is managed; the agent will have taken some of the responsibility—and perhaps the risk—associated with the choice. Intermediation may be direct—the intermediary is the primary link between buyer and seller—or indirect—a Rembrandt engraving will have been through many hands before yours. Trading transactions are typically impersonal, agency relationships typically personal.

All of these distinctions—between agency and trading, between transparent and managed intermediation, between direct and indirect intermediation—are significant, and will play a role in the chapters that follow. But none is necessarily clear-cut. An established trading relationship will begin to seem like an agency relationship: there is a sense of mutual obligation, and the seller will seek out goods or services which he or she thinks will be particularly suitable for the buyer.

The distinction between buyer/seller transactions and agency relationships has important legal and regulatory aspects. The American Legal Institute spells out the common law obligations of an agent to his or her principal.[1] The core obligations are those of performance and loyalty, and the requirements of loyalty are demanding—not to acquire a benefit from, or to act on behalf of, a third party, not to use information derived from the relationship for one's own purposes or benefit. Conflicts of interest should be avoided, or where unavoidable disclosed.

A degree of trust is essential to any intermediary relationship. We do not want to be advised by doctors who put *caveat emptor* on their brass plates. When trust is absent but products complex, as between buyers and sellers of used cars,[2] markets do not function well. The intermediary relationships we value most—the services of a capable doctor, access to a good supermarket, the reliability of a Google search—are those where trust in the intermediary is the result of our past experience. Trust can be established in both the trader and the agency model, but in markets where transactions are large and infrequent, regulation aimed at consumer protection can help support the development of reputations for honesty and reliability among producers. Well-conceived regulation can create an environment in which the twin mechanisms of regulation and reputation reinforce each other.

Transparency is a mantra in the modern world of finance. But the demand for transparency in intermediation is a sign that intermediation is working badly, not a means of making it work well. A happy motorist is one who need never look under the car bonnet. A good lawyer manages our problem; a bad lawyer responds to every issue by asking us what we want to do. When ill, we look for a recommended course of action, not a detailed description of our ailments and a list of references to relevant medical texts. The demand for transparency in finance is a symptom of the breakdown of trust.

Agency was the traditional norm in finance. Investors employed a broker or asset manager to handle their money. These were agency relations. Those old-fashioned bank managers were paternalistic, notorious for their caution. Company directors have specific legal duties towards shareholders and creditors. And agency stockbrokers did their best for their clients.

Regulated, managed agency, imposed by law and buttressed by regulation and practice, is the natural model for financial intermediation, but any strict application of the law of agency was overtaken by changes in regulation and practice. By the 1980s the broker–dealer was the norm. The temptation to do what is not the best for one's principal was to be handled not by refraining from placing oneself in such a situation but by denying that there was an agency relationship. Regulatory rules encouraged financial conglomerates to 'manage' conflicts of interest. We shall see that they did not try very hard.

The history of the mortgage market illustrates the transition from agency to trading that was a central characteristic of financialisation. From the 1980s subjective assessments based on the knowledge of both properties and borrowers which was held in branches of savings institutions were largely swept away in favour of computerised credit-scoring. Then the mortgages were packaged into securitised instruments which were themselves subject to credit evaluation by rating agencies using models derived from historic databases. Transactions replaced trust, trading replaced agency. US mortgage lending was probably the most extensive attempt to substitute mechanised assessment processes for face-to-face assessment.

The experiment ended badly. A systematic chain of misrepresentation developed from borrower to mortgage adviser, from adviser to lender, from lender to ratings agency and from sellers of mortgage-backed securities to suppliers of capital. The immediate impact was to lower the price and increase the availability of credit, since volume mattered more than quality. But in the long run, the effects were the reverse: price was higher and availability less. Lending institutions involved had deprived themselves of the trust, knowledge and skills necessary to manage mortgage provision effectively.

The costs and scale of intermediary activity grew very rapidly, the calibre and intellectual sophistication of people employed increased sharply, and new technologies became available to support their decisions. Yet the quality of intermediation was worse—much worse. This paradox was repeated across the whole financial sector. The explanation is that the new skills that were developed were skills that were related not to the needs of end-users but to the process of intermediation itself. People who traded mortgage-backed securities knew about securities, but very little about mortgages, and less about houses and home-buyers. People who traded shares knew about stock markets, but not about companies and their products. People who traded interest rate derivatives knew about derivatives, but not about politics and government finance.

The forces that led to these extensive failures in credit markets in 2007–8 had been evident earlier elsewhere. Robert Shiller received the Nobel Prize in economics for providing in the early 1980s the first careful demonstration of a proposition that seems intuitively obvious to anyone who watches stock markets: volatility is far greater than can be explained by changes in the fundamental value of securities. The 'explanations' provided nightly by market commentators and newspaper headlines are little more than rationalisation of the noise generated by this market volatility.[3]

Equity markets experienced more and more activity in secondary markets, while primary issuance had become less and less important.[4] Intermediaries in these markets knew less and less about the companies in which funds were invested, and expertise rested in knowing what 'the market thinks'.

It is common to anthropomorphise the market—to describe 'the mind of the market'. The market does not think, and the market knows only what individuals who trade in the market know. Anyone who comes from outside the financial sector to the world of trading is likely to be shocked by the superficiality of the traders' general knowledge. Those who deal in currencies often have knowledge of countries that barely

extends beyond national stereotypes of innovative Americans, indus-
trious Germans and lecherous Italians. Traders in government bonds
know little of finance or politics, and asset-backed securities are often
bought and sold in ignorance of the nature, and even greater ignorance
of the quality, of the underlying assets. Fund managers and investment
bankers deal in shares—or even buy and sell companies—with only a
rudimentary understanding of the businesses concerned, or of concepts
of business strategy.

Many senior executives talk privately with contempt of the analysts
who follow their company. The chief financial officers and investor relations personnel of large quoted companies engage with these analysts—
who are themselves one step removed from traders—in a process of
earnings guidance and earnings management that bears little relationship to the underlying business of the company.[5] Most of what is called
'research' in the financial sector would not be recognised as research
by anyone who has completed an undergraduate thesis, far less a PhD.
We do not fly an aeroplane by consensus of the views of the passengers:
instead we put our trust in a highly trained, skilled and well-informed
pilot. The failure of the mortgage market is only the most conspicuous
example of the consequences of replacing knowledgeable intermediation in favour of the supposed 'wisdom of crowds'.[6]

The aggregation of inconsequential information across large numbers of people amounts not to the 'wisdom of crowds' but to not very
much at all: the more so since the opinions that are aggregated are not
independently formed. The crowds that clamoured for the crucifixion
of Jesus, watched the tumbrels roll to the guillotine and stood to attention at Nuremberg rallies were not wise, but baying mobs reinforcing
the ignorant opinions of their neighbours. The trader typically knows
very little about the underlying characteristics of the securities he or
she trades, but a great deal about other traders, and what they currently
think. What 'the market thinks' may be little more than an accumulation of other traders' estimates of what other traders think—the process
famously satirised in Keynes' metaphor of the beauty contest, in which
judgements are based not on what is beautiful but on what others think
others think is beautiful.[7]

The misunderstanding of the nature of information processing in
markets is the fundamental flaw in the 'Greenspan doctrine', which sees

trade in risk and securities as similar to trade in milk and coffee. Financial economics mistook transactions based on differences in information and its interpretation for transactions based on differences in preferences and capabilities. Policymakers thought traders were in an alpine village when they were in Lloyd's coffee house.

Credit-scoring and carefully formulated accounting rules are valuable tools for financial intermediaries. The ability to compile, access and analyse large databases can, if properly harnessed, improve our understanding of both economic developments and the role the individuals and firms play in these developments. But these sources of information must complement, not replace, the traditional and still indispensable interpersonal skills of the effective financial intermediary. We need a modern intermediary sector that combines the experience and knowledgeable judgement of expert bankers and asset managers with the power of information technology. That is a very different environment from that of well-educated young white men baying for money and praying for liquidity.

## Liquidity

> And, sure, the reverent eye must see
> A Purpose in Liquidity.
>
> RUPERT BROOKE, *Heaven*, from *1914 and Other Poems*, 1915

In the Edinburgh of fifty years ago fresh milk was delivered daily. Except at Christmas. The milkman would make a double delivery on Christmas Eve. My father would ask each year how the cows were persuaded to produce twice as much milk. This feeble joke was part of our family Christmas ritual.

The dairy's problem was not, in fact, very difficult. The fresh milk was not so fresh: it had not come from the milking shed that morning. Stocks could be built up, or run down. In the days before Christmas milk that would normally have been sent to manufacture other dairy products was diverted to household use.

At ordinary times our demand for milk was stable. But sometimes we would have visitors and need extra milk. My mother would usually tell the milkman the day before, but if she forgot, the milkman would have extra supplies on his float to meet our needs. Of course, if all his customers did this, he wouldn't have been able to accommodate them. But that was never likely to happen—except at Christmas, and the dairy made contingency plans for that.

The ready availability of everyday produce is, in this sense, an illusion. But the concept of liquidity can be transferred from milk to finance. Bankers discovered that they need keep only a fraction of the deposits placed with them in ready cash. Depositors would believe that they could access their money whenever they liked, although if they all did so at the same time, they could not. The liquidity illusion in finance has a variety of forms and different names—maturity transformation, fractional reserve banking, and even 'money creation'. These esoteric terms contribute to the widespread notion that there is something mysterious and different about money, banking and finance.

Yet there is nothing special about the idea of a service available on demand if, and only if, not many people take advantage of that availability. My mother could always obtain an extra pint of milk; but if everyone on the milkman's round tried, most of them could not. I believe—correctly—that I can find a seat on a train to Edinburgh more or less any time I choose. Yet if any substantial fraction of the people who might board a train to Edinburgh actually did so, the platforms would be overwhelmed. If everyone in the country turned on their kettle simultaneously, none of them would be able to enjoy a cup of tea. The modern economy makes all kinds of promises that could not be fulfilled if many people chose to call on them. The fallacy of composition—inferring the properties of the whole from the properties of parts—is one of the most common errors in popular discussion of economics. What is feasible, or beneficial, in the small may be infeasible, or harmful, in aggregate.

And so it is with liquidity. The word is widely—almost obsessively—used in financial markets, but often without any precise or particular meaning. A casual search of investment dictionaries and encyclopaedias for definitions of liquidity will reveal as many definitions as sources. The concept of liquidity I will use draws on the homely analogy of the Christmas milk. Liquidity is the capacity of a supply chain to meet a sudden or exceptional demand without disruption. This capability is achieved, as it was by the milkman, in one or both of two ways: by maintaining stocks, and by the temporary diversion of supplies from other uses. When the supply chain lacks liquidity, consumers need to maintain stocks for themselves—they keep a spare pint of milk in the fridge. The financial analogue of the spare pint is the necessity for businesses and households to maintain monetary balances. In extreme cases of illiquidity, households end up hoarding cash under the bed. These supply chain inefficiencies may be costly, in both the milk supply chain and the money market.

The panic that ultimately closed the entire US banking system in 1933 was the result of widespread attempts by depositors to withdraw their deposits before the cash in the vaults was exhausted. But financial services are not unique in their vulnerability to runs. If people suspect there is not enough milk, they will queue to obtain whatever milk is available, and the fears of shortage will prove—temporarily—justified. This does happen for non-financial commodities, but not very often. Such dislocations are rare because consumers are confident, on the basis of experience, that there are sufficient stocks to meet even their exceptional needs. In the Soviet economy there was no such confidence, and queues were routine, not just because there was an actual insufficiency of supply—though there often was—but because consumers would rush to obtain whatever supplies were available.

And so with banks. A run on a solvent, liquid, well-capitalised and well-managed bank, in which unfounded panic among depositors creates an unnecessary crisis, is a theoretical possibility: but in practice it is as rare as a milk panic.

Even in times of financial distress there are widely dispersed supplies of cash and short-term credit available—in the hands of the public, and with large financial and non-financial corporations. Financial crises were traditionally handled by mobilising these resources. The central bank might provide funds itself as 'lender of last resort' and/or help orchestrate a rescue operation by other financial institutions. But as the sector became more aggressive and competitive such co-operation diminished. Perhaps the last great co-ordinated rescue operation—which involved much official twisting of private-sector arms—was the support package for the racy and absurdly named hedge fund Long-Term Capital Management in 1998. (The foul-mouthed Jimmy Cayne, of Bear Stearns, who refused to participate, would receive his come-uppance a decade later when the Federal Reserve took pleasure in forcing a fire-sale of his failing business to J.P. Morgan.)

But when banks came under pressure during the global financial crisis the problems were generally in the reality of the business, not in the imagination of depositors. The runs were the result of uncertainty about the underlying solvency of the companies and the quality of their assets. Lehman had run into trouble in commercial property (and in many other places), Fannie Mae was embroiled with sub-prime mortgages, HBoS and RBS had vied with each other to make terrible loans in the property sector, AIG had insured large quantities of complex securities that were destined to implode, and Sandy Weill's sprawling Citigroup had made mistakes all across its activities. All these companies had managed their businesses badly, and their capital bases were so small relative to the scale of their activities that they could not absorb even the most modest trading set-back.

In each case, the executives of the businesses concerned claimed that their problems stemmed not from solvency but from liquidity—that they were short of cash but that their business was basically sound. Similar claims are made by the executives of most failed organisations—if only our creditors and shareholders had shown sufficient patience, we would have survived. Businesses typically fail when the patience or credulity of creditors or shareholders is exhausted, and that was what happened to these financial companies.

Were these businesses solvent? Nobody knew: not depositors, not shareholders or regulators, not the management of the companies themselves. As we will see in Chapter 6, by 2008 the assets of banks were principally the liabilities of other banks, and vice versa. If the assets of banks are presumed to be safe, the liabilities of banks are secure. But such a structure is necessarily precarious; once the assets of banks cannot be presumed to be safe, the whole structure unravels, as it did in the global financial crisis. But before the crisis traders simply assumed that banks would always meet their obligations: and (to the limited extent that they thought about the matter at all) they expected that the government would stand behind these liabilities. This latter assumption proved to be generally correct. The scale of financial market activity today would be impossible without the expectation—now proven to be reality—that both the liquidity and the solvency of banks are underpinned by government.

Yet if the government were able and willing to intervene to provide milk when there was a possibility of shortage, milk suppliers would have less reason to maintain stocks of milk. Intervention would therefore frequently be required, and it would appear that the supply of milk was unreliable. The necessity of intervention would be self-justifying and the policy of intervention would be not a stabilising factor but a destabilising one. Broadly speaking, this is what has happened in the banking system. It is the moral hazard that Timothy Geithner seemed unable to see, which was present before 2008 and is pervasive today.

If a supply chain—for milk or for money—lacks sufficient liquidity to meet surges and panics, then the available supply can be rationed by queue or by price. Both mechanisms operate in most markets. When there is a surge in demand for cash from banks the available cash is allocated by queuing: the people at the front of the queue get their money in full; those at the back risk having to wait or losing out altogether. When there is a sudden surge in demand for milk, the same happens: there is a queue and those who are late to join the queue get no milk. If the surge is more sustained, dairies probably raise the price and the available supply is allocated differently. The queue rations by rejecting some demands, the market uses the price mechanism to ration by discouraging some people from buying or selling.

Most securities markets—in contrast to deposit-taking institutions—ration by price. If too many people want to realise their investment in a company, the price of that company's shares falls. The ability of savers to buy and sell shares enables companies to raise permanent capital without locking shareholders into holding their investments indefinitely. As in the banking system, there is a process of maturity transformation, and an illusion of liquidity: savers believe, generally with good reason, that they can get their money back whenever they want, even though if all, or even very many, tried, most would be unable to do so. And—as with milk or train tickets or bank deposits—this desirable illusion can continue so long as confidence is maintained and there is sufficient slack in the system to cope with temporary surges in demand. Prices fall until existing holders are ready to wait a bit longer for their cash or new holders are found who believe the shares are cheap.

Speculators can be helpful here: they act, in effect, like pawnbrokers, taking temporary custody of an asset to satisfy people who have an urgent need for cash. Such speculation can be stabilising and profitable, just as pawnbroking is. Speculators may be the providers of capital to the market, enabling forced sellers to realise cash, at a cost, until willing permanent buyers can be found. In this way, short-term traders can provide liquidity to the market.

If you raise the issue of how well markets are functioning with market participants, the conversation will within a few minutes—possibly seconds—turn to liquidity. There is little exaggeration in saying that one question dominates assessment of proposed regulation, technical innovation or change in market practice: what will be the effect on liquidity?

Nothing illustrates the self-referential nature of the dialogue in modern financial markets more clearly than this constant repetition of the mantra of liquidity. End-users of finance—households, non-financial businesses, governments—do have a requirement for liquidity, which is why they hold deposits and seek overdraft or credit card facilities and, as described above, why it is essential that the banking system is consistently able to meet their needs.

But these end-users—households, non-financial businesses, governments—have very modest requirements for liquidity from securities markets. Households do need to be able to realise their investments to deal with emergencies or to fund their retirement; businesses will sometimes need to make large, lumpy investments; governments must be able to refinance their maturing debt. But these needs could be met in almost every case if markets opened once a week—perhaps once a year—for small volumes of trade. As the milkman has discovered, surges in demand for cash are mostly either the result of uncorrelated decisions—car purchases or round-the-world cruises—or predictable events. Christmas reduces our capacity to save as it increases our thirst (not just for milk).

The considerable volatility of prices in modern securities markets leaves much room for doubt as to whether the real requirement of end-users for liquidity in securities markets—confidence that holdings can be mobilised reasonably quickly at appropriate prices—is being fulfilled better, or perhaps at all.

The need for extreme liquidity, the capacity to trade in volume (or, at least, to trade) every millisecond, is not a need transmitted to markets from the demands of the final users of these markets but a need, or a perceived need, created by financial market professionals themselves. People who applaud traders for providing liquidity to markets are often saying little more than that trading facilitates trading—an observation which is true, but of very little general interest.

The high-frequency trader employs computers that constantly offer to buy and sell securities—from other computers. High-frequency traders claim to account for a large proportion—perhaps more than half—of all dealings in stocks and shares in Britain and the USA. Exchanges pay to attract this 'liquidity', while the traders pay to locate their computers next to those of the exchange to minimise the time it takes for trading or regulatory news to reach their machines. Spread Networks' link through the Appalachians serves these traders. A millisecond is a long time in the life of a high-frequency trader.

But high-frequency traders make no contribution to market liquidity in the sense in which the term liquidity is used in this chapter; they cannot enhance the capacity of the market to meet a sudden or exceptional demand without disruption because they provide no capital to the market. Mostly, they 'close their books' at the end of every trading day.

Liquidity is sometimes measured by the effect on 'the spread'—the amount you would lose if you simultaneously bought and sold the same security. Since this is one trade no one is likely to make, the relevance of this measure is not apparent. What matters is the overall cost of trading, which depends not just on the spread but on the level of prices themselves.

Speculators can help provide liquidity when they bring capital to the market and the scale of their activity is moderate relative to the activities of long-term investors. Matters are quite different when the dominant mode of market trading involves short-term speculators trading with each other. Ticket touts can serve a useful role at popular sporting events when demand may exceed supply: but when the majority of tickets are in the possession of ticket touts, the price will be volatile—determined mainly by the expectations of other ticket touts about future prices—and the needs of genuine fans ill served.

Liquidity is in a sense an illusion, but a rewarding illusion not only for those who provide it but also for society as a whole. Yet many people have confused the provision of liquidity with the volume of market activity. The apparent liquidity provided by short-term traders is itself an illusion because it is only available when it is not needed. In the global financial crisis, panic led to an increased requirement for safe short-term assets, and traders, in aggregate, did not have and could not have had the capacity to meet this requirement. As for the milkman, his supply was readily available only so long as not many people needed it; the capacity to meet demand is fundamentally limited by the volume of milk—or, in money markets, patient capital—available.

Only intervention by governments could provide that patient capital. But the effect of official intervention was to aggravate moral hazard: to sustain a fragile structure that could continue to exist only by the implied promise of further intervention in the future. The liquidity to which Rupert Brooke referred was the liquidity of the Flanders battlefields, which gradually sucked in the lives of Brooke himself and many of his compatriots. They were victims of short-term actions, which seemed appropriate at the moment of decision, but cumulatively had long-term consequences that had never been envisaged. And so it has been with government responses to the global financial crisis. By supporting an industry structure not well adapted to the needs of users, policymakers preserved not just the financial system but also the institutions that had given rise to the instability. The adverse consequences for business, for households and for economic growth and economic policy will be described in later chapters.

## Diversification

> Behold, the fool saith, 'Put not all thine eggs in the one basket'—which is but a matter of saying, 'Scatter your money and your attention'; but the wise man saith, 'Put all your eggs in the one basket and—WATCH THAT BASKET.'
>
> MARK TWAIN, *Pudd'nhead Wilson's Calendar*, 1894

Financial intermediation can facilitate diversification. A small share of several projects is less risky than a large share of a single one. If you toss a coin once, you either win or lose: if you toss a coin thirty times, you will have ten or more wins 98 per cent of the time. Sharing the risks and rewards of a pool of assets with a group of people with similar objectives means that you can derive the same average return with lower risk of major loss (but correspondingly reduced possibility of substantial gain). Individuals can—and should—use this principle in building their own portfolios. Professional intermediaries can provide a service by offering ready-made diversification, so that savers can acquire a share in a portfolio with the purchase of a single security in a mutual fund or investment company.

The coin-tossing game reduces risk effectively because the results of successive throws are independent of each other. Diversification is most effective if the values of the assets in a portfolio are uncorrelated. For example, the risk that interest rates will rise sharply is unrelated to the risk that a cancer drug will fail its clinical trials, or the risk that Apple's new product range will flop. A conservative investor—like me—can invest in very risky things so long as the investment is part of a well-diversified portfolio. Correlation is the statistical term for the extent to which two distinct variables—such as the values of Apple shares and those of long-term bonds—move together. Understanding correlation, and judging it, is critical to effective portfolio management by intermediaries.

A fairly small number of securities is enough to provide effective diversification if the risks those securities carry are completely different. On the other hand, even a very long list of securities with similar characteristics provides little real diversification. Investing in companies in different economic sectors and different countries was once an effective route to diversification. But large corporations today operate in many businesses and are global in their scope. They have common sales profiles, so that Pfizer and Glaxo, Exxon and Shell, have fortunes very similar to each other. Not very much diversification is therefore achieved from a portfolio of big multinational companies like these.

The Gaussian copula—the 'formula that killed Wall Street'—was a method of calculating how the correlation between defaults on the components of an asset-backed security determined its overall default probability. But the answers a formula provides are only as good as the numbers fed into it. Correlations change with changing economic conditions. When the economy is booming, house prices are rising and credit is easy, then mortgage defaults are rare. The usual cause of arrears is some catastrophic event, such as severe illness or family break-up. As Tolstoy famously observed, all unhappy families are different, and these events will be independent of each other. Alan Greenspan explained in his 2008 congressional testimony how the data the rating agencies used to assess mortgage-backed securities were drawn from this benign overall economic environment. But when house prices stalled and credit tightened, these factors affected the ability of *all* home-buyers to meet their mortgage obligation. Defaults were not isolated events because the same economic forces were at work everywhere.

Correlation is a mathematical term, but understanding the sources of correlation requires qualitative as well as quantitative knowledge. A computer and a large dataset are not enough: you need local knowledge, and an understanding of the economic processes at work. What you learn in the local branch, or at the nineteenth hole, may be as useful as the ability to solve difficult mathematical problems.

The distinction between general economic risks that affect all firms and households (interest rates and the state of the housing market) and problems that are specific to individuals (divorce and illness) is central to the capital asset-pricing model, that keystone of financial economics. Business risks are partly attributable to the specifics of a particular business and partly related to the prosperity of the general economy. The CAPM describes them as specific risk and market risk respectively. Specific risk arises when a badly managed business loses share to its competitors, or a major project suffers from cost overruns. A well-diversified portfolio will accumulate a variety of specific risks. (CAPM implies that the lower risk achieved by constructing such a portfolio will be reflected in lower returns: I recommend readers to ignore this advice and build a diversified portfolio anyway.) Market risk is usually measured by $\beta$, which measures the correlation between the value of a particular stock and the movement of general share price indexes. I will return to this Greek alphabet soup in Chapter 7.

But selecting uncorrelated investments is not easy. The problem of selection has been aggravated by the degree to which, in a trading culture, prices have come to represent the shared opinions of other traders with little reference to underlying fundamental value. Successive waves of credit expansion driven by central banks—and especially the programmes adopted by the Federal Reserve, European Central Bank and the Banks of England and Japan after the global financial crisis—pushed up all asset values. The resulting common volatility of security prices has provoked a search for 'alternative assets' which would not be correlated with existing portfolios.

Traditionally 'alternatives' were investments such as gold, art, vintage cars and fine wines: but these exist only in limited quantities. And as investor interest in them grew, their prices became increasingly correlated with those of mainstream assets. From the 1990s private equity—which invested in a diversified collection of new businesses—and hedge funds—which adopted unconventional investment strategies—were favoured as diversifying 'alternative assets'.

The original hedge funds were run by legendary names such as George Soros and Julian Robertson: Long-Term Capital Management was the most famous of all. But after the New Economy bubble burst in 2000, pension funds and large investors poured money into these so-called alternative investments. But as demand for 'alternative assets' increased, the resulting increased supply of 'alternative assets' came more and more to resemble repackaging of existing assets. Hedge funds built portfolios of derivatives, or packages of securitised loans, which tracked general economic developments, while private equity invested in larger, established businesses little different from those listed on public markets. The newer hedge funds were, in fact, little more than trading funds with high fees: typically 2 per cent of assets as annual management fee plus 20 per cent of profit. Some sought-after funds charged more. Taken as a whole, although some particular hedge funds have been very successful, the hedge fund industry has been very profitable for hedge fund managers, but not for their investors.[8]

Diversification by financial intermediaries is nevertheless valuable and may be cheaper for investors. This was the initially persuasive rationale for pooled investment funds, which enabled small investors to take shares in a diversified fund which they could not possibly have built for themselves. A simple, lazy and therefore inexpensive way of constructing a diversified portfolio is simply to buy all the available stocks. In the 1970s computers made it easy for intermediaries to offer funds that held a proportionate share of every security. Academic research around the efficient market hypothesis—which encouraged scepticism about the reality of manager skill—led to the creation of the first index, or passive, funds. Within a few years passive funds, which simply held all the shares in the Standard & Poor's or other index, had captured a growing share of the market for intermediation, not just in stock markets but also among bond and even property investors. I will discuss the growth of passive funds further in Chapter 7.

A new twist of complexity was added with the development of Exchange Traded Funds (ETFs), an indexed security that is itself tradable. The next stage of development was the synthetic ETF, which does not actually hold the assets to which the value of the ETF is related. Today there are hundreds of different ETFs, and the market value and volume of trading in some ETFs is greater than the market value and volume of trading in the underlying securities. The financial world can never have too much of a good thing.

Above all, it can never have too much profit. In the next chapter I examine a key feature of financialisation: the rise in the reported profits of the financial sector, and the remuneration of those who work in it. But first a look at a key tool for that purpose—the use of leverage.

## Leverage

> When you combine ignorance and leverage, you get some pretty interesting results.
>
> WARREN BUFFETT, on the global financial crisis, 2008

Every savings or investment decision involves both the supply of capital and the assumption of risk. When you place a deposit in a bank, you run the risk that the bank will not repay you. When you invest in a business, you provide funds to the business, but you can never be certain how and when you will be repaid. When you buy a share, you are uncertain what dividends it will pay or what the share will be worth if you come to sell.

Leverage is a means of adjusting the combination of risk and savings to meet the particular needs of borrowers and lenders. Businesses that need funds for investment will typically look for a combination of loan and equity financing. The lender provides capital for the business—but takes less risk. The owner of the equity—the shareholder—provides less of the capital but assumes more of the risk. A mortgage on a property works in just the same way: the lender provides most of the required funding, and the home-owner must find the balance—the equity—and accept (most of) the risk. Higher return is generally associated with higher risk, and vice versa.

It is possible, but inadvisable, to separate completely the assumption of risk from the provision of capital. The traditional organisation of the Lloyd's insurance market did just that. A conventional insurance company maintains reserves to provide against claims. Lloyd's 'names'—the well-heeled subscribers to the institution—simply agreed to meet the losses, or receive the gains, from insurance underwriting. The trading of mortgage-backed securities was an attempt to separate risk-taking from the provision of capital in the mortgage market. And credit default swaps appeared an effective means of separating the risk of a loan from the provision of capital. None of these developments ended well, and it is important to understand why.

When securitisation began, in the 1980s, the idea was simply to take a bundle of loans and group them into a package. But with the development of collateralised debt obligations (CDOs) in the following decade, the package was divided into tranches of different levels of priority. As payments of interest or principal were made on the loans in the package, they would go first to meet the obligations on the senior tranches of the CDO. The claims of the junior or mezzanine layers would be met next, and finally, if all the underlying loans were paid in full, the holders of the lowest or equity tranches would be repaid. The lower the position of any security in this hierarchy, the greater the risk—and therefore the greater the promised, but not necessarily delivered, return. In Don Kohn's description of 'the Greenspan doctrine', this dicing and slicing enabled institutions 'to choose their risk profiles more precisely'.

But, as with simpler mechanisms of leverage, the overall risk attached to the portfolio of loans could not be changed by this repackaging. There was no alchemy through which a collection of loans on weak security to unreliable borrowers could be anything other than just that.[9] The simple observation that the list of banks which bought these securities was little different from the list of banks that sold them should have provided a warning that the Greenspan doctrine was not the whole story—or even a large part of it.

The development of asset-backed securities and subsequently collateralised debt obligations vastly expanded the market for credit ratings. Soon the majority of debt securities that qualified for the highest 'triple

A' rating were not, as traditionally, the bonds of Exxon Mobil and the government of Germany but tranches of asset-backed securities. The value of credit default swaps (and hence the bonds that they insured) depended on the credit rating of the guarantor. Thus a downgrading of the status of AIG was devastating in its consequences for the safety of bond portfolios.

What was it all for? To find explanations of the attractions of these various forms of leverage to investors, and their prevalence, it is best to move outside the confines of standard finance theory. Leverage enables a modest risk to be divided into two components: a debt element, which offers predictable returns with a low probability of substantial loss, and an equity element, with high volatility of return. But both of these structures are problematic, inviting errors of valuation.

Many people and organisations find it difficult to manage situations with low probabilities of large loss. I drive frequently on French autoroutes, where tailgating is a common driving strategy. Drivers, travelling at high speed, position themselves on your rear bumper, flashing their lights to demand you give way. Tailgating works on most occasions: the impatient driver arrives at his (usually his, though not always) destination marginally earlier. Sometimes, of course, the tailgating driver does not arrive at his destination at all.

Tailgating offers repeated modest gains, punctuated by infrequent disasters. The tailgater persuades himself, and perhaps others, that his success is the result of his skilful driving. Crashes occur, but an element of cognitive dissonance creeps into accounts of the crash. The accident victim blames someone else for his misfortune: usually with some justification. The accidents that result from tailgating are triggered by some other immediate cause—an obstruction on the road, a mistake by another driver. The same cognitive dissonance enabled many bankers to persuade themselves—and some others—that the global financial crisis was not caused by their imprudent behaviour.

The distribution of returns from tailgating shows a high probability of small gain and a low probability of large loss (picking up dimes in front of a steamroller). Financial economists characterise this type of transaction as 'writing heavily out of the money options'. Such distributions are difficult to evaluate or manage. Accountants have always struggled to find a good way to report events that might occur, but probably will not, in financial statements. It was this tailgating phenomenon that Raghuram Rajan had described to the unreceptive audience at Jackson Hole.[10]

Most traffic authorities believe that the costs and consequences of the accidents that follow tailgating exceed the benefits to successful tailgaters. However, this proposition could be definitely established only by many observations over a long period of time. And such an investigation would probably not dissuade many tailgaters from their foolish conduct. They would continue to suppose that, whatever the statistics might show for the driving population as a whole, the result did not apply to drivers as skilful as them. They might even be right to think this.

The 'out of the money option' is only one example of a security which people find difficult to value appropriately. After debt has been removed from a package, what is left is an equity component with high volatility. These distributions are inherently uncertain. Such valuation inevitably involves mistakes. Sometimes we overestimate the value of an asset to us; sometimes we underestimate. But it is easier to sell a fake Rembrandt to someone who believes it is authentic than it is to sell a real Rembrandt to someone who believes it is fake. So mistakes do not cancel out. The owners of assets are much more likely to be people who have overestimated their value than people who have underestimated them. This problem is known as the 'winner's curse'.[11]

Whenever there is uncertainty about the characteristics, or value, of an item, many purchasers will be people who bought it because they made a mistake. And there is always uncertainty in securities markets. That is why so much trade occurs. No one can be certain what a share is worth. No one can be sure that a loan will be repaid. The value of a commodity or a currency is always uncertain.

Every time you buy a share, you are buying it from someone who wants to sell. Many other people have chosen not to buy the share at the price you have agreed to pay. That should always give you pause for thought. HSBC bought Household's low-quality lending business because it was willing to pay more for it than any other bank in the world. Before long, the bank was writing off its investment, signalling the beginnings of the global financial crisis. The winner's curse is a general, and pervasive, problem, but one particularly relevant to the highly volatile distributions of outcomes created by the rise of leverage. Even small misjudgements of the pay-offs, or the probabilities attaching to them, can give rise to fundamental misjudgements of values by traders.

Tailgating and the winner's curse explain many of the follies created by leverage. But others are the result of the opportunity to bet with other people's money. While many remuneration schemes in the financial sector offer uncertainties—supposedly to align the interests of principal and agent—there is an overwhelming tendency to reward the upside of a trade more than the downside. This, in turn, creates a bias towards activities with high volatility of outcome.

There are other reasons why leverage might be advantageous. Differences in the tax treatment of interest and capital gain mean that some people wish to take gains and deduct interest, and others do not. This creates trading opportunities that are valuable for the parties to them, though the advantage to the parties is offset (perhaps more than offset) by disadvantage to taxpayers at large.

Leverage has been central to almost every modern financial crisis. The use of leverage can promote efficiency by enabling risk to be held and managed more efficiently. But the use of leverage provides opportunities for tailgaters and gamblers with other people's money, and creates many opportunities to fall victim to the winner's curse. And these opportunities were exploited to the full during the 'Great Moderation'. By the time of the global financial crisis, Deutsche Bank had liabilities more than fifty times its equity capital—and, as I shall describe in Chapter 6 even this calculation underestimates the extent of leverage.

What did Bernanke, Greenspan, Geithner and others think was really going on, as risk built up in the banking system? Perhaps Upton Sinclair had provided the answer: it was more convenient, politically and ideologically, not to look or analyse too closely. And even now politicians and the public are ready to believe that the bewilderingly complex transactions entered into by clever and very highly paid people are the product of profound understanding rather than ignorance and confusion. Surely that sophisticated mathematics is being put to good use?

Yet there was and is little justification for this confidence. The affairs of large financial institutions were impenetrable; the instruments being traded were hard to understand and often impossible to value. The risk models that were employed were essentially irrelevant to understanding the impact of extreme events (the situation, of course, for which risk models ought to be designed). David Viniar, CFO of Goldman Sachs, claimed as the global financial crisis broke in August 2007 that his bank had experienced '25 standard deviation events' several days in a row. But anyone with a knowledge of statistics (a group that must be presumed to include Viniar) knows that the occurrence of several '25 standard-deviation events' within a short time is impossible. What he meant to say was that the company's risk models failed to describe what had happened. Extreme observations are generally the product of 'off-model' events. If you toss a coin a hundred times and all the tosses are heads, you may have encountered a once in a lifetime statistical freak; but look first for a simpler explanation. For all their superficial sophistication, the masters of the universe had no real understanding of what was going on before them.

# CHAPTER 4

# Profits

## Smarter People

> Though the principles of the banking trade may appear somewhat ab-
> struse, the practice is capable of being reduced to strict rules. To depart
> upon any occasion from these rules, in consequence of some flattering
> speculation of extraordinary gain, is almost always extremely dangerous,
> and frequently fatal to the banking company which attempts it.
>
> ADAM SMITH, *The Wealth of Nations,* 1776

The year is 1995, and I am sitting at a massive octagonal table on the top
floor of the large modern building that dominates the town of Halifax,
West Yorkshire. The location is the boardroom of the Halifax Building
Society. The proposal before the board was that Group Treasury, which
managed the cash held by the Society from day to day, should no longer simply serve the needs of the business—taking deposits from savers
and making loans to home-buyers. Treasury should take active positions
in money markets, and become another profit centre. The plan was to
trade debt instruments: usually either government stock or the liabilities
of other financial institutions. The Society would take full advantage of
Lew Ranieri's revolution in the promotion of markets in fixed-interest
securities. Nick Carraway had given way to Sherman McCoy, and the
Halifax was lusting after its share of the action.

In the years that followed, many financial institutions continued (and still continue) to report profits from their trading activities. The mainspring of investment banking profits in recent years has been trading in fixed-income, currency and commodities (FICC). But the aggregate value of debt securities and currencies is fixed, and although commodity prices fluctuate, the long-run trend has been downward. Individual businesses and traders can make profits at the expense of each other, but this cannot be true for the activity taken as a whole.

That raised a question in my mind. Where would Treasury profits come from? Who would lose the money we expected to make? The reaction to my question was not polite. I was sent for re-education so that the traders could resolve my confusion. I did not find this experience enlightening. We would make money, I was told, because our traders were smarter. But the people I met did not seem particularly smart. And not everyone could be smarter than everyone else.

Still, some people plainly are smarter, and in a variety of ways. There are people who are good at understanding the fundamental value of securities: traders who are adept at predicting the changing moods and mindsets of other traders; individuals who are skilled at analysing the massive volumes of data generated by securities markets. These three broad styles of financial intermediation may be respectively described as investment, trading and analytics, and the groups of people who engage in them as investors, traders and quants. Stock markets provide the clearest, and perhaps most important, illustration of these approaches and the changes in the nature of intermediation in the era of financialisation.

Warren Buffett is the most successful investor in history, having parlayed modest beginnings into a fortune that has made him one of the richest men in the world. Berkshire Hathaway is now one of the largest US companies. Berkshire Hathaway owns the world's largest re-insurance company, GEICO, businesses as diverse as Netjets (which charters executive jets), Equitas (the insurance company created to handle the fall-out from the Lloyd's debacle) and See's Candies. Berkshire also holds substantial stakes in major quoted companies, such as Coca-Cola and Procter & Gamble. Buffett is distinguished by the extreme simplicity of his methods, his disdain for the conventional wisdom of the finance industry and his refusal to invest in anything he finds difficult to understand. Buffett describes his investment philosophy in folksy, annual letters to Berkshire Hathaway shareholders, written in conjunction with Carol Loomis, a doyen of business journalism. He has said his favourite holding period is for ever.[1]

There are some comparable European businesses. The Swedish company Investor AB, the investment vehicle of the Wallenberg family, owns a similarly wide range of businesses, including substantial stakes in most global companies with Swedish roots (such as AstraZeneca, Ericsson and ABB) and, somewhat improbably, the NASDAQ exchange. Buffett's success has not provoked significant imitation, however, in Britain or the USA.

The most successful of those investors who stress fundamental value are those who, like Buffett, have a deep knowledge of and engagement with the companies they choose. Stock-pickers have more modest aspirations, but nevertheless base their decisions on thoughtful assessments of the prospects of companies. Bill Miller and Peter Lynch acquired stellar reputations with sustained out-performance of market indexes through successful stock-picking. But both have retired (and Buffett himself is now over eighty). The era of the superstar stock-picker seems to be at an end, although a few individuals—such as Dennis Lynch—maintain strong reputations.

But there are few instances of sustained long-term success in stock-picking, and the number of fund managers is so large that a few will seem to demonstrate sustained success through chance alone. The reputations even of Peter Lynch and Bill Miller had faded somewhat by the time they left the investment scene. Analysis of the performance of mutual funds—which offer small investors diversified stock portfolios—show not only that they on average under-perform the market but that the degree of persistence of out-performance is very low.

Almost alone among the legendary hedge-fund managers who emphasise economic fundamentals in their judgements, George Soros has been persistently successful. Julian Robertson and Victor Niederhoffer, who had made billions for their clients and themselves in the 1990s, were eventually burned by substantial losses. John Paulson, whose famous 'big short' earned billions by anticipating the collapse of sub-prime mortgages in the global financial crisis, subsequently made large losing wagers on the price of gold.

Buffett has said that he buys stocks on the basis that he would be happy if the stock market shut down for ten years.[2] Buffett himself can get away with it because his track record is so lengthy and impressive, but his successors cannot. While the fundamental value of a security determines the returns available from it in the long run, over shorter periods the returns depend on the assessments of other traders.

As the value horizon—the time taken for an event to be accurately reflected in the value of a business—has lengthened, with business becoming more complex, the performance horizon—the period of time over which the performance of asset managers is measured—has shortened. Hence the rise of the trader chronicled in Chapter 1: the smartness that is rewarded is the smartness of the person who is adept at predicting the changing moods and mindsets of other traders. Simultaneously, the distinction between agent and trader, between broker and dealer, was eroded and effectively eliminated. The new 'smartness' was located, not in the service of investors through the medium of asset management firms such as Fidelity (which had employed Peter Lynch) or Legg Mason (Bill Miller), but for the benefit of the investment banks which had come to dominate market-making.

The shift fed into the behaviour of companies. The market impact of imminent announcements mattered to traders; the competitive strengths and weaknesses of the business mattered little. Companies became locked into the activity of quarterly earnings guidance and earnings management, in which business was directed towards 'meeting the numbers': achieving results slightly ahead of market expectations. This cycle of guidance and management became more and more divorced from the underlying realities of the business.

Investors look at economic fundamentals; traders look at each other; 'quants' look at the data. Dealing on the basis of historic price series was once described as technical analysis, or chartism (and there are chartists still). These savants identify visual patterns in charts of price data, often favouring them with arresting names such as 'head and shoulders' or 'double bottoms'. This is pseudo-scientific bunk, the financial equivalent of astrology. But more sophisticated quantitative methods have since proved profitable for some since the 1970s' creation of derivative markets and the related mathematics.

Profitable opportunities may be provided by arbitrage: observing regularities in the price movement of related securities. Rather obviously, for example, the price of a derivative based on a stock will follow the price of the stock itself. Arbitrage involves taking matched positions—buying one security, selling another, when the price differential moves outside its normal range. Such arbitrage strategies were widely used by Long-Term Capital Management, the hedge fund that collapsed spectacularly in 1998. LTCM, best known for its association with the two Nobel Prize-winning economists Robert Merton and Myron Scholes, was founded by John Meriwether, who had headed the trading operations of Salomon Bros in the 1980s (those described by Michael Lewis in his book *Liar's Poker*) which pioneered the explosive growth of FICC trading. The fund was largely staffed by his former colleagues, and insiders often described it as 'Salomon North'. In the end, the LTCM trades were settled profitably by the investment banks which had taken them over: a telling illustration of Keynes' (possibly apocryphal) dictum that 'markets can remain irrational for longer than you can stay solvent'.[3]

More recently, the mathematical analysis of trading patterns has enabled some algorithmic traders to make returns from minute movements in the prices of securities. The most persistently successful of these quantitative-oriented funds are the Renaissance Technologies funds of Jim Simons, which have over more than two decades earned extraordinary returns for investors while charging equally extraordinary levels of fee. Simons was a distinguished mathematician before taking to finance.

The early and successful practitioners of this quantitative style could use sophisticated methods to identify recurrent patterns in data, and arbitrage anomalies in the manner of LTCM. High-frequency trading uses computers to make, or offer to make, small trades at very frequent intervals. It may be illegal to trade on the basis of actual knowledge of the buying or selling intentions of other investors, but it is legal if you do not know but guess, or if your computer can deduce their intentions from their responses to the trading offers it makes. All the dealings of these funds are undertaken by computers, and the skills of the traders, which are considerable—the typical employee will have a maths or physics PhD—lie in programming the algorithms that the computers employ.

Analysis of price data can, by itself, yield no information about the underlying properties of the securities—foreign currencies, commodities, companies—which are traded or on whose values the derivative products that are traded are based. Although speeding the flow of information from Chicago to New York by a millisecond may be privately profitable, so long as this access can be sold selectively to enable some traders to profit from their exclusive access, the world as a whole derives no benefit from this infinitesimal increase in the speed of dissemination of information. Since FICC trading, taken as a whole, cannot be a profitable activity, the profits of the traders who are recipients of the information are necessarily earned at the expense of other market users: in effect, these profits represent a tax that other users can best avoid by keeping trading to minimal levels. So what was to be the source of these Treasury profits?

## Competition

> 'We must have a bit of a fight, but I don't care about going on long,' said Tweedledum.
>
> LEWIS CARROLL, *Through the Looking Glass*, 1871

There are traders who are smart, though not many: Buffett, Soros, and Simons are people of outstanding intelligence who have used that intelligence to earn billions in securities markets. Many others have simply been lucky. The extraordinary sums that the most successful investors have earned have encouraged many others of more modest talents to enter the field. This gives rise to a paradox. The profits of the smart are the losses of the less smart. But the existence of some smart people in the financial sector may increase profits for everyone—whether they are smart or not.

Here's why. When you buy some products, you want the best. As the surgeon picks up his scalpel, you may regret having searched for someone who will do the job more cheaply. If you plan to sell your house, it is worth paying extra for a negotiator who will get you a better price. If you risk a long term of imprisonment, you want the best attorney.

You can't be sure you will survive the operation, get the best price for your house or stay out of prison by paying more, but you suspect that you have a better chance. For many such products, haggling over price appears not only unseemly but unwise, implying that the purchaser does not really want a top-quality job. In activities like these, a business strategy that emphasises cheapness is not likely to be successful. If some people have skills that are worth paying for, but it is difficult to determine who they are, everyone will be able to charge more.[4] This mechanism is part of the explanation of high profits—and high remuneration—in the finance sector.

Price competition is also often ineffectual when the item in question represents only a small part of the overall cost of the transaction. People will drive to another store to save a few pounds on their grocery bill, but not to save the same amount on their furniture. When you think it through, this makes little sense: but it is certainly the way many of us feel. Yet small percentages of very large amounts can be large amounts. You might not think a 1 per cent annual fund management charge is very high—and by current standards it is not—but 1 per cent of $100,000 is $1,000. On a $50 billion takeover bid, a fee equivalent to one quarter of 1 per cent seems insignificant but amounts to $125 million. Fees of this level would not be unusual: chief executives want the best, and generally what they are spending is other people's money.

Yet perhaps the most surprising source of high fees for corporate advisory work is in the new issue market, since the percentages are not small and the money often comes from the pockets of founders and early shareholders. In the USA, 7 per cent is a standard fee for an IPO (initial public offering), and rarely discounted (European fees are typically lower and more variable).[5] But no evidence of a cartel has been produced, and probably none exists—there is simply a strong perception of collective interest in maintaining the status quo.

Regulation is often the enemy of competition. Where regulation prescribes the conduct of business in considerable detail, it is inevitable that all firms will behave similarly: a particular conception of 'best practice' will be shared between regulators and regulatees. Incumbent firms with close links to agencies may use regulation to resist innovation and raise barriers to new entrants: I will describe this phenomenon of regulatory capture more fully in Chapter 8. Moreover, there are economies of scale in managing regulation. Established firms employ professional regulatory staff: a large bank may have tens of thousands (J.P. Morgan reported hiring an additional 11,000 compliance and regulation staff in 2013 alone), and smaller firms can access this expertise only to a limited extent by hiring consultants. Similar economies of scale apply to lobbying regulators and legislators.

But simple consumer reluctance to switch providers is a major obstacle to competition in retail financial services. It is a well-known joke in the industry that customers change their spouses more often than their banks. They all seem the same: why transfer your loyalty from Tweedledee to Tweedledum? This inertia on the part of retail buyers is common across all financial products. Credit cards have consistently been one of the most profitable retail banking products. Bank of America, 'first mover' in this industry, continues to hold a strong position, despite aggressive attempts by entrants to solicit new business. Many people just do not like buying financial services, and minimise the time and effort they devote to their purchase as a result.

The days when retail customers of financial services were rewarded for their loyalty are long gone. The replacement of a relationship-based culture by a transaction-based one means that the best deal is almost always obtained by shopping around aggressively rather than by building trust. Customer perceptions have lagged behind this harsh reality.

But the profits of customer inertia and price insensitivity were not enough—and certainly not enough to seem to justify high levels of remuneration for senior employees. The aim of most financial companies has been to increase profits by establishing 'the Edge' in wholesale financial markets. This was the aim of the discussion around that Halifax board table.

## The Edge

The goose that lays golden eggs has been considered a most valuable possession. But even more profitable is the privilege of taking the golden eggs laid by somebody else's goose. The investment bankers and their associates now enjoy that privilege. They control the people through the people's own money.

LOUIS BRANDEIS, *Other People's Money*, 1914

Sen. Collins: 'Did you consider yourself to have a duty to act in the best interest of your clients?'

Mr Sparks: 'I had a duty to act in a very straightforward way, in a very open way with my clients. Technically, with respect to investment advice, we were a market maker in that regard. But with respect to being a prudent and a responsible participant in that market, we do have a duty to do that.'

Sen. Collins: '. . . did the firm expect you to act in the best interests of your clients as opposed to acting in the best interests of the firm?'

Mr Sparks: 'Well, when I was at Goldman Sachs, clients are very important and were very important and so . . .'

Sen. Collins: 'Could you give me a yes or no to whether or not you have a duty to act in the best interests of your clients?'

Mr Sparks: '. . . believe we have a duty to serve our clients well.'

SENATOR S.M. COLLINS (R-Maine) and D.L. SPARKS,
former partner and head of mortgage department,
Goldman Sachs, Congressional testimony, 27 April 2010

Philip Augar, a perceptive commentator who is himself a former investment banker, calls it 'the Edge'—the advantage investment banks gain from being at the centre of the financial system.

> The large investment banks know more than any other institution or organisations about the world's economy. They know more than their clients, more than their smaller competitors, more than the central banks, more than Congress or Parliament, more than the Chancellor of the Exchequer and more than the Secretary of the United States Treasury.[6]

A striking claim: but is it true? I have been to most of these places, talked to these people, heard their presentations and read their research materials. Investment banks may know more about the world economy than Congress or Parliament—though the House of Commons library produces some impressive briefing documents, and I expect the Library of Congress does the same. But I don't think the knowledge of the world economy found in investment banks compares favourably with that of the other institutions Augar describes—or with the knowledge that could be found in a consultancy such as McKinsey, the newsrooms of *The Economist* or *Financial Times*, the offices of the best asset managers or the common rooms of many academic research institutions.

Augar goes on to quote a fund manager as saying, 'Even though they [the investment banks] have all the information, they don't join up the dots.' Though Augar remains in awe of the information processing capacity of these institutions, I think that the sceptic has the better of the argument; investment banks have little reason to 'join up the dots', even if they had the capacity. In markets of today, what matters is not so much knowledge of the economy—knowledge of business, economic development, global politics—as knowledge of the activities of other market participants. That is the knowledge investment banks do have, and it is what gives them the Edge.

'The Edge' is a gambling term. While the Swiss villagers insured, the English gentlemen gambled. John Paulson and the Goldman customers who bought asset-backed securities wagered on opposing outcomes of the same event. 'Fabulous Fab' Tourre made the 'book'.

Typically, only the bookmakers and 'the house' find wagering profitable in the long run. Operators design products that appeal to the particularities—some would say, weaknesses—of human attitudes to risk. Slot machines have flashing lights, casinos employ attractive croupiers. The spin of the roulette wheel, the turn of the card, creates a moment of high drama. Punters are encouraged to believe their skill and knowledge give them the Edge. The professionals who run the house 'make books'. They design the mathematics of the game so that it is likely that, whatever the outcome, they will come out ahead. All of this is as true of financial markets as in the casino or at the racetrack.

If you were to bet on all the horses in a race, or if you bet on all the numbers on the roulette wheel, you would be certain to lose money. The bookmaker's objective is to create a 'Dutch book'—to set odds such that, whatever the outcome, he will win. He achieves this by adjusting the odds to reflect the amount of money placed on each horse. Successful bookmakers once required the ability to do complex arithmetic, very quickly, in their heads: today computers make these calculations much faster than any human.

The bookmaker gains an edge from his knowledge of his customers. Their judgements of horses are imperfect. They suffer from a variety of misapprehensions. They like the name of the horse or have received a tip from a friend. The consequence is that, on average, too much money backs hopeless horses and not enough is placed on those which are likely to win. Knowing this, the bookmaker will adjust his odds accordingly and tends to lose when outsiders romp home and to make more profit when favourites run as expected.

This is not because the bookmaker knows more about horses than other people; he might, but this illusion is potentially as costly to a book-maker as it is typically costly to a punter. The knowledge that is valuable to the bookmaker is knowledge of his customers, and of the mathematics of making a book, rather than knowledge of horses. A few people even make a profitable living out of betting on horses, but they are exceptions. The knowledgeable punter is the bookmaker's enemy: not because he will outsmart the bookmaker (who makes the odds on the basis of the money that is placed), but because fear of more knowledgeable punters may drive the ill-informed majority away. There is thus an intrinsic con-flict between the objective of attracting business into 'the house' and the transmission of knowledge about the underlying character of the risks that are the subject of the wager.

Before financialisation, the market-maker held 'the Edge' that is al-ways due to the house: he made a turn on the difference between buying and selling prices, benefited from his general knowledge of the habits of clients and put little capital of his own at risk. Sometimes, even a cau-tious market-maker may be hit by an unexpected event—a sharp market correction might, for the market-maker, be the equivalent of the long-odds winner for the bookmaker.

The rise of the broker–dealer, however, gave the market-maker spe-cific, as well as general, information about the positions and intentions of clients. And as both broker–dealers and traditional market-makers were absorbed into financial conglomerates, the information base avail-able to the market-maker became wider still. The modern investment bank derives a considerable edge not so much from its wide knowledge of the global economy as from its wide knowledge of financial markets: the identities, positions and intentions of the principal players. These are 'the dots' that the bank can—and does—join up.

The use of this information for the benefit of the investment bank and its traders creates an inherent conflict of interest. But such conflicts are not confined to the problematic broker–dealer relationship. The modern investment bank typically issues securities in the primary market, makes a secondary market in securities, gives corporate advice, undertakes asset management on behalf of retail and institutional investors, and engages in proprietary trading on its own account. Each of these activities is potentially in conflict with the others. Goldman was excoriated not only by Senator Collins; Chancellor Leo Strine, the leading judge in Delaware (the principal forum for corporate litigation in the USA), lambasted the firm for its multiple conflicts of interest in the acquisition of the El Paso oil business by Kinder Morgan.[7] Broadly, the bank advised El Paso, its client, to accept a sharply lowered offer from Kinder Morgan, a company in which the firm held a material shareholding and the partner advising a large personal stake.

The first business principle in Goldman Sachs' Code of Business Conduct and Ethics is 'our clients' interests always come first',[8] and there was, perhaps, a time when this was true. Gus Levy, the firm's senior partner in the 1970s, coined the slogan 'long-term greedy' to emphasise that the firm's success depended on maintaining the confidence of its clients.[9] But the demise of the partnership structure reduced the appeal of a philosophy of 'long-term greedy'. As 'Fabulous Fab' practiced his 'intellectual masturbation', he had little interest in the long-term health of Goldman Sachs, much more in his own bonus.

The cyber cafés of Lagos are home to the scammers who invite you to facilitate an illicit transaction in return for a large commission. The criminals call those who fall for their entreaties 'mugus'—people who believe they are the beneficiaries of impropriety when they are in fact the victims. There is always a supply of mugus. Some of Bernard Madoff's clients suspected he was operating illegally, but supposed he was improperly using the information he gained from his other activities to secure exceptional returns. So clients of investment banks often believe that 'the Edge'—the inside information about markets obtained by undertaking a wide range of financial services activities—is used for their benefit.

But even clients who are sceptical about the extent to which 'the Edge' benefits customers rather than insiders may find there is no practical alternative to dealing with these heavily conflicted firms. Or they may be drawn in by the advantages of scale in market-making. Buyers and sellers are attracted to the venues where there are most sellers and buyers. This is equally true of farmers' markets, Hollywood—the place where film-makers meet stars—and trading in foreign exchange futures. In consequence, market-making is intrinsically oligopolistic, and incumbent advantages are hard to displace. Leading investment banks have successfully established dominant positions in market making in FICC. That dominance allows them to take full advantage of 'the Edge'. And there are profits to be earned from another 'edge': the advantage the financial institution enjoys over the regulator.

## Regulatory Arbitrage

Fantastic grow the evening gowns
Agents of the Fisc pursue
Absconding tax defaulters through
The sewers of provincial towns.

W.H. AUDEN, *The Fall of Rome*, 1940

The benign opinion that Mr Potts delivered to the International Swaps and Derivatives Association in 1997, and the enthusiasm of US policymakers, set the scene for the explosive growth of the markets in credit securities—credit default swaps and collateralised debt obligations—which were at the centre of the financial crisis. But if credit default swaps were neither wagers nor insurance contracts, then what were they? In 1997 there was an answer to this question, although perhaps understandably it was not one on which Mr Potts chose to dwell. Much of the complexity of modern financial services is the result of regulatory arbitrage. Such arbitrage is a process by which you avoid or minimise regulatory restriction by engaging in a transaction with more or less identical commercial effect but more favourable regulatory treatment. This was the origin, and initial purpose, of the credit default swap.[10]

The idea was to exploit differences between the regulation of banks and insurance companies. Banks were required to hold reserves against loans. Such reserves were calculated as a proportion of the amount of the loan. Insurance companies were also required to hold reserves, but these were calculated as a proportion of the expected losses on the policies.

Exxon Mobil was a corporate borrower—and loans to companies carried a high risk weight in computing the reserves of banks. But Exxon Mobil was an extremely safe credit, so that the expected loss on the loan was negligible. Hence there was scope for profitable trade between bank and insurance company.

But it is always possible to have too much of a good thing. By 2008 the market for credit default swaps had extended far beyond loans to Exxon Mobil and included guarantees on complex packages of securities whose contents no one really knew or understood. AIG, America's largest insurance company, had by 2008 underwritten $500 billion of credit default swaps, mostly not against the bankruptcy of Exxon Mobil but on the viability of tranches of asset-backed securities. The leader of its financial products group, Joe Cassano, had told investors as late as August 2007 that it was hard 'to even see a scenario within the realm of reason that would see us losing $1 in any of these transactions'.[11]

Cassano was wrong. In September 2008, with widespread loan default in prospect, AIG was liable to pay around $12.9 billion to Goldman Sachs, America's leading investment bank, money that AIG could not afford to pay but which Goldman Sachs could not afford not to receive. To the relief of both parties, the US government came to the rescue, providing an extraordinary $85 billion to the failing insurer, which was thus able to meet its obligations in full. Significantly, Goldman had separately insured itself against the failure of AIG.[12]

But regulatory arbitrage was in place long before Blythe Masters, an executive at J.P. Morgan, invented credit default swaps. An early example of regulatory arbitrage was the circumvention of interest rate restrictions on current accounts under Regulation Q through the Eurodollar market. A different mechanism of regulatory arbitrage was created for retail customers—the money market fund. An investor in a US money market fund holds a share in a portfolio of debt, while the manager of the fund is expected to redeem the share at a fixed price and the income from the portfolio is paid to the investors (in effect, the depositors). Cheques can be written on the money market fund, so that in the eyes of the saver, but not of the regulator, the money market fund is a bank account. In the USA these funds have come to rival conventional bank deposits in scale. The role of money market funds is almost entirely confined to countries that have, or once had, significant restrictions on interest on current accounts. In the UK, where no equivalent of Regulation Q has ever existed, money market funds have negligible market share.

Since money market funds were not technically deposits, they did not qualify for deposit insurance. However, when the very large Reserve Primary Fund—which held some Lehman debt—'broke the buck' (was unable to offer redemption at the fixed price) in 2008, pressure from aggrieved investors and fear of a run on other funds led to an extension of government guarantees of deposits to such investments. Since 2008 there has been extended—and still inconclusive—discussion of an appropriate new regulatory framework for money market funds.

Regulation Q was gradually weakened and became ineffective after 1980, although it was not finally abolished until 2011. But regulators rarely remove otiose or ineffective regulations. The more usual response is to elaborate the regulation in an attempt to remove or reduce the arbitrage opportunity. Thus begins a game of cat and mouse, in which the financial services companies are generally one or more steps ahead of the regulator. The outcome is regulation that becomes progressively more complex but which is rarely fully effective in achieving its intended purpose.

Both the Eurodollar market and the market in credit default swaps had origins in regulatory arbitrage, but both acquired a life of their own. This is also a recurrent pattern. The 'repo market' is an example of a financial investment that began as a mechanism of regulatory arbitrage and has survived and prospered despite extensive attempts to remove its arbitrage benefit. A repo agreement is the means by which many large corporations make deposits with banks and other financial institutions. The depositor 'buys' a security, such as a government bond, from the bank. The bank signs an agreement to repurchase it the following day, at a small premium which is equivalent to one day's interest. The mutual intention is to repeat this transaction every day.

What is it all for? If you ask a corporate treasurer, you will be told that repos offer companies slightly better returns than simple deposits. But why? Regulatory arbitrage is one reason for trading in this way: repo transactions were treated differently in accounting reports and the calculation of regulatory capital (and, in the familiar cat and mouse game, more elaborate rules to counter this are followed by more elaborate arbitrage). The inquiry into Lehman's bankruptcy emphasised the extent to which the defunct bank had used a complex form of arbitrage known as 'repo 105' to flatter its accounts for regulators and customers.

There are also opportunities for fiscal arbitrage—transactions with similar commercial effect may be taxed in different ways. And for accounting arbitrage—two transactions have similar commercial effect but are treated in different ways in company accounts. Just as regulators respond to regulatory arbitrage by developing ever more complex rules, so tax authorities respond to fiscal arbitrage by adding pages to the tax code, and accounting standards bodies respond to accounting arbitrage by elaborating more detailed accounting standards. Arbitrage and reaction to arbitrage are the principal reasons why regulatory rulebooks, tax legislation and accounting codes become progressively more complex.

Repo 105 had benefited from jurisdictional arbitrage. If a transaction is prohibited in one country, or is regulated or taxed or accounted for in a manner you don't like, perhaps you can make the transaction somewhere else. Lehman had shopped for a legal opinion that supported its treatment of these instruments and found a more appealing one in London than in New York. The relevant transactions were therefore routed through London in order to be governed by English law.

Countries may invite jurisdictional arbitrage. In the years before the global financial crisis, policymakers in both Britain and the USA understood well that Britain was using looser regulation as a tool to attract business from New York to London. Locations such as the Cayman Islands may be more accommodating still. These offshore locations ('treasure islands'[13]) are often described as 'tax havens', but they are every bit as much regulatory havens as tax havens. The Grimaldis of Monaco were the first to discover the potential profitability of such activity when they set up the Monte Carlo casino a hundred and fifty years ago, and jurisdictional arbitrage has since become a major revenue source for many small states.

Regulatory arbitrage, fiscal arbitrage and accounting arbitrage all cost money. From the perspective of the non-financial economy, the resources devoted to arbitrage are a dispiriting waste. Some of the cleverest minds in the country are devoted to activities whose objective is intentionally damaging to the goals of effective regulation, efficient taxation and honest and transparent accounting. In addition to the fees that go to the lawyers and accountants who devise these schemes, businesses pay traders for sows' ears to be turned into silk purses which receive more benign regulatory, fiscal or accounting treatment. Arbitrage is therefore a significant contributor to the trading profits of financial institutions.

But what is the source of these profits? This is not a simple question. The answer seems clearest in the case of fiscal arbitrage. Arbitrage is worthwhile if the tax saved is greater than the cost of engaging in the avoidance transaction. The company that saves tax gains, the advisers gain, the trader gains: the taxman loses a corresponding amount. Fiscal arbitrage is a means of taking money out of the pockets of the public and transferring it to advisers, traders and the firms that employ them.

With regulatory arbitrage, the loser is the potential beneficiary of the regulation. If the regulation is useless, as may often be the case, the costs of regulatory arbitrage simply represent a transfer from the operating profits of the business to the financial professionals who make the arbitrage possible. If the regulation would have benefited customers, or protected taxpayers or other firms from potential loss, then these customers or taxpayers are losers from the efforts to avoid regulation.

Accounting arbitrage yields profits at the expense of those who rely on the integrity of accounts. Enron was an extensive user of accounting arbitrage, and Arthur Andersen's involvement in auditing this process was the cause of the accounting firm's demise. J.P. Morgan and Citigroup each agreed settlements of around $2 billion to settle claims made by Enron investors who alleged they had been duped by misleading accounts facilitated by transactions the banks had arranged.

Regulatory arbitrage is an inevitable outcome of the detailed prescriptive regulation of financial services. The only means of avoiding it is to ensure that transactions with similar economic effect are always treated in the same way. This is a generally accepted regulatory objective, but not realistically achievable in the context of the complexity of the financial and regulatory system we have today. An alternative allows regulators more discretion, so that they feel confident in implementing the spirit rather than the letter of the rules. But this would require a dramatic and permanent shift in both the calibre of regulatory staff and the balance of political influence between regulators and regulated activities. A better response is to find far more robust and easily implemented principles of regulation. I return to this issue in later chapters.

## I'll Be Gone, You'll Be Gone

'We are investment bankers. We don't care what happens in five years.'
VINCENT DAHINDEN, head of global structured products,
Royal Bank of Scotland, *Institutional Investor*,
12 February 2004[14]

The claim that 'our people are smarter' was implausible in a world that contained Buffett and Soros, Simons and Harding. But the events that followed provide a clue to the answer to my Halifax question. Soon after that debate, the board took what was seen (perhaps wrongly) as an even more momentous decision. The Society would end a hundred and fifty years of mutuality and become a public company. Four years after that (and, for the record, after I had left the board), Halifax plc took over the Bank of Scotland. In 2008 HBoS, as the new organisation was called, failed and was rescued by the British government.

Part of the explanation of the profitability of FICC is that the activity is not as profitable as it seems. In the first decade of the twenty-first century, banks announced that they had made large profits and paid a substantial fraction of those large profits to their senior employees. But the profits had been imaginary. Their shareholders were more or less wiped out, and the banks looked to governments to support their creditors and restore their capital.

In the words of Nassim Taleb, 'their profits were simply cash borrowed from destiny with some random payback time'.[15] But by the time payback time arrived, many of the principals had departed: the architect of the HBoS merger, Sir (but again to be Mr) James Crosby retired from his position in 2006 at the age of fifty. Profits are measured year by year, or quarter by quarter. But the time-scales of business projects—such as a loan or a mortgage—are usually much longer than a year or quarter—and often longer than the tenure of the officers responsible for them. 'I'll be gone, you'll be gone', as they say in the trading room. This disjunction of time-frame is challenging for accountants.

Not all my school contemporaries who did not go on to university found secure employment in the then conservative Bank of Scotland. Others—often those better at numbers and worse with people—became accountants. Accountants were notoriously dull. And, like bank managers, prudent. Values were based on cost, unless assets were no lon-ger worth their cost, in which case they had to be written down. Banks were encouraged to understate their profits and create hidden reserves. A bird in the hand was worth more than any number in the bush: only when the bird emerged from the bush were you permitted to count it at all.

Like finance, and for similar reasons, accounting became cleverer, and worse. Britain never had business schools on an American scale. Nor (outside a few global corporations) was there internal management training of the kind characteristic of Japanese or German corporations. By the 1980s accounting had become the principal means by which Brit-ish graduates prepared for business. Many of these trainees found jobs in the finance sector; others took jobs in non-financial business—and many rose to senior positions. Young accountants were smarter, greed-ier, less schooled in prudence and better schooled in economics. 'Fair value' increasingly replaced conservatism as a guiding principle. But this route to the 'true and fair view'—the traditional holy grail of the accountant—often led to an outcome that was just the opposite of fair. At first sight, the adoption of mark-to-market accounting seems obvi-ously sensible. Historic cost is just history—the market recognises cur-rent reality. Twenty-five years ago I co-authored a book on economics and accounting,[16] and at that time I was in no doubt of the superiority of mark-to-market procedures. But twenty-five years is a long time.

In 1990 a young McKinsey partner named Jeff Skilling was lured away from the world's most respected consulting firm by a small, sleepy Texas energy business. Skilling and his colleagues thought that gas contracts could be traded in the way in which banks like Halifax were learning to trade fixed interest, currency and commodities. Lucy Prebble's musical play *ENRON* achieved the remarkable feat of bringing mark-to-market accounting to the stage.[17] The opening scene is set in Skilling's office on 30 January 1992, as he and his colleagues held a champagne party. The occasion was the arrival of a letter from the Securities and Exchange Commission (SEC): the regulator had agreed that mark-to-market ac-counting might be used for gas contracts. Prebble's play has the struc-ture of a Shakespearean tragedy. In Act III Skilling rises to become chief executive of the company, and almost rivals Jack Welch as one of the most admired business people in America. In Act V he is sentenced to twenty-four years in prison.

A long-term gas contract, such as an agreement to supply gas over twenty-four years, should yield a steady stream of profits over the life of the contract. Just as a sound loan from a bank will yield a steady stream of profits over the life of the loan. Traditional accounting procedures would report these profits year by year. But if the contract or loan is tradable, the transaction might be treated differently. If you were to sell the contract, the price the buyer would pay would reflect all the profits that might be expected to accrue in future. Marking to market enables you to credit the entire value of these profits immediately to your profit-and-loss account. Enron had explained the rationale to the SEC. A trading business 'creates value and completes its earnings process when the transactions are finalised'.[18] Enron was no longer an energy company, but a 'Gas Bank'.

More than half a century ago, J.K. Galbraith presented a definitive depiction of the Wall Street Crash of 1929 in a slim, elegantly written volume. Embezzlement, Galbraith observed, has the property that 'weeks, months, or years elapse between the commission of the crime and its discovery. This is the period, incidentally, when the embezzler has his gain and the man who has been embezzled feels no loss. There is a net increase in psychic wealth.' Galbraith described that increase in wealth as 'the bezzle'.[19]

In a delightful essay Warren Buffett's business partner Charlie Munger pointed out that the concept can be extended much more widely. No illegality need be involved to create this psychic wealth: mistake or self-delusion is enough. Munger coined the term 'febezzle',[20] or functionally equivalent bezzle, to describe the wealth that exists in the interval between creation and destruction of the illusion.

The critic who exposes a fake Rembrandt does the world no favour: the owner of the picture suffers loss, as perhaps do potential viewers, and the owners of genuine Rembrandts gain little. The finance sector did not look kindly on those who pointed out that the new economy bubble, or the credit expansion that preceded the global financial crisis, had created a large febezzle. It is easier for both regulators and market participants to follow the crowd. Only a brave person would stand in the way of those expecting to become rich by trading internet stocks, or who denied people the opportunity to own their own homes because the buyers could not afford them.

The joy of the bezzle is that two people each ignorant of the existence and role of the other can enjoy the same wealth. The champagne that Skilling drank was paid for by Enron's shareholders and creditors, but they would not know that until ten years later: most had not even heard of the company at the time. Households in US cities received money in 2006 that they could never hope to repay, while taxpayers had never dreamed that they would be called on to foot the bill. Shareholders in banks—including the hapless recipients of the ultimately worthless windfall shares from the Halifax, and the Bank of Scotland shareholders who exchanged their holdings for Halifax paper—could not have understood that the dividends they received were money they had borrowed from themselves. Investors congratulated themselves on the profits they had earned from their vertiginously priced internet stocks. They did not realise that the money they had made would melt away like snow in a warm spring. Stores of transitory wealth were created that seemed real enough to everyone at the time. Real enough to spend. Real enough to hurt those who were obliged to pay the money back.

There are many routes to bezzle and febezzle. The accounts of financial institutions were once opaque and conservative. They are still opaque, but generally the opposite of conservative. Estimates of future gains—'mark to market'—are registered as current trading gains.[21] But what if there is no market? You might estimate what the price would have been if there had been a market—'mark to model'.

Skilling toasted the opportunity to recognise future profits which might—or might not—materialise. The shift from a conservative regime to its opposite created a transitional era in which reported earnings were higher than they had been in the past, or were likely to be in future: a transition much to the benefit of those who happened to be around at the time.

If you measure profit by marking to market, then profit is what the market thinks it will be. The information contained in the accounts of the business—the information that should illuminate the views of the market—is derived from the market itself.[22] And the market is prone to temporary fits of shared enthusiasm—for emerging market debt, for internet stocks, for residential mortgage-backed securities, for Greek government debt. Traders need not wait to see when or whether the profits materialise. I'll be gone, you'll be gone.[23]

The tailgating problem arises whenever there is an activity that combines a high probability of a small profit with a low probability of a large loss. But that is the nature of lending. Most loans are good and make a modest return for the bank; many such transactions are needed to offset occasional ones that go sour. As with tailgating, the profitability of lending can only be assessed over the long run, and then with difficulty. Loss accounting for banks has always been problematic. What provision, if any, should be made against profit today for loans believed to be sound?

Suppose there is a 1 per cent probability that a loan of $100 will not be repaid. A 'mark to market' or 'mark to model' approach might value the loan at $99. But the loan is not worth $99. Like Schrödinger's cat, which is either dead or alive, the loan is either good or bad; it is either worth $100 or nothing. 'God does not play dice with the universe', Einstein said of problems like Schrödinger's, but bankers do play dice with the financial universe. Traditionally, banks would squirrel profits away in anticipation of hard times: more recently, however, their senior management has had the opposite concern, seeking to justify their bonuses by declaring the largest profits possible.

One answer to the dilemma of how to account for loan losses is to wait and see: the need to take a long view in measuring bank profitability was an important reason why employment in 'the Bank' and 'the Royal Bank' was a career. A managerial position in a bank was a job for life, and much of the reward was deferred: the bank manager would expect to retire with a generous pension and enjoy many golden years on the golf course on which he had schmoozed his clients. Because of this mutual long-term commitment between bank and employee, those who made lending decisions would be concerned for the total consequences, and not just the immediate impact, of what they did.

That was still the prevailing culture in Halifax in the early 1990s. That institution was responding more slowly than most to the changing times, but it was responding. As I submitted to re-education by the traders, with their culture of 'I'll be gone, you'll be gone', I realised how critical tailgating was to their success—or apparent success. Much of the profit the Halifax Treasury hoped to make would be derived from 'carry trades'—transactions that would secure an interest rate premium by offsetting loans of different maturities (and different interest rates), or matching a good credit with a poorer credit.

A few years later the opportunities created by the formation of the Eurozone gave rise to one of the largest of carry trades—and one that would have political as well as economic consequences. Financial institutions could buy southern European assets financed by funds raised in northern Europe. This opportunity was exploited so extensively by traders in French and German banks that the differential between interest rates on German and Greek bonds almost disappeared. The regular profits—the seconds shaved off the tailgater's journey—were credited to the banks—and, crucially, to the bonuses of the traders. As with the tailgaters, the losses to be incurred were assumed, correctly, to be far down the road.

The martingale is a betting strategy which responds to every loss with a larger bet. Imagine a 'fair' gamble in which you stake $5 to win $10 for a head, and nothing on a tail. If you win, you walk away with a $5 profit. The martingale proposes that if you lose, you should bet $10 on the next throw of the coin. If you win, you will now gain $20, recover the $15 (the $5 on the first throw + $10 on the second) you have laid out on the game, and will walk away with a $5 profit. If you lose, you repeat the strategy, doubling up after every losing bet. The paradox of this game, which has intrigued statisticians and attracted gamblers for centuries, lies in its two seemingly incompatible properties. The game is certain to be profitable if you play for sufficiently long, but if you play it regularly you will eventually be ruined.

From time to time 'rogue traders' grab the headlines. The term came into popular language after Nick Leeson, a 28-year-old employee in the Singapore office of the venerable London investment bank of Barings, vanished overnight from his desk. The losses he had incurred led to the bankruptcy of the bank, and prison for Leeson. More recent 'rogue traders' include Jérôme Kerviel, that former employee of the French bank Société Générale (now in prison), who was ordered to repay €4.9 billion, and J.P. Morgan's 'London whale' (Bruno Iksil), whose irregular trading was said to have lost the US bank $6 billion.

Perhaps the largest of such excesses were those reported by 'Howie' Hubler, a once respected trader at Morgan Stanley, whose activities in 2007 were reported to have resulted in losses of $9 billion.[24] A rogue trader is one who has run out of money, or scared his employer, before his number came up. Hubler, like the other rogue traders, had followed a martingale strategy: he increased the size of his bets on collateralised debt obligations based on mortgage-backed securities in a collapsing market.

Rogue traders normally protest that the activity would eventually have been profitable if the bank had not closed its position, just as the gambler dragged home from the casino tells his wife and the world that he would have come out on top if only he had been allowed to stay longer. Often these claims will be correct. At Long-Term Capital Management the banks that took over the positions of the failed fund ultimately made a profit on the transaction.

A collateralised debt security often had a structure in which the issuer promised to respond to any inadequacy of collateral by 'topping up' the contents to maintain the value. 'Payment in kind' securities similarly buttressed their value with additional debt of the same kind: the reality of much Third World debt, where promises to pay were simply rolled forward into the future, was similar. Like the gambler in the casino with a martingale strategy who always plays another hand, the borrower defers the due date of payment whenever it falls due. Warren Buffett famously said of these structures that 'it is impossible to default on a promise to pay nothing'.[25]

The Ponzi scheme is closely related to the martingale. This approach to thinking yourself rich is named after Charles Ponzi, who told investors (correctly) in the 1920s that international reply coupons, used by the world's postal authorities, were mispriced. Profits could be earned by buying in one country and selling in another. Sadly the supply of coupons was insufficient to meet the demand of investors.

So Ponzi resorted to fraud. The theft was not complicated—high returns to savers were achieved by paying any withdrawals out of the funds subscribed by new investors. The new investors were attracted by the success of those who had been in the scheme from the beginning. Ponzi schemes break down when the supply of new investors is insufficient to meet the withdrawals of the old.

The greatest of all Ponzi schemes in history was that perpetrated by Bernard Madoff,[26] who claimed high returns with low volatility from an investment strategy using derivative securities. In fact, no investment activity took place. During the global financial crisis the demand for redemptions increased and incoming funds shrank. Unable to meet withdrawals, Madoff turned himself in to the FBI and was duly sentenced to 140 years in prison. Some of those who invested with Ponzi and Madoff made money. Even if you know, or suspect, a Ponzi scheme, you might hope to get out in time, with a profit. I'll be gone, you'll be gone.

Ponzi and Madoff went to prison because they lied. But the new economy bubble of 1999–2000 was a—perhaps legal—Ponzi scheme. Early investors made large profits, but it was later investors, attracted by the prospect of similar gains, who provided the funds that made these profits possible. Securities with no intrinsic value were bought and sold repeatedly by people whose motive for buying was knowledge of the profits that had already been made in such stocks and the expectation (fulfilled in many cases) that they would make similar profits by selling these stocks on at higher prices still. Eventually, as in all Ponzi schemes, the supply of fresh buyers ran out, the bubble burst and the share prices of internet stocks collapsed. The boundaries between scam, deception, self-deception and mistake are fuzzy.

In the new economy bubble some early-stage investors made money, but most stayed on in the hope of making still more. Even highly intelligent people overestimate their ability to time the correction of market mispricing. Legendary investors such as Julian Robertson and George Soros misjudged the new economy bubble and damaged their reputations. Warren Buffett stayed resolutely on the sidelines, and was derided for his failure to 'get it'. Isaac Newton famously lost money in the South Sea Bubble, an early Ponzi scheme. As the new economy bubble expanded, I asked myself often, 'Do people in financial conglomerates selling products really believe these things, or are they cynical in their deception?' I came to realise that the truth lay somewhere in between: neither naïveté nor fraud provided sufficient explanation. It was convenient to repeat the received opinions of organisations and colleagues. In the self-referential world of finance, reiteration appeared to validate these opinions.

The persistence of bezzle and febezzle is the product of a casual lack of concern for truth. When I naïvely asked the Halifax question, 'Where do the profits come from?' a striking feature of the response was that most people within the finance sector did not think the question either interesting or important. Their attitude was not the comprehensive immorality of the overt fraudster but the wilful blindness of those who do not ask questions when it would be embarrassing, or at least inconvenient, to know the answer. Upton Sinclair's remark is again relevant: 'it is difficult to get a man to understand something, when his salary depends on his not understanding it.'

## How Profitable Is the Financial Sector?

> Lucky fools do not bear the slightest suspicion that they may be lucky fools.
>
> NASSIM NICHOLAS TALEB, *Fooled by Randomness*, 2001

The herd instinct and associated competitive pressures led businesses to imitate the disastrous strategies of their rivals. Chuck Prince had encapsulated the problem: 'As long as the music is playing, you've got to get up and dance.' The self-referential values and practices of the industry reinforced false beliefs. Commitments to the interests of clients, loyalty to institutions, were replaced by the aggressive pursuit of individual self-interest and the culture of 'I'll be gone, you'll be gone'. All this activity was sustained by the illusion of profitability: the belief that financial innovation was adding great value and securing exceptional returns when the reality was that traders were borrowing from the future to fill their own pockets.

The possibility that financial institutions do not really make lots of money is difficult to grasp. Look at the salaries, the bonuses, the marbled reception areas, the corporate jets. All the trappings of an exceptionally profitable industry are there. Can it really be the case that the industry is not, in fact, exceptionally profitable?

Conglomerate banks take the view that their retail operations are relatively unrewarding. But conglomeration permits—even encourages—cross-subsidy between activities. When competing groups are jostling for overall control of the enterprise, such cross-subsidy will tend to favour the group that is, for the moment, in charge. There have been substantial cross-subsidies from the retail division to the trading operations of financial conglomerates—of such magnitude, in fact, that it is difficult for these trading operations to compete effectively without the support of retail banking.

That recognition was an important part of the conglomeration that was central to financialisation. Salomon Bros, which had done so much to promote the rise of the trading culture, became part of Citigroup; Warburg, the City of London's most innovative investment bank, was acquired by UBS. Retail banks such as Barclays and J.P. Morgan developed their investment banking activities. Some smaller investment banks, such as Lazards, withdrew into specialist niches, while John Meriwether—Lew Ranieri's boss at Salomon—founded his own firm: Long-Term Capital Management.

This conglomeration and associated complexity increased the difficulty of assessing profits. In 2005 Citigroup announced profits of $25 billion, one of the largest amounts ever reported by any company. (In the USA only Exxon Mobil and Apple have exceeded this figure.) But this claim was spurious. By 2008 Citigroup was effectively bust: the company survived because the US government provided it with capital and the Federal Reserve Board provided it with cash. Over any recent ten-year period, shareholders in Citigroup lost money. They would have been better off depositing their money in a bank account with Citigroup, but only because the US government ensured that the bank's depositors were paid in full.

Before the global financial crisis, governments (strictly speaking, the deposit protection schemes they sponsored) were known to stand behind deposits, up to a limit: but in principle larger depositors, and other bank creditors, were at risk. But not in reality. The collateral for trading activities provided by the retail deposit base proved crucial in 2007–8, when three of the five major independent investment banks failed— Lehman falling into bankruptcy, and Bear Stearns and Merrill Lynch into the arms of large retail banks—while the other two, Goldman Sachs and Morgan Stanley, survived only because they reconfigured themselves as bank-holding companies so that the Federal Reserve could open to them the channels to liquidity available to troubled retail banks. After 2008 governments made more or less explicit the assurances of support that had earlier been more or less implicit.

The largest bank at risk—the largest bank in the world, Citigroup— was supported through the US Treasury's *ad hoc* 'troubled assets relief program'. Shareholders of 'the Bank' and 'the Royal Bank,' of Bear Stearns and Lehman, and of all Irish and Icelandic banks lost virtually

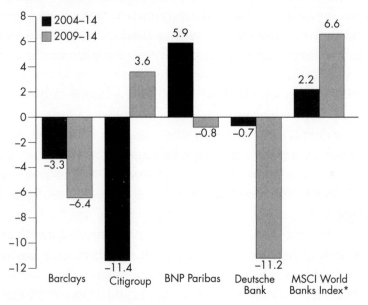

Figure 3: **Annualised shareholder returns of major banks, August–August (per cent per annum) (Total shareholder return, including dividends)**

*Composed of large and mid-cap stocks across twenty-three developed markets. US dollar return.
Source: Morningstar, MSCI

everything. The US government made good the phenomenal losses at AIG, Citigroup, and Fannie Mae and Freddie Mac, leaving some value for shareholders. Shareholders in Bank of America and Barclays also lost most of their investment.

Shareholders in financial companies were victims, not beneficiaries, of the boom and bust of the first decade of the twenty-first century. Over the fifteen years prior to 29 August 2014, the annual compounded gross return on the MSCI World Bank Index was 3 per cent. Within diversified financial conglomerates, many activities were profitable in that period— market-making, securities issuance, asset management and some retail products. Much of that profit was paid to senior employees. The remainder was more than offset by overall losses on wholesale financial market activities. The bezzle and febezzle, the money borrowed from destiny, was paid to senior employees of banks. Large financial conglomerates were run for the primary benefit of the people who manage them—and, in the main, they still are.[27]

Of course, apologists will explain, the global financial crisis was a once-in-a-lifetime event. In the sense that the tailgater experiences a crash once in a lifetime, the gambler who uses a martingale strategy capitulates once in a lifetime, the perpetuator of the Ponzi scheme is exposed once in a lifetime. The crisis was a product of the events that preceded it; and the losses incurred were inseparable from these earlier profits.

In the years before the global financial crisis, bank CEOs competed like schoolboys to demonstrate that 'my return on equity is larger than yours'. The display was led by Josef Ackermann, chief executive of Deutsche Bank from 2002 and chairman from 2006 to 2012, who announced a target of 25 per cent return on equity. In 2008, as the global financial crisis broke around him, he proudly announced that this target had been achieved.

Return on equity (RoE) is a ratio of profit to shareholders' funds, and there are two ways to increase a ratio. You can raise the numerator—the profit—or you can reduce the denominator—the equity capital. Reducing equity is easier. RoE is a seriously misleading measure of profitability. For businesses that are not very capital-intensive—such as asset management, or other professional service firms such as accountants, high returns on equity are achievable because the capital requirement is so small. Capital-intensive businesses—in the modern economy they are principally banks, utilities and resource companies—can achieve high returns on equity only through extreme leverage, as Deutsche Bank did.

Even as the thinly capitalised Deutsche Bank was benefiting from state guarantees of its liabilities, it was buying back its own shares to reduce its capital base. And whatever return on equity was claimed by the financial officers of Deutsche Bank, the shareholder returns told a different, and more enlightening, story: the average annual total return on its shares (in US dollars with dividends re-invested) over the period May 2002 to May 2012 (Ackermann's tenure as chief executive of the bank) was around minus 2 per cent. RoE is an inappropriate performance metric for any company, but especially for a bank, and it is bizarre that its use should have been championed by people who profess particular expertise in financial and risk management.

Banks still proclaim return on equity targets: less ambitious, but nevertheless fanciful. In recent discussions of the implications of imposing more extensive capital requirements on banks, a figure of 15 per cent has been proposed and endorsed as a measure of the cost of equity capital to conglomerate banks.[28] If these companies were really likely to earn 15 per cent rates of return for the benefit of their shareholders, there would be long queues of investors seeking these attractive returns. In practice, most European and some American banks are unable to raise any capital at all from investors, and the new capital which has been needed to restore bank balance sheets following the losses of 2008 has principally been supplied by governments or by customers. Modern financial conglomerates are not so much engines generating large profits as institutions that suck up public subsidy.

The accounts of major banks are lengthy and impenetrable. No one really knows the profitability of banks, year by year, business segment by business segment, or in aggregate. The proliferation of poorly understood complexity in the financial sector was intentional: complex products were a source of profit, and these products would have been less rewarding for the sellers if they had been better understood by the buyers. But this complexity would in the end overwhelm the management of financial institutions, as the requirements of oversight increased faster than the capabilities of executives and regulators entrusted with that oversight.

The key to a high return on equity is to have little equity in your capital base—to have very high leverage—and Deutsche Bank achieved this to more dramatic effect than any large company in history. At the onset of the global financial crisis equity represented less than 2 per cent of the liabilities of Germany's largest bank. How could anyone suppose that a trading entity with liabilities twenty, thirty, even fifty times its capital would remain stable, far less be an appropriate repository for the savings of individuals and the credit system of a nation? No other industry operates on such a thin capital base, and no financial institution would lend to a non-financial institution whose finances were so insecure. But Deutsche Bank was thought to be impregnable, like Citigroup and AIG—and, thanks to the German government and European Central Bank, it is. When government stands behind you, it is not necessary to be profitable, to be politically and economically powerful or to be well placed to provide handsome rewards to senior employees.

Governments too have become tailgaters, taking risks in support of the financial system that will probably pay off, but which may entail immense costs if they do not. Some governments will announce that the measures they took in 2008 had no cost, or even yielded a profit. Such claims have already been made for the US government's TARP programme. But guarantees are not free.

The provision of loan guarantees—whether by the relative of a borrower, the founder of a business, or a government—is an archetypal tailgate strategy. Mostly the guarantees are not called, and the result is a small benefit with no apparent cost. Sometimes the guarantees are called, however, and the costs may be very large. The Irish government foolishly made an explicit promise to meet the liabilities of what were in fact insolvent (in the case of Anglo-Irish Bank, hopelessly insolvent) banks: the costs of this operation will be a burden on the Irish economy for a decade or more. Yet Ireland is not the worst imaginable case: Ireland's banks were not very large, and their losses were substantially attributable to bad lending within Ireland itself. That the bail-out was essentially a redistribution within Ireland to the spivs, speculators and ordinary opportunistic Irish folk who had taken advantage of the country's property bubble, from Irish taxpayers (thus relieving foreign lenders to Irish banks of their potential losses).

The European Central Bank's support for the liabilities of the financial system of the Eurozone is the largest martingale in history. Each official intervention encountered pushback in markets, and after a few months Europe's institutions returned with intervention on a larger scale. Finally, in 2012, the newly appointed ECB governor, Mario Draghi, promised to do 'whatever it takes'[29]—his bank would stay at the table for as long as was needed to walk away from it successful. Perhaps this will turn out to be true.

Attempts have been made to measure the scale of public subsidy to the banking sector from the implicit or explicit underwriting provided by the taxpayer. There are two—similar—approaches. One asks how much borrowing costs for banks would rise if there were not state support; the other uses the market in credit default swaps to assess what it would cost them to buy privately the insurance that is provided publicly. (Of course, no market on that scale could credibly exist.)

The most well-founded estimates of the subsidy are the measures of the likely impact on bank financing costs from the implementation of the UK's Independent Commission on Banking's recommendation that retail banking should be ring-fenced from other aspects of bank operations.[30] The Commission put these costs at between £4 billion and £7 billion annually.[31] More speculative estimates for the international banking sector as a whole have been made by Andrew Haldane of the Bank of England, who put the overall figure in 2007—before the global financial crisis—at $37 billion and in 2009—after the global financial crisis—at $250 billion.[32] A similar calculation by the IMF for the fiscal year 2011–12 came up with a range of figures from a low of $150 billion to as much as $500 billion (much of the latter figure relating to the euro area).[33]

The scale of subsidy described is very large, both in absolute terms and relative to the reported profits of banks,[34] but it is unproductive to become engaged in discussion of the detail. In practice, the cost to the general public of supporting the financial sector is likely to be much less than these figures, but might be considerably more. That wide dispersion of possible outcome is the nature of tailgating.

The more important point is that, if banks had to pay for the insurance provided by the doctrine of 'too big to fail', the trading activities in which they privately engage simply would not take place, or at least would not take place on the current scale. Much, perhaps all, of the profitability of these institutions comes from the willingness of lenders (including other financial institutions themselves) to make finance available on terms that would, in the absence of such public support, be regarded as too risky.

No one in that Halifax boardroom doubted that the essence of the proposal was to use the strong balance sheet established by routine deposit-taking and mortgage-lending activities to compete in a market populated by less creditworthy individuals and institutions. But at that time no one imagined that the scale of these trading activities would— as we will see in Chapter 6—come to completely overshadow the core business. 'If it seems too good to be true, it probably is.' That maxim for investors applies equally to the profitability of the financial sector.

## PART II

# THE FUNCTIONS OF FINANCE

*Part I described what the modern financial system does, how that has been affected by financialisation and the consequences for the non-financial economy. Part II is concerned with the necessary underlying functions of a modern financial system. Economies need finance to facilitate payments, to channel the savings of individuals into fresh investment and to enable households to manage their finances over their lifetimes and to transfer wealth between generations. These next chapters describe how, and how well, these core purposes of search for new opportunities and stewardship of existing ones are achieved. Chapter 5 reviews the central mechanism of a capitalist economy—the translation of household wealth into productive assets. Chapters 6 and 7 look at the two primary mechanisms that facilitate that process—the deposit channel and the investment channel.*

# CHAPTER 5

# Capital Allocation

## Physical Assets

> The price or money-form of commodities is, like their form of value generally, a form quite distinct from their palpable bodily form.
>
> KARL MARX, *Capital*, Volume I, 1867

In an ill-judged interview with the *Sunday Times* in 2009, Lloyd Blankfein, CEO of Goldman Sachs, claimed that his company was doing 'God's work'.[1] The Deity's purpose was 'to help companies to grow by helping them to raise capital. Companies that grow create cash. This, in turn, allows people to have jobs that create more growth and more wealth. It's a virtuous cycle.' If you asked the occupants of the executive floors of the buildings on Wall Street or in the City of London to explain what the finance industry contributed to the real economy, their answers would echo Mr Blankfein's (although perhaps without the divine blessing). The financial sector raises and allocates capital.

A central function of financial markets is to direct money from savers to businesses, home-owners and governments. They in turn use these savings to build, own and operate houses, shops, offices, warehouses and factories, to buy plant and machinery, and to develop the nation's infrastructure and civil works, its roads, bridges, electricity and telephone cables, pipelines and sewers. Or so it should be.

Each generation inherits a stock of assets from the one that preceded it. Each generation makes use of that stock and sees it depreciate. Each generation adds to it, and passes an augmented capital stock on to the generations that follow. An effective financial system aids businesses, households and governments to achieve these objectives—and enables them to leave behind a better country than the one they found. Or so it should be.

I will describe these two key functions of the financial system as search and stewardship. Search is the pursuit of new investment opportunities, stewardship the management of long-term assets that have already been created. This chapter will mainly be concerned with search, and Chapter 7 principally with stewardship. The distinction between search and stewardship in capital allocation is well established in the commercial property sector. Property developers look for sites and possibilities of refurbishment and reconstruction, and investors hold property as long-term investment, and they have different skills, expertise and, often, corporate structures. Of course, some firms will fulfil both development and investment roles, and the twin functions are never wholly distinct, but the dichotomy is familiar and useful.

If we look at the financial sector today with that distinction in mind, many of the people who work in it do not really seem to be engaged in either search or stewardship. The central paradox of this chapter is the intensification of the dichotomy that Marx described, between the physical assets themselves and the securities that represent them. Financialisation diverted more and more resources to what was described as the process of capital allocation. But that expertise was, in the main, not devoted to search, the promotion of new tangible investment, or stewardship, the care and management of assets. It was not directed to the building of new houses, the creation and maintenance of infrastructure, the development and organic growth of businesses. The expansion was in trade in securities related to existing houses, infrastructure and businesses. The new generation of financiers knew less, not more, than their predecessors about the needs of households for accommodation, the utilities that make everyday commercial and social life possible, the competitive strengths and corporate strategies of new and established businesses. The world they inhabited was that self-referential one in which they talked, and traded, mostly with each other.

But to understand the role of capital markets, begin by understanding the nature of capital itself. If you want to measure the value of the nation's assets, there are two approaches. You might look at the assets themselves—the palpable, bodily form, to use Marx's nineteenth-century Germanic terminology—or you could look at the securities that represent these assets—'the price or money-form of commodities'.

To assess the assets themselves, you would travel the country and walk its streets, digging under them to find its pipes and cables, visiting offices, shops and factories, traversing roads and railways. At every stage you would estimate the values of the assets you identified. You begin with the assets you can see: a house, a rack of goods in a warehouse, an electricity line. But you will also want to include many assets that are valuable and even tradable, but which are not things you can easily touch and feel: a copyright, part of the radio spectrum, an entitlement to walk across someone's land or to emit smoke or extract water. Some assets—such as software—are on the borderline between the tangible and the intangible. Many goods and services have dematerialised. Possession of knowledge is as important as the ownership of physical property. These intangible assets have far greater significance today than Marx imagined (with wide-ranging implications).

But this extension of the concept of capital should not—at least for present purposes—be taken too far. Economists talk about 'human capital', derived from education and training, which although not tradable is manifestly valuable. Others have used the term 'social capital' to describe the value of trust and social bonds.[2] It is, perhaps, a minor side-effect of financialisation that so many commentators feel it necessary to use the language of finance to describe social institutions far distant from the world of finance. But the physical assets relevant to financial markets are those tangible or intangible things that you can, or at least might, buy or sell.

Another, quite different, approach to the measurement of capital assesses household wealth—in the language of Marx, it examines the price, or money-form, of commodities rather than their bodily form. To measure this you would knock on doors, ask people how rich they were, and add up the results. The respondents might tell you about their houses, their mortgages and other debts, the securities they hold, the cash they have in

Figure 4: **Physical assets of nations, end of 2012 (local currency in trillions)**

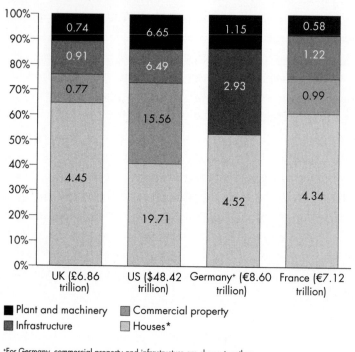

+For Germany, commercial property and infrastructure are shown together.

*Structures only (excluding underlying land) in France and Germany.

Source: OECD, Federal Reserve (US real estate)

their wallets and purses and bank accounts. They might value their pension expectations. Or they might not.

The statistics offices of developed countries conduct both these exercises—the assessment of physical assets and the measurement of household wealth. Not, of course, in quite the ways I have described. There is an element of subjectivity, an arbitrariness, about both procedures. The measurement of capital and wealth is not a precise exercise.[3]

The physical assets of the nation are mostly houses. As Figure 4 shows, residential property accounts for about 60 per cent of the value of the capital stock of Britain and France, 50 per cent of that of Germany, and 40 per cent of the physical assets of the USA. The balance is made up, in roughly equal amounts, by commercial property, infrastructure, and business assets.[4]

Since houses are much longer-lived than other assets, the composition of new investment is more equally balanced between these three

Figure 5: **UK investment* by asset class, 1990–2010 (£ billion at 2010 prices)**

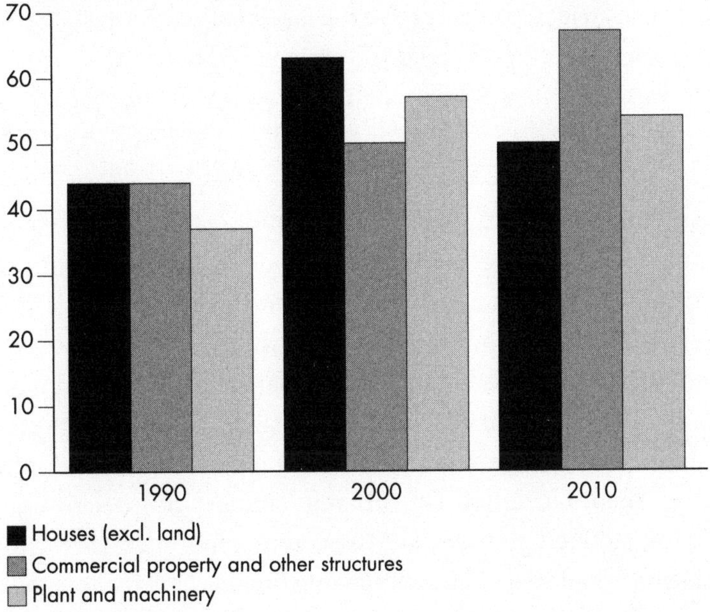
70
60
50
40
30
20
10
0
1990
2000
2010
Houses (excl. land)
Commercial property and other structures
Plant and machinery

*Gross Fixed Capital Formation.
Source: Office for National Statistics

broad categories than the stock itself (Figure 5). The pattern of investment varies considerably from year to year, reflecting housing booms and busts, and the ebbs and flows of public expenditure and business confidence.

The physical assets of the nation are financed by the wealth of its households. Where else could the resources come from? The complexities of financial markets sometimes obscure the central point that all capital originates in personal savings. People talk about 'new sources of finance' when what they mean is new ways of channelling existing sources of finance; they confuse the channels of intermediation with the origin of funds. The remainder of Chapter 5 describes the ways in which capital is deployed to build the physical assets of nations. Chapters 6 and 7 describe the two channels—the deposit channel and the investment channel—by which intermediation directs household wealth for these purposes.

## Housing

I believe the stars are aligned in a way they have not been aligned before. You have a political consensus that you have not had in decades.... You have both sides saying we have to do something about housing.

ANDREW CUOMO, secretary of Housing and Urban Development, remarks on housing policy in the new millennium, 2 October 2000

Financing the purchase of residential property is the largest element of the capital allocation mechanism of a modern economy. Until the era of financialisation, Wall Street, the City and other wholesale financial centres played only a minor role in funding housing. From the 1980s this changed, with disastrous results. Misallocation of housing finance was central to the global financial crisis. Mortgages did become cheaper, for a time, and then more expensive. Many individuals who had unwisely dabbled in the housing market suffered hardship or foreclosure. Every major bank suffered substantial losses, and some, such as Washington Mutual, which had specialised in housing finance, failed altogether. Fannie Mae and Freddie Mac, the two parastatal agencies that dominated US housing finance, collapsed. The share of owner-occupation in the housing stock declined for the first time in a century.

At the beginning of the twentieth century, most households—not just low-income households—rented their homes. But landlords have always been unpopular. A history of rent control, and legislation that limited the rights and extended the obligations of landlords, reduced the economic and political attractions of investment in housing, while tax advantages made owner-occupation an attractive means of saving. And owners tend to be better occupiers. By the end of the twentieth century owner-occupation had become the norm.

So today most houses are owned by the people who live in them. First-time house-buyers arrange a mortgage for a substantial fraction, usually between 60 and 100 per cent, of the value of the property. This is a highly leveraged transaction. But if house prices rise, the debt diminishes as a proportion of the total, and the equity of the owner—the difference between the value of the property and the debt—increases. In Britain and France, most of the value of the housing stock—around two-thirds—is owners' equity. In these countries this accumulation of housing equity is the main vehicle for household saving. In other countries—such as the USA—mortgage interest can be deducted from income for tax purposes. Perhaps for this reason, households in these countries tend to have larger mortgages, relative to the value of their properties, and more financial assets—stocks, funds, insurance and pension policies. The overhang of the sub-prime mortgage boom in the USA is also an explanation of the very high debt-to-value ratio in that country.

Germany is different. A majority of households rent, rather than own, the property they live in. Investment institutions—commonly, large insurance companies—own a substantial proportion of the housing stock. Such institutional ownership was once common in other countries. But with the growth of owner-occupation the private rented sector is today dominated by public and quasi-public agencies which provide social housing for low-income households. A few individual private landlords channel long-term savings into a property or a small portfolio of properties.

With the growth of owner-occupation across the twentieth century, specialist institutions—thrifts in the USA, building societies in Britain, *Bausparkassen* in Germany—grew rapidly through the provision of residential mortgages. But with financialisation, in both Britain and the USA a structure that had worked well for decades was dismantled. Deregulatory measures were motivated by considerations of general principle rather than specific adverse experience of the consequences of regulation. Ambitious financiers brought innovative techniques and imaginative structures into sectors about which they knew little. People who were capable managers of housing finance organisations imagined themselves great international financiers. Delusions of grandeur played almost as large a role in the era of financialisation as did avarice, as illustrated by men such as Fred Goodwin and Sandy Weill, Robert Campeau and Jeff Skilling. American savings and loan deregulation was enlivened by a sprinkling of crooks. The housing finance system wasn't broken, but we fixed it, and then it broke.

The new methods of housing finance, like the old, relied largely on local representatives, but these representatives were sales people, not loan officers. Often in collusion with borrowers, they exploited a central system operated by people who devised clever structures but knew very little of the fundamentals that underpinned what they were doing. The growth of markets in residential mortgage-backed securities led not to an intensification of knowledge about housing markets but to its dissipation. Thrifts and building societies disappeared, and when new institutions entered the industry, as they did in the US sub-prime sector, they were essentially mortgage-selling businesses, not specialist lenders. The paradox is that, while the resources diverted to financial intermediation in the housing market increased, housing expertise diminished.

The thrift industry was deregulated in 1980. Because of the structure of the US mortgage market, with rates paid by borrowers fixed for the term of the mortgage, thrifts had been hit hard by the abrupt rises in interest rate engineered by the Fed under Paul Volcker. Deregulation would, it was hoped, allow them to earn their way out of financial difficulty through profitable expansion. The opposite proved to be the case. The reform was followed immediately by extensive diversification by thrifts and soon after by widespread failures. The Resolution Trust Corporation was established in 1989 to manage failed thrifts. The rescue package financed by the Federal Government was the most expensive financial bail-out prior to the global financial crisis.

The gap left by the collapse of thrifts was filled partly by established banks but also by the development of new specialist lenders. By 2006 the largest and eventually most notorious of these, Countrywide Financial, under its aggressive and well-connected CEO, Angelo Mozilo, accounted for 20 per cent of all US mortgage lending. With similar excess, Northern Rock accounted for 19 per cent of new British mortgage funding in 2007. Countrywide was bought by Bank of America in July 2008 in one of the worst corporate acquisitions ever made.

Deregulation and new industrial structures were accompanied by financial innovation. Thrifts, building societies and similar organisations matched deposits and loans, but some were good at raising deposits and others better at selling mortgages. Wholesale markets could make up the difference. But mortgage securitisation created new opportunities.

Securitisation received a boost from the Basel agreements on bank regulation from 1987. Mortgages packaged into bonds and graded by rating agencies were effectively treated as less risky than the underlying mortgages. Mortgages could be further tranched or rebundled into more complex packages which would also be assessed by the agencies. The pace of securitisation, packaging and repackaging, tranching and re-tranching grew increasingly frenetic. The demand for mortgage-backed securities was such that in the USA sales people on commission pressed mortgages on anyone who could sign their name on an application.

In the revisionist account of the global financial crisis, excesses in mortgage securitisation were the result of US government measures to widen home-ownership.[5] There is something in this explanation, but not much. The great expansion of owner-occupation occurred when there was almost no secondary trading of mortgages—the lender retained the mortgage, and security on the property, until the loan was repaid. In the USA the transition from renting to owner-occupation had more or less been accomplished by the 1960s, while Britain also pushed home-ownership above 60 per cent in the 1980s as a result of the sale to tenants of much of the social housing stock under the Thatcher government.

Experience around the world suggests that 70 per cent may be a natural limit to the sensible proportion of owner-occupation; beyond that point, people are drawn into the housing market whose financial affairs or financial competence may be too precarious to support the obligations involved. The USA pushed towards and sometimes beyond that limit as the seemingly insatiable demand for mortgage-backed securities led lenders to lower standards of assessment.

Despite the efforts of mortgage sales organisations such as Countrywide, the volume of low-quality mortgages was still insufficient to satisfy the demands of those who wanted to trade in mortgage-backed securities, leading to the development of a market in 'synthetic mortgage-backed securities'. These were simply wagers on the value of packages of mortgages that had already been bought and sold by other people.

Some individuals made a great deal of money out of the process. Lew Ranieri, who first sold residential mortgage-backed securities, and John Paulson, who used credit default swaps to bet that many of these instruments would fail, both became billionaires. Angelo Mozilo, CEO of Countrywide, the world's worst mortgage lender, and Franklin Raines, CEO of Fannie Mae, the world's worst mortgage insurer, were rewarded for their efforts with hundreds of millions of dollars. More modest fortunes were made by the 'financial advisers' such as Lee Farkas, who will reappear in Chapter 10, who persuaded indigent borrowers to take on mortgages they could never repay, by bond salesmen who peddled tranches of mortgage-backed securities and by rating agencies which gave their stamp of approval to complex securitised products. What was lost, in the end, was mostly other people's money. By 2007–8, it became apparent that even the most senior tranche of a package of mortgages sold to people who were in default and whose houses were difficult to sell was likely to be worth very little.

The story of that collapse has been told in detail in many places.[6] Mozilo would settle charges levelled against him by the SEC with a payment of $67.5 million. With the cognitive dissonance of the tailgater, he would explain that the considerably larger amount he had received for his services as chief executive of Countrywide was justified by the profits that his company had reported from the sale of mortgages before the borrowers failed to pay them back. I'll be gone, you'll be gone.

With the decline of thrifts, bank examiners had assumed the role formerly played by the Office of Thrift Supervision (although this famously incompetent regulator continued in existence; AIG Financial Products, issuer of credit default swaps, discovered a loophole that enabled it to operate under the Office's feeble oversight). But as the focus of mortgage-lending in Britain and the USA shifted to banks supervision was, if anything, more intense and was certainly administered by stronger regulatory institutions than those which had done the job two or three decades earlier. If there was a shortage of equity capital to support housing lending, it was because the reorganisation of the industry had led to capital dissipation in demutualisation windfalls and unwise diversification.

The fundamental causes of the crisis in housing finance were to be found in changes in the structure of the housing finance sector. The lengthening of the chain of intermediation, and the growth in secondary market activity, did not improve the efficiency of capital allocation. Capital allocation was worse—much worse. The weakening of the line between lender and borrower led to low-quality underwriting and poor management of delinquent mortgages. Lenders lost their money, and borrowers their homes. Badly designed capital requirements on lenders encouraged securitisation and off-balance sheet activities. Rating agencies were given a monitoring role by regulators that they were not equipped to perform and which they lacked an incentive to perform well.

The saga of US housing exemplifies what has gone wrong in the global financial system, and what needs to be done to put it right. The problems originated in structural changes in the industry which followed from financial innovation (notably securitisation) and the removal of restrictions on diversification by financial institutions—measures which were well intentioned but in practice proved to be damaging, They were aggravated by related changes in individual and business incentives which rewarded trading volumes rather than productive long-term commercial relationships.

The success or failure of any system of housing finance should be judged by whether we have the houses we need, in the locations where they are needed, and whether the houses are well matched to the needs of the people who live in them. It would require a whole book to answer the question of whether or not we are better housed, and this book is not it.

What is relevant for this book, however, is that the question 'Are we better housed?' is not a question that would occur to most people now engaged in housing finance today. Some of those involved—such as Mozilo—paid lip-service to the claim that they were housing the nation even as they built mansions for themselves: but most of those involved in trading in residential mortgage-backed securities had no knowledge of or interest in housing at all, beyond a hunch that house prices usually went up. When housing finance was the province of building societies, thrifts and *Bausparkassen*, the people who ran these organisations understood that their role was to help meet the housing needs of the communities in which they operated. The shift in focus from the *purposes* of intermediation to the *process* of intermediation was also evident in other areas of capital allocation.

## Property and Infrastructure

> Secretary Summers, that was a fine speech, and I agree with all of it. Just one thing—why should any of the students believe you when there is paint chipping off the walls of their classroom? . . . There is no chipping paint at any bank.
>
> ANONYMOUS TEACHER, in conversation with Larry Summers,
> reported by Summers in the *Huffington Post*, 14 April 2014

Shops, offices and warehouses are the main forms of commercial (investment) property. Other non-residential buildings include factories, schools and hospitals. Most commercial property is privately owned and occupied, but government occupies considerable office space and public agencies play a large role in health and education. Infrastructure includes roads and bridges, airports and railway lines, pipes and sewers, telephone wires and electricity cables. Historically, most infrastructure was owned and operated directly by government. But a large part of it is now privately 'owned', although the 'ownership' is, essentially, a licence to operate that infrastructure on terms determined by a regulator.

Property and infrastructure are long-term assets which provide relatively predictable and stable returns over an extended period. Businesses are subject to competitive pressures and may suffer or benefit from rapid technological change. Their equity is risky; their loans may not be repaid. But shops and offices, factories and warehouses, bridges and sewers, schools and hospitals, are always there and always necessary. Populations shift, shopping areas go in and out of fashion, and new technology has altered the design of office space. But such change is mostly gradual.

Both these asset classes benefit from specific, relevant expertise. Many property agents know both how to manage buildings and how to advise investors on the financial returns. Architects, surveyors and builders have experience in construction. Infrastructure is more idiosyncratic, but consultants offer project management capabilities around the world, and many engineers are highly knowledgeable about the development and use of infrastructure assets.

Property and infrastructure are natural homes for the long-term savings, and particularly the retirement funds, of households. Before financialisation, infrastructure was mostly funded in this way, with government bonds purchased by insurance companies and pension funds on behalf of long-term savers. Some commercial property was—and is—funded similarly, through direct ownership of buildings by these institutions. But financialisation has changed—and complicated—these structures. Direct investment in property by institutional investors has declined in overall significance, and the processes of financing infrastructure have been substantially changed by the privatisation of many utilities and the adoption of a variety of public–private partnerships.

The relatively stable pattern of underlying yields on property can be transformed by the use of leverage, which divides the overall return on the investment into a debt component and an equity element. Such use of leverage has always been a common means of financing property development and purchase. Lending on the security of property carries a small probability of significant loss, in return for which it commands a higher yield—a classic tailgating structure. But since property lending in good times appears to offer enhanced returns with no apparent risk of loss, competitive imitation occurs whenever economic growth is fast and prices are buoyant. Banks and other lenders, seeing their rivals steal volume and report profits, relax lending criteria. Conventional wisdom holds that property values always go up—and indeed in the long run, that conventional wisdom is often true. But time horizons in the finance sector are shorter: I'll be gone, you'll be gone.

The equity element of a leveraged property transaction has high volatility. The upside may be large, the downside limited to loss of the equity investment, with further losses borne by the debt providers. When economic conditions are benign, almost everyone who gambles in the property market with highly geared equity makes money. And, like all gamblers, they interpret their success as evidence of their skill. In the run-up to the global financial crisis many people persuaded themselves that the profits they had made from rising house prices were evidence of their financial acumen: numerous books on 'how to become rich by flipping properties' were listed on Amazon. Even after the crisis and its consequences, some of the books are still in print.

Speculation in property has created great fortunes but also spectacular losses. In 2008 Sean Quinn was reported by the *Sunday Times* 'Rich List' to be the wealthiest man in Ireland and among the 200 richest people in the world, with a fortune of around €4 billion. In 2011 he was declared bankrupt. Equity investors in property, and the institutions that provide debt to them, are potential victims of the winner's curse. Properties are idiosyncratic, and the equity investor who buys a shop or office outbids other equally well-informed investors. The financial institution that finances the purchase has similarly undercut other lenders for the privilege of financing the transaction. For Anglo-Irish Bank, which had lent Quinn almost €3 billion, the winner's curse was indeed a curse. (Sean FitzPatrick, the bank's CEO, comfortably outranks Fred Goodwin for the title of world's worst banker, and Anglo-Irish, now owned by the Irish government, is in the process of being wound up.)

Commercial property values are correlated with each other, with economic conditions, and with the prices of many other assets. The potential for booms and busts is obvious. And realised, at regular intervals. The process of leverage, applied on a modest scale, might enable investors to pool and diversify the modest risks intrinsic in commercial property investment. The reality is that the packaging of property risk has turned commercial property into a significant and frequent source of economic instability.

Most infrastructure has been built by government or its agencies. There were exceptions—railroads, the US telephone network and even some subway lines were built and operated by private firms. But a history of political interference, lack of profitability, inadequate performance and wartime destruction meant that by 1950 most privately financed infrastructure had come into state ownership. Funds for public infrastructure were part of general government borrowing, although nationalised industries and other agencies were sometimes able to borrow on their own account. This borrowing was often explicitly government guaranteed, and even when it was not, it was assumed to be government guaranteed.

After Margaret Thatcher became UK prime minister in 1979, government control of infrastructure was reorganised, through the sale of state industries, contracting out of government services, public–private partnerships and the financing of infrastructure investment through private finance initiatives. Britain pioneered these reforms, but they were widely imitated in other countries. As an army of lawyers, accountants and other consultants offered advice around the world, expertise in these complex financial transactions became a British export industry.

Public-sector management of large infrastructure projects has often been poor, with substantial overruns and delays. Boston's 'Big Dig', a 3½-mile tunnel for Interstate 93 in Central Boston, was planned to cost $2.8 billion and be completed in seven years. The actual cost was $14.6 billion, and the project took fifteen years to complete. Large idiosyncratic construction projects often come in way over budget, but many of the most egregious examples have been government sponsored.

The pressing need to improve the management of public infrastructure has, however, become conflated with increasingly complex mechanisms of financing. Removing debt from the public-sector balance sheet was an objective of privatisation from the very beginning.

But accounting manipulation is a slippery slope. Off-balance-sheet financing was central to Enron's frauds. A complex transaction managed by Goldman Sachs flattered Greece's national accounts in order to ease its entry into the Eurozone. The aptly named SIVs—structured investment vehicles—were a primary mechanism by which banks hid the scale of their exposures in the years before 2008.

The ugly but iconic building on the corner of Parliament Square occupied by the UK Treasury is rented from a private company, Exchequer Partnerships, which is highly leveraged and has no other activities. This 'special purpose vehicle' is owned by a consortium created by Bovis (a construction company), Stanhope and Chelsfield (property companies), Chesterton (an estate agent) and Hambros Bank. The money was borrowed in a 'funding competition' at a premium of 1.63 per cent per annum to the government's own borrowing rate.

One purpose of these financing mechanisms is to disguise the extent of public-sector debt. What is not clear is from whom it is intended to be disguised. The political opposition, perhaps, but governments of all complexions have engaged in this chicanery. Are bond traders and rating agencies taken in by such transparent ruses? Perhaps. Or perhaps the purpose is to enable politicians and officials to deceive themselves.

In any event, the net cost of such arrangements to taxpayers around the world can be counted in many billions. To be fair, the bulk of this overpayment has gone to enhance the returns on our pensions and other long-term savings. But a large part has been creamed off along the way by a private finance industry which has an interest in continuing to complicate the essentially simple matter of raising long-term finance for government and its agencies.

The recent history of public infrastructure has seen a necessary attempt to achieve greater expertise in the planning and management of large projects hijacked by financial, legal and accounting interests in favour of progressively more—and unnecessarily—esoteric financial transactions. At present, governments of countries such as Britain, France, Germany and the USA can borrow more cheaply than ever before.

These market conditions provide an unprecedented opportunity to refresh the paintwork in the school as well as the bank, and more broadly to renew the crumbling public infrastructure that is particularly evident in the UK and USA. Yet instead of borrowing on spectacularly favourable terms, governments are aggressively buying back their long-term debt and cutting their capital expenditures in the name of austerity. Public finances are being shored up by costly short-term off-balance-sheet financing. I shall explain this conjuncture further in Chapter 9. But the common sense that sees the outcome as absurd contains more wisdom than technical explanations peppered with acronyms such as PPP, PFI, QE and SIV.

## Large Companies

> A bank is a place that will lend you money if you can prove that you don't need it.
>
> attributed to BOB HOPE

Lloyd Blankfein explained that the work his company engaged in was 'to help companies grow by helping them to raise capital'. There are two mistakes here. 'Helping companies grow by helping them to raise capital' was not, in fact, an important part of the business of Goldman Sachs. Raising capital for companies through underwriting and issuance of new debt and equity have together accounted for less than 10 per cent of the company's net revenues in the last five years.[7] Goldman's profits are mainly derived from secondary market trading in equities and FICC.

The other mistake is to think that the companies who are the typical clients of Goldman Sachs grow by raising external capital. While major corporations once used the London and New York stock exchanges and other capital markets to raise funds to expand their businesses, this has not been true for many years.

Exxon Mobil has been both the most profitable company and the biggest private investor in the USA. Massive expenditure on exploration and development and on infrastructure is necessary every year to exploit new energy resources and bring oil products to market. In 2013 Exxon

Mobil invested $20 billion. That figure was in itself a significant fraction of total investment by US corporations. Exxon got all of that money from its own internal resources. In 2013 Exxon Mobil spent $16 billion buying back its own shares, in addition to the $11 billion the company paid in dividends to shareholders. The company's short- and long-term debt levels were virtually unchanged. It raised no net new capital at all.

Nor was 2013 an exceptional year. Over the five years up to and including 2013, the activities of the corporation generated almost $250 billion in cash, around twice the amount it invested. Exxon Mobil did not raise any new capital in these five years either. Instead the company spent around $100 billion repurchasing securities it had previously issued.

Oil exploration, production and distribution are capital-intensive. Many modern companies need very little capital. The stock market capitalisation of Apple—the total market value of the company's shares—is over $500 billion. Although the corporation has large cash balances—currently around $150 billion—it has few other tangible assets. Manufacturing is subcontracted. Apple is building a new headquarters building in Cupertino at an estimated cost of $5 billion, which will be its principal physical asset. The corporation currently occupies a variety of properties in that town, some of them owned, others leased. The flagship UK store on London's Regent Street is jointly owned by the Queen and the Norwegian sovereign wealth fund. Operating assets therefore represent only around 3 per cent of the estimated value of Apple's business.

Apple shares have been listed on NASDAQ since 1980, when the corporation raised $100 million from investors. Even then, the purpose of the issue was not to obtain money to grow the business. As with most flotations of technology companies, the reason for bringing the company to market was to give early investors and employees of the business an opportunity to realise value. Forty members of Apple staff became (paper) millionaires that day, and Steve Jobs' wealth was estimated at over $200 million. Mike Markkula, who had invested $80,000 to enable Jobs and his partner Steve Wozniak to start making computers, was similarly enriched. Stock markets are not a way of putting money into companies, but a means of taking it out.

The opportunity to realise a return on investment is essential to an early stage investor such as Markkula. The ability to attach value to their shareholdings provides an incentive to Jobs and his colleagues and successors. Once a business becomes established, long-term institutional investors will pay for a share in the profit stream generated. This opportunity enables angel investors such as Markkula, and entrepreneurs like Jobs, to monetise their efforts. This opportunity for realisation fulfils an important economic function. But it is not the function for which stock markets originally developed, and the volume of trading needed to serve these functions is modest.

The first companies to obtain listings on modern markets were companies like railways and breweries, with large requirements for capital for very specific purposes. Building a railway is expensive, and once you have built it the only thing you can do with it is run trains. You cannot use a brewery except to brew beer. Early utilities and manufacturing corporations raised large amounts of money in small packets from private individuals.

But both the commercial world and the financial world have changed. Today most business premises are offices, shops or warehouses that can be used for many purposes. The companies that operate from these buildings do not need to own them and usually do not. As at Apple, the assets that matter to these businesses are largely intangible: the brands and reputation of the company, the skills and capabilities of the people who work for it. While railways, car manufacturers and brewers needed additional funds to build new plants as they expanded, new companies today—such as Apple or Google—commonly become generators of cash, rather than users, early in their lifetime. When Facebook, unusually, raised $16 billion in fresh funds in its initial public offering, the company stated in the prospectus that it had no real idea what it would do with the money.

And the nature of share ownership has changed. The external shareholders of companies are no longer dispersed private individuals, who needed a public market-place if they were to achieve liquidity and a fair price for their holdings. Shareholdings are, as I will describe in Chapter 7, now concentrated in large institutions and controlled by professional asset managers. A paradox of financialisation is that the need for an active share market has diminished at the same time as the volume of trading has grown exponentially.

In an economy dominated by large corporations, the allocation of capital to investment projects is not decided by investors or financial institutions. Nor should it be. Neither shareholders nor investment banks are competent to determine the scale and content of Exxon Mobil's capital expenditure programme. The decisions about how much to invest, and where to spend it, are made by the corporation itself: that is the job its senior executives have been trained and selected to do.

The stock market plays an indirect role in capital allocation—and more broadly in judging the efficiency of operational management and corporate strategy—by supporting, or failing to support, incumbent management. If the results of Exxon Mobil's investment programme do not meet the long-term needs of the business, then its management should feel external pressure and ultimately risk the sack. What is often called stewardship—the supervision of management by informed investors—is not incidental to equity investment but is its primary modern role. I will discuss this aspect of share ownership further in Chapter 7.

Large companies issue debt. Not in general because they need the money for investment: debt for investment purposes is largely confined to public infrastructure. In 2012 the rates Exxon Mobil and a handful of similarly strong companies needed to pay on their bonds actually fell below the rates obtainable by the US government. Commercial paper—a short-term borrowing instrument initially created to finance cargoes at sea and later employed to fund inventories and work in progress—is also widely used. In Europe large companies rely more on bank debt and less on tradable debt securities—although loan securitisation has blurred the difference between the two.

Why do big companies borrow when they don't need the money? The corporate treasurer used to be the person who paid the company's bills. But he gained status and by the 1980s aimed to be a financier in his own right, making money for the company by taking positions in credit markets and foreign exchanges, exploiting interest rate and maturity differentials. This was the path the Halifax decided, somewhat belatedly, to follow. In a company like Exxon Mobil, the Treasury is effectively the banking division of a conglomerate corporation. The strong balance sheet established by the company's oil assets means that the business is more highly rated than any bank.

Apple raised $17 billion in a bond offering in 2013. Not to invest in new products or business lines, but to pay a dividend to stockholders. The company is awash with cash, but much of that money is overseas, and there would be a tax charge if it were repatriated to the USA. For many other companies, the tax-favoured status of debt relative to equity encourages financial engineering. Most large multinational companies have corporate and financial structures of mind-blowing complexity. The mechanics of these arrangements, which are mainly directed at tax avoidance or regulatory arbitrage, are understood by only a handful of specialists. Much of the securities issuance undertaken by Goldman Sachs was not 'helping companies to grow' but represented financial engineering of the kind undertaken at Apple.

What does this capital market activity have to do with business—to return to the question Burrough and Helyar raised? How does it relate to pumping oil, or selling iPads? Very little. Almost none of it is necessary to enable companies to meet their investment needs, which can be fully financed from their underlying cash generation. The use of capital markets by large companies today is mainly driven by tax and regulatory arbitrage, and undertaken by corporate treasurers with other people's money.

## Financing Small- and Medium-Size Enterprises

> 'Is not commercial credit based primarily upon money or property?'
> 'No sir. The first thing is character. . . . Because a man I do not trust could not get money from me on all the bonds in Christendom.'
>
> J. PIERPONT MORGAN, testimony before the Bank and
> Currency Committee of the House of Representatives
> (the Pujo Committee), Washington, DC, 19 December 1912

In modern economies, large companies finance investment through cash generated from operations. Small- and medium-size enterprises (SMEs) need capital to grow. Initially, they must rent and fit out premises, buy stocks of materials, install plant and equipment. But assets have become more fungible and companies less capital-intensive. These changes in the nature of business are as relevant to new businesses as to established small- and medium-size ones. The principal requirement for funding in small- and medium-size enterprises is to meet operating losses incurred as new businesses define and develop their products and establish a market position.

Obtaining finance for a small business has never been easy. A lending bank would require security, and property was the preferred collateral—the assets of the business might serve for this purpose, but often the bank would place a charge on the homes of the founders. Bank finance was, and continues to be, more suitable for businesses that needed to buy plant and fit out premises than for new companies which need to spend money to develop products or test them in the market-place.

But as financialisation gathered pace, and the traditional bank manager retired, or was made redundant, business lending operations were removed from bank branches and transferred to regional offices. More professional analysis of business plans replaced information gained at the nineteenth hole. The *Moneyball* phenomenon—the substitution of statistical methods for gut instinct and conventional wisdom—has improved outcomes in fields such as medicine, on which no baseball is played; dispassionate analysis of numbers is often more reliable than the conventional wisdom of people who emphasise the value of experience and know the value of little else.[8]

But the financing of small business is not only, or primarily, a matter of judging the numbers, as J.P. Morgan recognised. The success or failure of a new business depends very largely on the personality and capabilities of the individuals who run it, and these are difficult for a computer to assess. But the most important source of change was in the priorities of banks. The traditional bank took deposits from retail customers and lent them to businesses and, to a smaller extent, to government and individuals. The financial conglomerates of today retain the names of these institutions—Barclays, Citibank, Deutsche Bank. But traditional banking functions, and in particular the support of SMEs, represent only a small part of what these modern financial conglomerates do.

As banks gave less emphasis to the funding of business investment in SMEs, money was channelled to small start-up companies through venture capital, which was pioneered by rich individuals and a few imaginative asset managers. Some early investments in information technology—such as Markkula's backing of Apple—enjoyed spectacular success. If he had retained his shareholding, that investment alone would have made him the world's richest man. Markkula's investment in Apple was followed by specialist venture capital funds such as Sequoia Capital. Observing these exceptional returns, many institutional investors were earmarking funds for unlisted investments by the 1990s.

But the result was the transformation of what had once been called venture capital into private equity. Venture capital had been devised for start-up and early-stage businesses, such as the Apple of the 1970s: the focus of private equity was on buy-outs of existing businesses from large corporations, or the refinancing of established companies with additional leverage. The high fee levels appropriate for investments of small size which required careful monitoring were applied to the much larger sums of money deployed in financial engineering. The industry drifted from its initial purposes, in ways that generated more revenue for intermediaries but less economic value.

Apple, along with many other transformational new companies, was founded in the small area of California now known as Silicon Valley. Some other companies—such as Facebook—moved there at an early stage in their life. Yet other new businesses—such as Amazon and Microsoft—are based in Seattle or other locations on the West Coast.

The new businesses that have emerged in 'the Valley' are strongly, though not exclusively, focused on information technology and biotechnology. These industries benefited from heavy investment in basic research by the US government in the post-war era. Responsibility for such funding was divided among a range of bodies—the National Science Foundation, the National Institutes of Health and agencies of the US Defense Department. The resulting (and unintended) pluralism of approach was productive if also duplicative. The choice of location for these activities seems to have been the result of a combination of the aftermath of the war in the Pacific and the agreeable weather. The proximity of a major research-based university at Stanford is also significant, and many successful entrepreneurs have been Stanford alumni.[9]

The success of some early ventures established a pool of individuals with both considerable personal wealth and experience of the application of new technologies to infant businesses. These individuals supported fresh start-ups. Markkula had retired from Intel as a multimillionaire at the age of thirty-two. Another Intel veteran, John Doerr, was an early supporter of Amazon and Google. Peter Thiel, a founder of PayPal, was the first external investor in Facebook.

The activities of these and other entrepreneur financiers were aided by small financial advisory firms (the 'four horsemen': Alex Brown, Hambrecht & Quist, Montgomery Securities and Robertson Stephens) which acted as conduits for institutional investors to put money alongside business angels. Since the funds financed start-up losses, the finance involved necessarily took the form of equity, and initially neither investment banks nor retail banks were involved.

When the new economy bubble inflated in the 1990s, investment banks aggressively sought mandates to take Silicon Valley business public. Morgan Stanley's 'internet goddess', Mary Meeker, was a pioneer, and Frank Quattrone of Crédit Suisse First Boston was another prominent figure. The 'new economy' bubble burst in 2000, and Quattrone would soon spend more time in court than in investor presentations. The operations of the 'four horsemen' were subsumed into other divisions of the banks that had acquired them.

But by this time 'the Valley' had a life of its own, and it continued to be vibrant even after Wall Street interest shifted from high technology to mortgage-backed securities. Fresh venture capital firms took the place of the 'four horsemen'. The new businesses that continued to emerge were mainly focused on information technology and biotechnology, but the model has spread to some other sectors. Tesla Motors, the innovative electric car manufacturer, was founded by Elon Musk, another cofounder of PayPal.

But the popular obsession with Silicon Valley should not lead anyone to believe that all successful SMEs are made in California. The business writer Hermann Simon has identified around two thousand firms he calls 'hidden champions', distinguished by a combination of modest scale (revenues below $4 billion) and world-dominant positions in niche markets.[10] Most of their products are sold to other industrial firms and are items that most readers have never imagined buying. Characteristic examples include: Tetra, based in Blacksburg, Virginia, the global leader in food for ornamental fish; Saes, located in Lainate, north-west of Milan, which has 85 per cent of the world market for barium getters (chemically reactive materials which help maintain a vacuum); and Hamamatsu Photonics, a Japanese world leader in light sources for medical applications. These firms generally operate in sectors where customers attach much greater significance to quality than to price.

Although there are niche producers such as these in the USA, Italy and Japan, two-thirds of the 'hidden champions' come from Germany and the German-speaking areas of Switzerland and Austria. These 'hidden champions' are the stars of the *Mittelstand*, the small- and medium-size companies that are the basis of Germany's extraordinary strength in manufacturing exports. German exports per head are four times those of the USA and more than ten times those of China. The businesses of the *Mittelstand* are predominantly family-owned. 'Hidden champions' have little need of external capital—like quoted companies, they typically generate more than sufficient cash for their investment needs from their internal resources. But all businesses were once start-ups, and in need of early-stage finance.

Public equity markets play a more limited role in continental European countries than in the English-speaking world. The stock market value of German companies is around 40 per cent of German national income, compared with over 100 per cent in Britain and the USA. Business finance in Germany is mainly provided through its distinctive banking system, which has three elements, of broadly similar domestic scale. Global financial conglomerates, of which Deutsche Bank is by far the largest, are now similar in structure and behaviour to such conglomerates in other countries. Savings banks are owned by municipalities and regional governments. Within the savings bank sector, *Landesbanken*, owned by the provinces, began, in effect, as local central banks for the savings banks of the area but diversified their activities to become commercial and international banks. Co-operative banks, locally based mutuals, are the third element in the German banking system.

Financialisation has not passed Germany by. The global ambitions of Deutsche Bank will be discussed more fully in the next chapter, while the credit expansion of 2003–7 wreaked havoc among *Landesbanken*. Germany had more than its share of men like Fred Goodwin, successful provincial bankers with far grander visions of themselves. The German banking system was a prime dumping ground for the paper created by the securitisation and tranching of US sub-prime mortgages. WestLB, the *Landesbank* of North Rhine-Westphalia, was one of the prime European casualties of the global financial crisis, and the federal government took control of Commerzbank, the second-largest German bank. Yet the co-operative and savings bank sector, which provides around two-thirds of lending to the *Mittelstand* and is willing to provide long-term debt finance of a kind and on terms virtually unavailable to small business in Britain and the USA, emerged largely unscathed.

Throughout financialisation, global investment banks have sought to promote the development of capital markets in debt and equity in Germany and have frequently found support for this objective from the European Commission. The fragmented nature of German banking, and Germany's low level of capital market activity, has been the subject of criticism, even derision. Yet the German banking system has funded what is certainly the most effective SME sector in Europe, and possibly the world.

The *Mittelstand* has shown little interest in being brought to public markets. The normal pattern has been one of continued family ownership, with founders and their families being succeeded by professional management, a structure that fits with the German division between supervisory and executive board.

This pattern extends even to larger companies. BMW exists today because Herbert Quandt, a major hereditary shareholder, decided in 1959 to reject the absorption of the failing business into Mercedes and give new management authority to revamp its product range. The reclusive family, and their Quandt Foundation, profited by billions of euros. As noted in Chapter 1 a consequence of this concentrated ownership and governance structure, and the success of family controlled *Mittelstand* companies, is that Germany has a less egalitarian income and wealth distribution than other continental European countries.

Banks commonly hold equity stakes in German companies. Unlike venture capitalists and private equity investors in countries with high levels of trading activity, banks are willing to retain these stakes for decades. In Britain and the USA successful medium-size businesses grow by acquisition or are themselves acquired. But this 'hollowing out' of the middle of the size distribution of companies has not occurred in Germany.

The distance between Palo Alto and Germany's industrial heartland is much more than a geographical one, yet these provide the two main paradigms of successful small business finance. But it is Silicon Valley that governments around the world have attempted to emulate. With little success. Silicon Valley's particular combination of imaginative state support for core research and the training of highly qualified individuals, along with dynamic private sector innovation and enterprise—strikingly free from the influence of either established large corporations or conventional financing mechanisms—has not been effectively imitated. Perhaps the closest approximation is found in the development of a high-technology start-up sector in Israel, focused on (though not confined to) electronics. These achievements appear to rest in large part on the personal relationships and technical skills acquired in the Israeli defence forces.

The very different environments of German-speaking Europe, California and Tel Aviv demonstrate that there is no single formula for success in nurturing SMEs and providing the necessary finance. Each of these industrial groups—the *Mittelstand*, the Valley, the Israeli electronics cluster—has proved effective in global competition, but each is the product of particularities of history, culture and environment which are probably irreproducible elsewhere.

Nevertheless, there are common features. Government, innovative financiers and wealthy individuals with relevant industrial experience all have a role to play. Geographical concentration and personal relationships matter. The notion that securitisation is a useful approach to the financing needs of SMEs is another illustration of the misconception that the solution to most problems is found in complex financing tools. SME funding cannot be effectively rated by a computer. The growth of financial conglomerates has been at the expense of the locally focused institutions that remain critical to Germany's *Mittelstand* and which have played an equally crucial role in the evolution of Silicon Valley.

Perhaps the most useful initial role for government is to promote the creation of new financial institutions directed to providing the mix of loan and equity finance and advice needed to help SMEs grow. That development should be conjoined with a brief for asset managers that is less focused on public markets. I will discuss these issues further in Chapter 7.

Throughout the capital allocation process, expertise in investment has been supplanted by expertise in the mechanics of financial intermediation, an activity that requires greater intellectual capabilities and the capacity to do complicated mathematics, rather than the convivial conversation of the nineteenth hole. In the housing sector, local knowledge of property and people has been replaced by model building and securitised product design. In the markets for listed securities, knowledge of companies has been eroded and the greatest rewards are now earned by those who design and implement sophisticated trading algorithms. Banks have centralised small business lending, and venture capital investors have shifted their attention to the refinancing of established businesses. These are the means by which financialisation has created a world of people who talk to each other and trade with each other, operate in a reality of their own creation, reward themselves generously for genuine if largely useless skills and yet have less to offer the real needs of the real economy than their less talented predecessors.

# CHAPTER 6

# The Deposit Channel

## Household Wealth

> If we command our wealth, we shall be rich and free; if our wealth commands us, we are poor indeed.
>
> EDMUND BURKE, *Letters on a Regicide Peace*, 1796

Capital and wealth are surprisingly elusive concepts. The last chapter described two approaches to the measurement of national capital: the aggregation of household wealth, and the appraisal of physical assets. This chapter is about the channels of intermediation—the ways in which the savings of households become the physical assets of the nation. These channels, once clear and direct, have become complex and clogged.

Some household wealth is immediately connected to physical assets. Most households own their homes, and some small-business owners personally own offices, shops and other trading assets. Some statistics offices include certain household durables, such as cars, in their calculations of the value of physical assets. Households also lend to each other, mostly through intermediaries—the savings of the prudent fund the mortgages and credit card debts of the needy. However, in aggregate, these transactions between individuals cancel out.

But directly owned assets represent only around half of personal wealth. Most personal saving is intermediated. Households entrust their money to companies, financial institutions and government, which in turn hold assets on their behalf. All the physical assets of the nation are legally owned by someone—an individual or an institution. But if the ownership is institutional, we can always, in principle, follow the chain of intermediation to its end and identify individuals and households as beneficiaries. All the assets and claims of institutions represent other people's money.

If I had been writing this book before financialisation, the explanation of how household savings are intermediated into physical assets would have been much simpler. A deposit channel, operating through banks and thrift institutions, directed savings which were repayable on demand or at short notice into finance for house purchase and loans to business. An investment channel provided equity finance for business and the development and purchase of commercial property. Infrastructure was mostly built by government or its agencies, which financed this activity through the issue of bonds; these securities in turn were held by banks and directly by investors. With short, simple chains of intermediation, savers and investors could identify the type of asset their savings funded and often the specific project.

Today the channels of intermediation are longer and more complex. There are many obstructions and diversions and detours and flows in and out, and intermediaries who levy tolls. But the total value of national physical assets and the total value of national household wealth are—necessarily—similar, as Figure 6 shows. The average household has wealth of between $100,000 and $200,000; Germany (with low home-ownership) is towards the bottom of this range and the USA towards the top. These averages, of course, conceal very wide dispersion across households in each country; Bill Gates has $80 billion—500,000 times the average—while others own little more than the clothes they wear.

The USA and Europe have markedly different savings cultures, the result of differences in history and in the structure of intermediating institutions. In Britain, France and Germany investment in housing (net of mortgages) accounts for about 40 per cent of household wealth. The US figure is lower, reflecting in part the tax deductability of interest and the lower level of house prices but also a higher level of mortgage debt relative to property values, a legacy of the indiscriminate lending that preceded the global financial crisis. The USA is the only country in

Figure 6: **Household wealth by asset category, end of 2012 (US $000 per capita at purchasing power parity)**

|  | UK | US | Germany | France |
|---|---|---|---|---|
| Housing wealth (property value less housing loans) | 63.7* | 32.7* | 43.7 | 51.0 |
| Net cash and deposits | 25.2 | 16.9 | 30.6 | 23.8 |
| Net long-term savings | 64.0 | 159.2 | 38.6 | 44.0 |
| *Insurance and pensions* | *52.9* | *64.2* | *27.6* | *28.8* |
| *Directly held in securities* | *11.1* | *95.0* | *11.0* | *15.2* |
| TOTAL | 152.9 | 193.1 | 112.9 | 118.7 |
| Population (in millions) | 63.7 | 313.9 | 81.9 | 63.5 |
| Total value of household wealth (US$ trillion at PPP) | 9.74 | 65.54 | 9.25 | 7.54 |
| Total value of physical assets (US$ trillion at PPP) | 9.29 | 45.32 | 10.95 | 8.34 |

*Includes land
Source: OECD, author's calculations

which direct holdings of securities by individuals form a large proportion of household assets; in the other three countries, most long-term savings are channelled through intermediaries.

While in the USA long-term savings products in the investment channel are almost ten times assets in the deposit channel, in Germany the two figures are nearly equal, with Britain and France somewhere in between. Consumer debt is much higher in the USA than elsewhere: British households owe much less, while levels of consumer debt in France and Germany are negligible. Pension funds appear much less significant in France and Germany than in Britain and the USA. But this is misleading. Pension provision is more generous in these continental European countries than in the Anglo-Saxon ones, but largely unfunded—paid from current revenues. And, as will be explained below, only funded pension commitments are included in the reported figures for household wealth.

Intermediaries intermediate, but they cannot create wealth. So we need to explain why the equivalence of the value of physical assets and the total of household wealth is only approximate. The reasons fall into three broad categories. The most fundamental is the direct impact of financialisation—the creation of an extensive nexus of financial claims whose value only loosely corresponds to the value of the physical assets that underpin them. The second is the particular status of government assets and liabilities. The third is the globalisation of capital flows. I'll review each of these in turn.

Half a century ago, the key to valuing a company was to 'look through' to the underlying value of its physical assets. That was the practice on which Ben Graham, Warren Buffett's mentor, built his investment strategy: but, as Buffett has well understood, securities valuation must now be approached in a different way. The transition is partly the result of a change in the nature of modern business (Apple) and partly the result of the deliberate proliferation of complexity for the benefit of modern financiers and their hangers-on (Enron).

In the last chapter I described how the value of Apple stock reflected not the negligible value of its operating assets—the book value that would have interested Ben Graham—but the expectation of its future profits. And this expectation is a real asset, created by the activities and record of the business, even if it is an asset of uncertain value. Apple's future customers do not, however, report any matching liability, and perhaps they should not, since they will buy the company's products only if they are delighted to do so. The difference between the value of Apple as a company and the value of its physical assets might be quantified as an 'intangible asset', the value of the 'Apple brand'. But this reasoning is essentially circular. The 'Apple brand' is no more, or less, than the company, its products and its operations. The 'brand value' is simply a number calculated to make the stock market value of the company and the book value of its assets the same.[1]

To attach value to Apple stock far in excess of Graham's book value is to recognise that a modern economy rests on design and ideas rather than on physical activity. Expectations of continued profitable success by Apple appear well founded, but expectations are necessarily subjective. The same reasoning was alleged to hold for Enron's capitalisation of anticipated future earnings on energy contracts, and for optimistic assessment of the likely returns from mortgage-backed securities. Valuations of financial claims based on beliefs about the future give opportunities for bezzle and febezzle, and the greater the volume of such tradable claims, the greater the likely volume of bezzle and febezzle. Spurious claims about the value of the financial claims held by Enron were translated into household wealth through Enron's elevated share price.

But that elevated share price was used in valuation of share portfolios and the pension funds and investment companies that held Enron stock. If official statisticians had asked Madoff's clients to declare their wealth, his victims would have reported the amounts printed on the statements he issued to them. When the value of financial claims rises, the value of household financial assets increases. Only time will tell whether these movements in securities prices represent a rise in the actual value of physical assets, well-founded expectations of future profits or, as at Enron and Madoff Securities, bezzle and febezzle.

Many people have criticised the growth of public and private debt in the years before the global financial crisis. But this critique, though not irrelevant, does not get to the heart of the matter. Financialisation has created a vast edifice of financial claims built on top of a slim foundation of physical assets: that is how it came about that the value of outstanding derivative exposure far exceeds the value of all the assets in the world. Taken as a whole, these financial claims cancel out, but their existence leaves all the individual holders of these claims exposed to both market risk (changes in the market value of the claims) and credit risk (inability of the counterparty to pay). These exposures far exceed the net value of the positions. To be a millionaire is to enjoy a comfortable financial situation. To be in the position of owning $100 million of assets while owing $99 million of debt is another matter altogether. The more so if there is some uncertainty about the value of that $100 million and a tendency, via the winner's curse and other mechanisms of bezzle and febezzle, for valuations to be biased upwards.

Several other factors prevent an equivalence between financial claims and physical assets. Most financial claims are, in principle, matched by someone else's obligation to pay, but sometimes it is not clear on whom that obligation falls. This is true, in particular, of the financial claims represented by government debt and for some pension rights, both of which are claims of substantial magnitude. The taxes that will redeem public debt and pay state pensions when they fall due are a liability of future taxpayers. But the taxpayers who will eventually have to meet these obligations do not treat the obligation as a debt. Many of those indebted individuals have not yet been born.

Institutions and households certainly regard their holdings of government bonds as an asset, but the treatment of pension rights, both in household budgeting and official statistics, is less certain. Someone aged sixty-five with a pension of $10,000 per year owns a financial asset currently worth between $150,000 and $200,000. If the pension may be increased in the course of payment, perhaps reflecting inflation, the value of pension rights will be considerably more. But households do not necessarily think in this way.

And nor do official statisticians. Most surveys of household wealth include pension rights to the extent that, but only to the extent that, the pension entitlement is matched by financial assets. So if you have your own personal pension fund, its value will be counted in household wealth. If you are a member of a company pension scheme that has a trust fund backed by investments, your share of that fund will be included in reported household wealth as well, even though you have probably never stopped to think about its value. But the value of state pensions, which will be financed from future taxation, is not included in wealth. Nor does reported household wealth include unfunded promises by employers to pay pensions in future, the main mechanism of pension provision in France and Germany.

While future taxpayers do not tend to think of government debt as their own personal liability, a corollary is that people do not think of government-owned assets as part of their personal wealth. As individuals and households we share and derive benefits from the road network, the pictures in the National Gallery and the National Parks, but we do not report that benefit when we are asked how rich we are. The assets and liabilities of government are assets and liabilities of everyone in general, but of no one in particular.

We live in a world of global capital. An increasing proportion of government debt—notably US government debt—is owed overseas. Multinational corporations are ubiquitous. Some domestic assets belong to foreigners, while households also own—directly and indirectly—assets overseas. Large countries, like big companies, are essentially self-financing. This is true of Britain and France.

Figure 7: **Overseas assets and liabilities, end of 2012 (as % of total national wealth)**

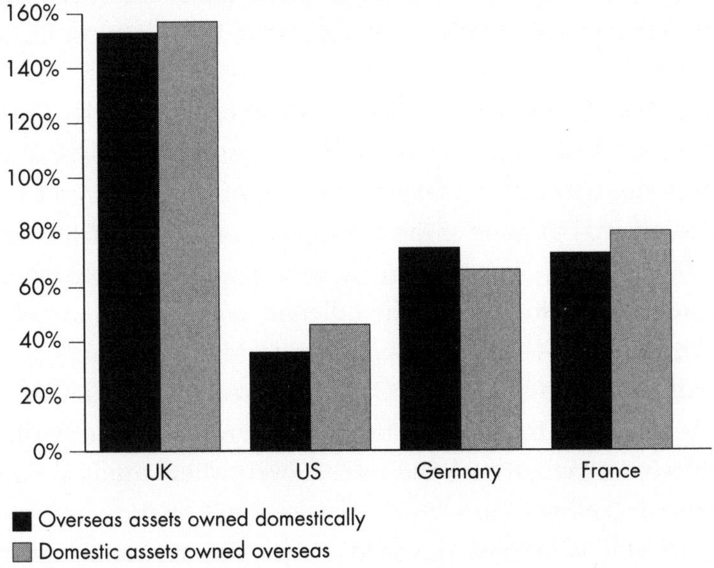

■ Overseas assets owned domestically
▩ Domestic assets owned overseas

Source: OECD, author's calculations

Germany, with persistent balance of payments surpluses, has more overseas assets than liabilities, while this position is reversed for the USA. A few small, wealthy countries such as Switzerland and Luxembourg, and the oil-rich states of the Gulf, are substantial net owners of overseas assets, relative to their size. Poor countries are mostly indebted: their governments have borrowed, often heavily, and much of their business is foreign-owned. This is also true of the former socialist countries of eastern Europe.

There are many benefits from these international flows of capital, quite apart from the opportunity to spend more than is earned by sucking in capital from Asia and the Gulf. US companies operate around the world, while inward investment by Japanese and European companies shake up the US car industry. Through these mechanisms, the spread of capital disperses both new technology and good management practice.

But the recent growth in global capital flows and balances—between 2000 and 2008 both the overseas assets and the liabilities of the UK grew almost fourfold—is the direct result of financialisation. Both asset and liability totals are dominated by the amounts financial institutions owe to each other.[2] This aspect of globalisation is the reason the collapse of Lehman was immediately not just an American problem but a global one.

I have described some of the many complications involved in disentangling the relationships between physical assets and financial claims, complications that have increased by orders of magnitude as a result of financialisation. But none of these complications detract from the basic truth that the assets of nations are the product of household saving.

Because of intermediation, the different savings practices of different countries do not have correspondingly large consequence for where the funds end up. In France and Germany direct intermediation, largely through banks and insurance companies, is the norm. The similarity of the underlying capital stock means that everywhere funds are directed to mortgage-lending, business and government finance, and property development. In Germany, the deposit channel is an important conduit to business. In the USA intermediation through securities markets is far more extensive and many activities are funded through bonds and equity. The UK, as often, lies somewhere in between the two. The remainder of this chapter is concerned with the functioning of the deposit channel (and the payment system that is inextricably linked to it), while Chapter 7 reviews the operation of the investment channel.

## The Payment System

> Money often costs too much.
>
> RALPH WALDO EMERSON, *The Conduct of Life*, 1860

Paul Volcker, the tall, laconic figure who preceded Alan Greenspan as Chairman of the Federal Reserve Board, has been reported as saying that the only useful recent financial innovation was the ATM.[3] Volcker is deeply sceptical of the developments in wholesale financial markets that excited the celebrants at Jackson Hole. What matters from the perspective of ordinary customers is innovation in retail financial services. The payment system, which all of us use every day, is the principal financial service that business and households need.

The first payment systems relied on physical units of exchange. Precious metals, particularly gold, were well suited to this task. Our ancestors came to understand that they could deal in credits against gold while allowing the gold to stay in the same place.[4] More recently they realised that gold was not necessary to this process at all. These conceptual discoveries facilitated the development of credit, but were also an invitation to fraud and instability. So governments first regulated and eventually monopolised the issue of paper money. The last vestiges of a link between paper money and precious metals disappeared when the USA abandoned the gold standard in 1971. And so for centuries there have been two principal means of making and receiving payment: the exchange of tokens and the transfer of credit.

Coins and notes issued by government or its agencies are used in everyday transactions for small amounts. Larger payments rely on debit and credit entries in the books of a bank or other financial institution. Contactless payment cards and mobile banking apps are simply the latest manifestations of these long established practices.

The payments system is one of the utility networks—the electricity grid, the telecommunications network, the water supply system—that underpin social and commercial activity. We use these networks every day. If they are out of action for even a few hours, commercial activity grinds to a halt and social lives are disrupted. We sit at home waiting for normal service to be resumed.

Perhaps we should not exaggerate this effect. In 1970 a strike by Irish bank workers shut down that country's payment system. Customers could not withdraw money from their accounts, and cheques were not cleared. The lesson of this bizarre experiment is that it did not seem to matter much. Business continued. Ireland's pubs operated on a credit system. Ireland in 1970 was not a particularly advanced economy, but it was hardly a primitive society. Perhaps being a small, socially homogeneous country with a high degree of mutual trust helped. In any event, the impact of the strike on the Irish economy through the freezing of its payment system was much less significant than the effect of the collapse of the Irish banking system during the global financial crisis in 2008.

Most utility networks are also natural monopolies. The twin characteristics of indispensability and monopoly explain why utilities are closely regulated. Public ownership by national government or municipalities has been the traditional mechanism of utility regulation. A major anti-trust suit resulted in the breakup in 1981 of AT&T, the company that had dominated American telecommunications for almost a century. In other countries, privatisation and liberalisation opened many networks to competitive access and transferred many of the utilities themselves to regulated private ownership. This reappraisal began in the UK but was imitated in many other countries. The new regulatory regimes for utilities gave competitor firms with innovative products access to these networks. The transformation of telecoms that brought us smartphones and the internet would probably never have happened without this state action to break the power of incumbent behemoths, private companies and state-owned businesses.

The physical networks of transport, telecoms and other utilities were planned by engineers. Resilience and robustness were design objectives from the beginning. Payments systems evolved in a more haphazard way and over a longer period of time. To the extent that there was design at all, such design was the work of financiers and administrators. This difference in historical evolution—a difference not only in the development of the payment system but also in the evolution of the financial system as a whole—is the primary reason why financial networks have repeatedly proved so much less stable than other infrastructure networks. Nassim Taleb has explained how system fragility creates profit opportunities, so that this instability serves the interest of many market participants.[5] I will return to these issues of system design in Chapter 10.

In Britain, and in most European countries, the payment system is controlled by a consortium of banks. When you write a cheque or make an electronic payment through the internet or via an automated transfer, your payment is aggregated in a clearing system with all other payments made by your bank and offset against the total of payments that your bank receives from other banks. The net amount of inter-bank receipt and payment is credited, or debited, to the bank's balance with the central bank—the bank for banks. Only a very few large and privileged corporations hold accounts directly with a central bank.

You can obtain government-issued notes from the ATM because your local bank draws cash from its deposits with the central bank, which prints the money.

The Bank of England is the central bank for the UK. In the USA banks hold deposits with the appropriate Federal Reserve Bank for the regions in which they operate. The New York bank, which Timothy Geithner headed, is the most important of these institutions. The national Federal Reserve System exercises overall responsibility for the structure under the supervision of the Federal Reserve Board, whose chairman, appointed by the president, is the nation's central banker. Similarly, in the Eurozone, a bank operating in Spain holds deposits with the Bank of Spain, which in turn holds deposits with the European Central Bank— the bank for central banks.

But there is a critical difference between the operation of the Federal Reserve System and the operation of the Eurozone. If someone in Kansas buys goods from a seller in New York, the money is debited from the accounts of the purchasers, transmitted by the Federal Reserve Bank of Kansas to the Federal Reserve Bank of New York and credited to the merchant's account in New York. In Europe that middle step need not take place. The Federal Reserve System does not allow its members to run large permanent overdrafts; the European Central Bank does. Germany is owed €500 billion, a sum broadly matched by outstanding liabilities within the system of almost €200 billion each from Spain and Italy and €100 billion from Greece. This indebtedness—around €6,000 per head of German population—is an effective transfer from Germany to Club Med. It is hard to see sources from which these liabilities are likely to be repaid, and the outstanding balances within the TARGET2 system, which manages indebtedness between Central Banks in the Eurozone, are one of the time-bombs beneath the European Monetary System.

International payments by individuals and businesses (including intra-Eurozone payments) rely on a Brussels-based clearing system called SWIFT—which, as most ordinary users will have discovered, it is not. Since the formation of the Eurozone, the European Commission and Parliament have exerted downward pressure on charges. But they have been less successful in prioritising modernisation and efficiency. To a surprising degree, the day-to-day mechanics of cross-border Eurozone payments operate as if little has changed since the adoption of a single currency.

Alongside the clearing system runs a 'real-time' payment mechanism in which funds can be credited or debited immediately. This is the method by which high-value transactions are processed—readers will probably have used it for house purchases. Although real-time processing accounts for only a small proportion of transactions by volume, it accounts for an overwhelming proportion by value. Most high-value transactions settle the trades financial institutions make with each other.

The payments system is the heart of the financial services industry, and most people who work in banking are engaged in servicing payments. But this activity commands both low priority and low prestige within the industry. Competition between firms generally promotes innovation and change, but a bank can gain very little competitive advantage by improving its payment systems, since the customer experience is the result more of the efficiency of the system as a whole than of the efficiency of any individual bank. Incentives to speed payments are weak.

Incrementally developed over several decades, the internal systems of most banks creak: it is easier, and implies less chance of short-term disruption, to add bits to what already exists than to engage in basic redesign. The interests of the leaders of the industry have been elsewhere, and banks have tended to see new technology as a means of reducing costs rather than as an opportunity to serve consumer needs more effectively. Although the USA is a global centre for financial innovation in wholesale financial markets, it is a laggard in innovation in retail banking, and while Britain scores higher, it does not score much higher. Martin Taylor, former chief executive of Barclays (who resigned in 1998, when he could not stop the rise of the trading culture at the bank), described the state of payment systems in this way: 'the systems architecture at the typical big bank, especially if it has grown through merger and acquisition, has departed from the Palladian villa envisaged by its original designers and morphed into a gothic house of horrors, full of turrets, broken glass and uneven paving.'6

The ATM has, as Volcker recognised, made a large difference to everyday experience of finance. As has the internet. More and more people now manage their finances through home computers and mobile devices. Yet bank customers do not seem to share the enthusiasm of other users of services transformed by information technology: music aficionados, users of social networks, readers of e-books, online shoppers.

The experience of these other industries provides an important clue to the explanation. In music, social media and books, industry disruption was led by new entrants in the face of the resistance of incumbents seeking—unsuccessfully—to retain control and preserve their existing business model. Napster and then Apple marginalised established music labels; YouTube, Facebook and Twitter sent newspapers into decline; Amazon redefined first bookselling and subsequently book production. But a combination of institutional complexity and bureaucratic inertia, buttressed by regulation, has prevented such disruptive change in money transmission.

As in music, social media and books, major innovation is the result of the development of new systems rather than the evolution of old. The plastic payment card is the key not only to the ATM but also to the reform of payments. The credit card was pioneered by Bank of America as a substitute for store-based credit. Instead of negotiating credit terms and limits individually with stores, the customer obtained a line of credit from a bank and used this facility in multiple stores. These stores would pay a fee to the bank for access to its customers and their spending power.

After false starts, the credit-card concept proved successful and was adopted by other banks. Issuers formed networks to enable merchants to process the cards of several different providers. This arrangement had the further advantage, at least for banks, of enabling them to reach mutual agreement on the fees they charged merchants. The two principal networks—VISA and MasterCard—emerged in this way from consortia led by Bank of America and Citibank respectively.

The rise of the credit card coincided with the technological development of electronic processing. As a consequence of this historical accident, the credit card became—and remains—a simple means of access to a fully electronic payment system that is distinct from, and in many respects more advanced than, the traditional payment system operated by the banks. Handling credit-card payments was largely outsourced to technology companies, of which First Data Corporation is the largest. However incumbent banks were able to sustain a position as gatekeepers of the networks.

In the USA and in Britain, where the credit card was first promoted, a single credit card serves the dual (and largely distinct) functions of providing a rolling facility for consumer credit and an electronic payment mechanism. This duality has proved very profitable—especially for the pioneers of credit cards, such as Bank of America and Citibank. The expensive credit offered by the cards is widely used, often by people who did not have any intention of borrowing and who could obtain credit much more cheaply.

Banks have been slower to promote debit cards, which integrate electronic payment systems with current accounts. We don't need to use paper any more, whether in the form of banknotes, cheques or bank statements. The use of transport smartcards has speeded the adoption of contactless payment, and you can readily see the resulting savings in time and staffing and reduced congestion. Transfers via mobile phones have been particularly important in some poor countries (famously Kenya's M-Pesa) where the mobile phone network is the most—perhaps the only—efficient component of the national infrastructure. PayPal, the largest internet payment system, is owned by the online auction house eBay.

It is not hard to visualise a world in which notes and coins have disappeared. You would wave a pre-loaded card to make a small payment, while larger payments would take place by direct electronic transfer between accounts. In Scandinavia, the Netherlands and Japan cheques are no longer used. Perhaps significantly, countries with large financial sectors—such as Britain and the USA—seem to have been slower to innovate in payment systems. Plans to eliminate the use of paper in Britain failed when it became clear that the banks had given little thought to the effect of the change on their customers.[7]

The revolution will come. Institutional inertia can slow technological change, but can rarely prevent it altogether. The complete dematerialisation of payments potentially deprives governments and established banking institutions of their traditional mechanisms of control: monopoly of currency issue and access to physical records. The invention of the credit card means that it is no longer necessary to have cash or deposits to make a payment, only a certificate of anticipated future resources sufficient to settle the transaction: a change that is potentially the end of money as we have known it.

The evangelists for bitcoin, the much-hyped digital currency that is a strange mixture of the visionary and the fraudulent—are, in a sense, not imaginative enough. They are simply trying to reproduce in the electronic world a commodity—currency—that has long existed in the material world. The larger question is whether currency as we have known it is any longer necessary at all. I once joked with beginning students that money existed because when a pipe burst it took too long to find a plumber in need of economics lectures—but today it is possible to locate that plumber.

It is improbable that in fifty—perhaps twenty—years from now the deposit channel will have the central role in the financial system that it has occupied for centuries by virtue of its link to payments. The payment system is ripe for disruptive innovation, but to date entrants—such as PayPal, Square and most recently Apple Pay—have preferred to shelter under the umbrella of the high charging structure established by inefficient incumbent banks. This cautious sharing of oligopoly profits will not persist indefinitely, and in time the payment system will become an inexpensive utility distinct from the deposit channel.

The evolution of payments will pave the way for wider change, both institutional and intellectual. Our understanding of money and banking will be fundamentally revised—indeed the notion of 'controlling the money supply' has already given way to much looser concepts of influencing the maturity profile of assets. As I shall describe in Chapter 9, interest rate policy today is directed more to the scale of subsidy to banks than to the terms on which borrowers and lenders deal with each other. Regulators and incumbent banks will resist these changes, and will succeed for a time, before they finally fail.

## The Activities of the Deposit Channel

> Robbing a bank's no crime compared to owning one.
> BERTHOLT BRECHT, *Happy End*, 1929

The deposit channel serves two purposes: facilitating the payment system and intermediating between borrowers and short-term savers. Few people want to take out loans that are repayable on demand, but lots of people want to make deposits that are accessible on demand. So the ability of intermediaries to provide liquidity is crucial. The deposit channel depends on the liquidity illusion—an illusion that can survive only so long as not many people take advantage of it.

But illusions are fragile. The belief that large financial institutions could always meet their obligations provided support for the growth of the extraordinary volumes of speculative trading between them described in the introduction. When the global financial crisis hit, the international financial system could not provide the liquidity on which it was predicated, and after a few hiccups governments provided it instead. Today the deposit channel is clogged—especially in Europe—by a doomed attempt to build up reserves of capital and liquidity sufficient to support the scale of these trading activities without the backstop of official support.

Figure 8 summarises flows through the deposit channel. Total deposits everywhere amount to about one year's national income. The differences between the USA and the three European countries are more apparent than real. In the USA money-market funds (which are effectively deposits) total around $4 trillion, and the main holdings of these money-market funds are very short-term securities issued by banks, or the quasi-banks that are the Treasury operations of large corporations such as Apple or Exxon Mobil. This American exceptionalism is one aspect of the general tendency for more intermediation to take place through securities markets in the USA than in Europe. Deposits are mostly savings and transactions balances of households, although the short-term cash holdings of businesses are also significant.

The deposits the real economy places with the banking system are approximately matched by the banking system's loans to the real economy. Mortgages are everywhere the largest component. Business lending is a particularly small proportion of the total in the UK. Anyone who supposes that financing business is the primary function of banking is mistaken. Most bank lending is residential mortgages for house purchase. Aside from business finance, the balance of lending is made up of commercial property finance and consumer credit. Banks also need to maintain reserves at the central bank, in order to facilitate inter-bank transfers in the payment system. Providing the functions of the deposit channel is not very complicated. George Bailey was well able to do it. But

Figure 8: **Flows through the deposit channel, mid-2014 (local currency (in trillions)**

|  | UK £ | US $ | France € | German € |
|---|---|---|---|---|
| Personal deposits | 1.09 | 8.74 | 1.23 | 1.89 |
| Non-financial business deposits | 0.39 | 1.04 | 0.44 | 0.45 |
| **Total deposits** | 1.49 | 9.79 | 1.66 | 2.34 |
|  |  |  |  |  |
| Mortgages | 1.06 | 2.78 | 0.85 | 1.03 |
| Consumer credit and other HH lending | 0.11 | 1.74 | 0.24 | 0.45 |
| Business lending | 0.43 | 3.53 | 0.87 | 0.91 |
| *of which commercial property* | *0.17* | *1.68* | *n.a.* | *n.a.* |
| Government lending | 0.01 | 0.00 | 0.22 | 0.36 |
| **Lending to non-finance sector** | 1.61 | 8.05 | 2.17 | 2.74 |
| Financial sector transactions | 5.53 | 8.93* | 5.82 | 4.85 |
| TOTAL ASSETS/LIABILITIES | 7.13 | 16.98 | 8.00 | 7.59 |

*As explained in Chapter 6, figures greatly understate the scale of derivative exposures. This understatement is much greater under US GAAP than European IFRS, so that the US figure is too low relative to the European ones.

Source: Bank of England (Bankstats table B1.4, C1.1, C1.2), Federal Reserve (Financial Accounts of the United States table L.109, L.204, L.205, L.215, L.218), European Central Bank (MFI Balance Sheets Online, tables 1 and 2).

operating the deposit channel has now become very complicated, and George Bailey could not do it today. The overwhelmingly dominant element on banks' balance sheets today are the claims financial institutions have against each other. What is it all for?

The debate in the Halifax boardroom recounted in Chapter 4 had been conducted in many financial institutions—earlier in most cases: Halifax came late to this particular game. Halifax had always held positions in fixed-interest securities, mostly government debt, and there were attractions to using the scale of the balance sheet and the strength of the credit rating to build a much larger portfolio and balance sheet. There was competitive pressure: other firms were already reporting significant profits from this source. Surely an opportunity was here for the world's largest mortgage-lender?

The confidence generated by a large balance sheet—both for traders and for those with whom they trade—is a major advantage and facilitates the production of bezzle and febezzle. The martingale—doubling up on losing bets—can be successfully pursued only by those with large resources. Tailgating—strategies with low probabilities of occasional catastrophic loss—produces a steady stream of profits for those whose credit rating can support the strategy. While the inevitable crashes put standalone hedge funds out of business—this is, in practice, their normal fate[8]—a big bank can attribute its exceptional losses to exceptional factors, pick itself up and start all over again.

The search for high returns on equity, led by Deutsche Bank, encouraged banks to build these very large balance sheets based on positions in FICC. At Deutsche, the pursuit of return on equity produced a balance sheet in which shareholders' equity amounted to less than 2 per cent of total assets and liabilities—a leverage ratio of over fifty to one. The risk capital available to Deutsche Bank—with shareholders' equity of €54 billion in 2012—is not much greater than the funds available to the largest hedge funds. In 2014 Renaissance had funds under management of $38 billion and Paulson $24 billion. (J.P. Morgan and Citigroup, with shareholder funds over $200 billion, are way ahead of any hedge fund, although these banks, like Deutsche Bank, are engaged in many activities other than trading.) But banks with large retail deposit bases have significant competitive advantages in trading, as a result of the size of the collateral they offer and the implicit or explicit government guarantee of their liabilities. The scale of their activities is altogether different—and with it the potential consequences of trading losses.

However this fifty-to-one ratio actually substantially *understates* the leverage at Deutsche Bank because derivative contracts create leverage. Suppose instead of buying a share for $100 I acquire a widely employed derivative instrument, a contract for difference (CFD) in respect of that share. Through the CFD, I promise to pay you, whenever I close the contract, the difference between the share price and its current value of $100. For all practical purposes, this is equivalent to borrowing $100 to buy the share, and the risk management processes of a bank will record an 'exposure' of $100. But so long as the share price remains around $100 the accounts will record this contract at its 'fair value'—which is zero.

Figure 9: **Deutsche Bank balance sheet, 2012 (€ billions)**

| Derivative exposure | 55,605 | |
| --- | --- | --- |
| Derivative value | positive 777 | negative 756 |
| Overall balance sheet | assets 2,012 | liabilities 1,958 |
| Lending operations | loans 397 | deposits 577 |
| Value of all assets in Germany<br>GDP of Germany | 8,600<br>2,500 | |

Source: Deutsche Bank Annual Report, 2012

The two global banks with the largest derivatives exposures are J.P. Morgan and Deutsche Bank. The derivatives exposure of J.P. Morgan is around $70,000 billion and of Deutsche Bank €55,000 billion. These figures are, respectively, about one-and-a-half times the total value of all the assets in the USA, and twenty times German national income. But the numbers in the balance sheets of these banks are much lower. Deutsche Bank declares its investment in derivatives at €768 billion: not a small amount, but only a modest fraction of the Bank's exposure. Deutsche Bank's financial position is set out in Figure 9.

The absurdity of these figures gives a clue to why Warren Buffett called derivatives 'weapons of mass destruction'.[9] But before making for the bomb shelters, readers should feel reassured that there is little possibility that J.P. Morgan or Deutsche Bank will actually lose trillions of euros or dollars. Many of these exposures are approximately or completely hedged—the positions they represent are offset by other positions—and while the euro or the dollar might fall precipitately, their values will not fall to zero. The risk models used by these banks, which do recognise exposures, are designed to limit the effective exposure to market risk, and while these models cannot bear the weight placed on them, they are not without value.

Credit risk is the supposed purview of regulatory capital requirements. And one response to the global financial crisis has been to require that more derivative contracts be cleared through exchanges. The objective is to enable assets and liabilities with the same counterparty to be offset. This measure is intended to reduce this risk in banks, at the price of creating new risk within the exchanges themselves. But whatever the extent of hedging, the sophistication of risk models and the impact of regulatory supervision, the scale of activity takes one's breath away. One-tenth of 1 per cent of €55 trillion is €55 billion, and a loss of that amount would destroy either bank.

Deutsche Bank draws up its primary accounts under IFRS (International Financial Reporting Standards), the European accounting standard.[10] Under US GAAP (Generally Accepted Accounting Principles), derivatives disappear almost completely from the balance sheets of American banks. The indefatigable ISDA (which commissioned that legal opinion from Mr Potts) naturally believes GAAP is superior, and has provided data comparing major banks under the two systems. Judged by size of balance sheet as reported in annual accounts, the five largest Western banks are all European, led by France's BNP Paribas. But if IFRS is used, the top places are taken by Bank of America and J.P. Morgan.

I suspect most readers—and certainly the writer—will simply feel at a loss to cope with these figures. €55,000,000,000,000 is a number beyond comprehension—beyond the comprehension of politicians, regulators or, importantly, the people who run Deutsche Bank. The scale of Deutsche Bank's everyday activities—deposits of €577 billion, and loans of €397 billion—are themselves extraordinary, yet insignificant relative to the bank's total financial exposure—only 1 per cent of it. The amounts of support that the British and US governments put behind their country's banking systems—estimated at £3 trillion and $23 trillion respectively—were sufficient to buy all the non-housing assets of these countries, yet far below the potential size of the indebtedness of these banking systems.

What does this fragile tower of assets and liabilities, reaching into the stratosphere, have to do with the core business of Deutsche Bank: managing the deposit channel, collecting those €577 billion of deposits and making loans to customers of €397 billion? Not much. Except in one key respect. The existence of these €577 billion of deposits, and the assumption that the German government stands behind them, enables those who contract with Deutsche Bank to do so with confidence.

When Halifax decided to enter the world of more aggressive trading of fixed-interest securities—and subsequently currency—the bank recognised that it would have to compete for the 'talent' (the word sticks in the throat, but is widely used to describe experienced traders) in salary levels and bonuses. Not only against other banks but also with stand-alone hedge funds. That meant high pay, and a bonus culture. These innovations proved to be a cancer which in little more than a decade spread through the once healthy institution and destroyed it.

The global financial crisis was primarily caused by placing on top of the deposit channel an elaborate and largely impenetrable superstructure of trading activities in FICC—impenetrable even by the executives of the institutions themselves. When that superstructure collapsed in 2008 in the face of abrupt recognition of the scale of counterparty risk, the collapse threatened to destroy the deposit channel—the mechanisms by which payments are facilitated and short-term savings directed to home-buyers and businesses.

Governments, of necessity, intervened in the only way possible to minimise immediate damage—effectively guaranteeing all counterparty risk. But this is not an appropriate long-term response. The appropriate long-term response creates a firewall, or ring-fence (there is a wide choice of metaphors), between the deposit channel and the trading activities of banks. This is the underlying intent of the Volcker Rule, which the venerable and venerated central banker successfully urged on President Obama.[11] Related measures have been proposed by the Vickers Commission in the UK and the Liikaanen Committee for the EU.[12] It is, of course, a response heavily resisted by the banks themselves. Ring-fencing of the deposit channel is discussed more extensively in Chapter 10.

# CHAPTER 7

# The Investment Channel

## Managing Wealth

> You never actually own a Patek Philippe. You merely look after it for the next generation.
>
> Advertisement for PATEK PHILIPPE, luxury watch manufacturer

Businesses and households use the deposit channel to facilitate their everyday transactions. They also utilise it for short-term savings when they require a high degree of confidence that their money will be available in full when needed. Long-term savers select the investment channel, where they assume a degree of risk in the hope of higher returns. Long time horizons and greater risk-tolerance fit together: the more extended the time-scale, the greater the likelihood that an investment strategy that on average yields a higher return will actually do so.

As I described in Chapter 5, the functions of the investment channel involve both search and stewardship. Through the search processes described there, capital is allocated through the investment channel to various long-term uses, in business, investment, property and infrastructure. But even if there were no investment, no depreciation and no replacement of the capital stock, there would be need for a stewardship function in nurturing and maintaining the existing stock of assets.

Although much of what is written about finance would give a different impression, you are not providing funds for business investment by holding a company's shares, directly or indirectly. As I have explained, companies large enough to be quoted on a stock exchange are, overwhelmingly, self-financing. The relationship between the long-term investor and Exxon Mobil is one of stewardship.

Exxon Mobil is the principal successor to the Standard Oil company which John D. Rockefeller established a century and a half ago,[1] and is likely to be around for many years to come. The managers who control it and the savers who hold its shares, like the wearer of a Patek Philippe watch, 'look after it for the next generation'. Exxon Mobil is a long-lived company, though there are many others. The Scandinavian resources company Stora Enso claims its origins in a charter granted by King Magnus of Sweden in 1347. General Electric, established by Thomas Edison, and Siemens, founded in Berlin by Werner von Siemens, have been major industrial conglomerates for more than a century. Perhaps modern companies have a shorter lifespan—will Google or Facebook still attract attention a century from now, or will they have gone the way of Pullman, Studebaker and Polaroid? The corporate sector may evolve through established companies developing new business activities—as GE and Siemens have—or by the formation of new corporations, but whatever the forms of business development there will still be a requirement to hold the assets of the corporate sector for the next generation.

Companies are long-lived, but most products are not. The bread we eat is bread that was baked today. We cannot store electricity, or haircuts or walks in the park. The electronic devices and software we use now will be obsolete within a few short years, perhaps even months. Yet we need to shift income and consumption over time and across generations. When young and when old, we consume more than we are capable of earning. We need mechanisms for transferring wealth over time, and trade in securities is one such mechanism: I will describe the full variety in Chapter 9. We can buy a share in Exxon Mobil's business and oil reserves now, and sell it when we age, and we can do this without disturbing Exxon Mobil's investment plans. We can create financial assets such as Apple shares, based on future earnings, and trade them in a similar way, with similar effect. By this means we can thank Steve Jobs for his efforts by giving him a share of Apple's future profits as well as its current ones.

The institutions that traditionally dominated the investment channel were: the investment bank, which searched for those in need of capital; the financial adviser—stockbroker, bank manager, insurance agent—who provided both search (fresh opportunities) and stewardship (continuing guidance) on behalf of individual savers; and investment institutions—principally insurance companies and pension funds and some other pooled investment funds—which engaged in stewardship as they gathered and placed substantial sums through the investment channel. Elements of this structure remain, but financialisation has brought about major changes.

The investment bank once played the primary role in search: the selection of investments. Investment banks would place some of their own funds in these activities, sharing the risks and using their reputations to attract funds from others. But such reputations were only of much value in an era in which long-term relationships—with companies and with investors—were the norm. Modern investment banks are institutions organised around transactions and trading. Their primary objectives now are to get 'the mandate' for the deal and then to 'get it away'.

Crooks such as Jeff Skilling and Bernie Ebbers (the former basketball coach who enjoyed a brief career as telecommunications titan at World-Com before moving on to federal prison) were aggressively courted by all major investment banks. J.P. Morgan, whose eponymous founder had once identified 'character' as the foundation of banking, paid $160 million to terminate an investigation by the SEC into its role in the frauds of Enron. Suits related to the bank's issuance of bonds were settled for a payment of $2 billion.

Even in the days before financialisation, investment banks never dealt directly with any but the richest of individuals. Savers normally gained access to the investment channel through advisers. Many people—then as now—lack confidence in their ability to manage financial affairs, often justifiably. They look for a trust relationship—a personal relationship with an individual financial adviser, who might often have been the local bank manager—or an institutional relationship with a respected organisation. When thrifty households set small sums aside, the life insurance company was the principal intermediary. More affluent individuals bought shares on the advice of a stockbroker, and had access to pooled investment funds—the vehicles of managed intermediation provided by investment companies.

But, for reasons explained in Chapter 1, the bank branch is no longer the natural port of call for the prudent saver. Those bank premises that remain now look like shops—and that is what they are. The place of the intimidating but trustworthy bank manager has been taken by friendlier sales people remunerated by commission and motivated by sales targets. The resulting pressures on staff have led to serious abuses in the provision of personal financial services: notably (in Britain) the extensive sale of largely worthless payment protection policies to borrowers and (in the USA) the marketing of mortgages with low teaser rates to people who had little prospect of ever being able to repay.

The personal stockbroker, full of bonhomie and (after lunch) alcohol, has more or less disappeared. The rise of the broker–dealer meant that most stockbroking firms were absorbed into financial conglomerates. Some independent stockbrokers remained, seeking to provide a range of advisory services to private individuals, in competition with the 'wealth management' services devised for the more affluent customers of retail banks. The 'execution only' stockbroker allows individuals to trade stocks without benefit of advice (if benefit it had been).

Throughout the investment channel, traditional intermediaries that had been serving the needs of either savers on the one hand or the users of capital on the other shifted their focus from advice to sales. This conflation of the roles of agent and trader is, in the investment channel as elsewhere, a key feature of financialisation. There are roles for both trusted adviser and sales people, but the customer needs to know which is which, and this becomes especially difficult if the supplier is himself confused about the nature of the role. Customers find it difficult to distinguish good from self-interested advice. And if the customer cannot tell the difference, advice tainted by conflict of interest tends to drive out unconflicted advice: conflicted advice is more profitable.

But even if the motives of advisers had been pure as snow, personalised and independent financial advice of quality cannot be provided to a mass market. In other retail sectors cost pressures have led to the replacement of skilled and knowledgeable advisers by pleasant sales personnel: all but the very rich pick their own groceries and select their clothes from racks or shelves; all but the most basic legal advice is priced out of range of ordinary people; individualised medical assistance is available, but is mainly paid for at public expense, and the cost absorbs a large and increasing share of national income.

Technology may come to the rescue. A computer can today establish a client's needs more effectively than a lightly trained 'financial adviser'. Since the logic of the computer is set out in its programmes, bias in its recommendations can be identified. There is less variation in the financial needs of different people than there is for more idiosyncratic purchases such as households and clothes. As I described in Chapter 1, the first intermediaries in the investment channel were investment companies and life insurers, and these continue to play a large role today. Insurance companies (and banks, often in collaboration with them) remain the principal vehicle of intermediation in continental Europe. Investment companies play a larger role in Britain and the USA. In the twentieth century, pension funds became a major part of the investment channel.

Pension funds and insurance companies—even small ones—would have their own investment offices, would trade infrequently and would base their decisions in large part on research on companies provided by friendly stockbrokers—friendly both to the investment officers of the funds and to the companies whose affairs they reviewed. But as these brokers were absorbed into investment banks, the conflict between agency and sales was evident here also. The 'research' that analysts produced became an advertisement for the products of other divisions of the bank. The Merrill Lynch analyst Henry Blodget's enthusiastic recommendation of a stock he thought was a 'piece of shit' was abnormal only in that he was unwise enough to put his true opinion in an email, with consequences to be noted in Chapter 10.

Specialist asset managers, such as Fidelity and Capital, developed their own research capabilities. 'Buy-side' analysts employed by these asset management institutions began to take the place of 'sell-side' analysts working for securities issuing houses, a development that gathered pace and urgency as the activities of analysts such as Blodget during the New Economy bubble were exposed. The sell-side analyst was passing his sell-buy date.

Insurers and pension funds have increasingly outsourced their investment management to specialist asset managers. The larger institutions established separate asset management divisions, which seek business from other intermediaries and directly from savers. Investment companies delegated investment decisions to asset management businesses (and most investment companies are now sponsored by asset managers). Financialisation has led to the emergence of large asset management companies.

Larry Fink, a pioneer of the securitisation boom of the 1980s, was fired from First Boston after making a large losing trade. Fink had tailgated and crashed. Recognising the phenomenon, he learned from it. 'We built this giant machine, and it was making a lot of money—until it didn't. We didn't know why we were making so much money. We didn't have the risk tools to understand that risk.'[2] Fink's subsequent career took a different course. Through an aggressive acquisition strategy BlackRock, the asset management firm he founded, became a corporation that today has around $4 trillion of assets under its control. The ten largest asset management companies today have total assets of around $20 trillion. A majority of these firms are American (Vanguard, State Street, Fidelity and BNY Mellon, as well as BlackRock, the largest, and the asset management division of J.P. Morgan). The asset management arms of the largest insurer and bank in France (AXA and BNP Paribas) and in Germany (Allianz and Deutsche Bank), respectively, take the remaining four places.[3] Fink is sometimes described as the most powerful man in finance whom most people have never heard of. BlackRock manages the largest pool of capital of any institution—more than any bank. If asset management firms do not today appear as powerful as conglomerate banks, that is because they act almost exclusively as agents, not principals. Whether asset managers are agents at law is, at least in Britain and the USA, a complex question: many of them write contracts that seek to exclude agency liability. But asset managers mostly behave as agents, whatever the formal position. The asset management sector today displays more awareness than most divisions of financial conglomerates that it deals with other people's money.

Life insurers, pension funds and investment companies traditionally functioned as managed intermediaries: as in the deposit channel, the saver had a financial interest in, and claim against, the intermediary rather than a direct interest in the underlying assets. The actuary would determine the payout from the insurer; the fund trustees would fix the level of pensions; the investor would own a share of the investment company. The saver would be informed from time to time of the progress of the assets the intermediary had selected.

But managed intermediation has always been open to fraud and abuse. Dickens, unimpressed by his visit to the United States, recorded it as the land whose fraudsters induced Martin Chuzzlewit to invest in swamps marketed as Eden, which became reality in the Florida land boom of the 1920s. Investment companies, launched principally for the benefit of the promoters, played a major role in the US stock bubble which preceded the 1929 Wall Street crash. The essay in which J.K. Galbraith introduced the concept of the bezzle has a chapter ironically entitled 'In Goldman Sachs we trust', which highlights that firm's role in the promotion of investment companies that were destined to fail.[4] The outcome was the virtual disappearance of investment trusts (closed-end funds) in the United States. Frauds and failures in US pension funds led in 1974 to tougher supervision and restrictions and mutual insurance. Similar provisions were introduced in the UK when the death of the flamboyant Robert Maxwell in 1991 exposed his theft of pension assets.

And so managed intermediation has largely given way to transparent intermediation. The saver has a direct interest in, and perhaps legal ownership of, the underlying securities, and can regularly establish—possibly on a daily basis—the value of that interest. The transparent intermediary takes no investment risk and therefore needs no capital to support that risk. The shift from managed to transparent intermediation is the result of regulatory pressures, ideological stances biased towards trading, and loss of trust by savers.

Transparent intermediation by asset managers is today encouraged by a raft of expectations and regulation. The dominant vehicle for pooled retail investment funds is now the mutual fund, subject to numerous restrictions on portfolio composition and disclosure. Insurance company regulation has increasingly driven the industry towards transparent rather than managed intermediation. Payouts were once determined by the professional judgment of an actuary, but common practice today credits the policyholder with an appropriately calculated share of the underlying assets. Pension provision is increasingly based on 'defined contribution' schemes, in which the pensioner receives a return based on the investments he or she has chosen. The investment freedom of pension

Figure 10: **The Investment Channel: total global investable assets, 2013 (US dollars in trillions)**

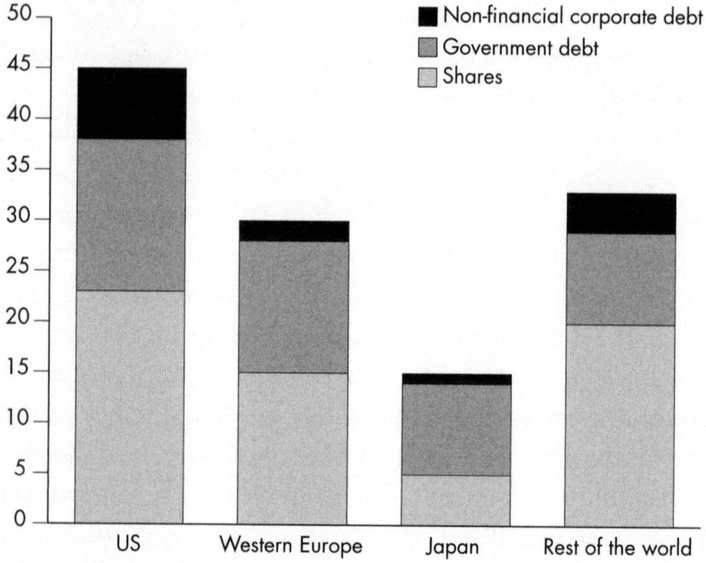

Source: McKinsey Global Institute

funds has been steadily eroded. Along with this goes a culture that puts increasing stress on disclosure and regular accountability.

These changes have gone furthest in Britain and the USA: in France and Germany traditional long-term insurance contracts are still common, although transparent investment funds (open-ended investment companies) are increasing in significance, and pension provision is largely unfunded. But if savers are to know the value of their funds on a daily basis, there needs to be at least the appearance of a market in which assets can be valued on a daily basis. This requirement substantially confines investment to securities whose market value can be readily computed and whose proceeds can be quickly realised.

So investment through intermediaries is mostly placed in the quoted shares of global companies. The 'universe' of investable assets for long-term investors totals around $125 trillion (figure 10),[5] so that around half of the value of all global assets can be intermediated in this way. These figures exclude securities issued by financial institutions—which are mostly part of the merry-go-round of transactions within the finance sector but include government debt held by financial institutions, which is a large fraction of total government debt. Transparent, liquid intermediation in the investment channel is heavily biased towards the shares of large global companies. Whether this bias serves savers well is a question to be considered below.

## A Bias to Action

> We don't get paid for activity, just for being right.
>
> WARREN BUFFETT,
> annual letter to the shareholders of Berkshire Hathaway, 1998

The economic functions of the investment channel are: to search for good investments for new savings; to secure the effective management of assets through stewardship; and to do these things while helping households transfer their wealth across their lifetime and between generations. These things are not, however, the things most people employed in the investment channel do. They rearrange the financial claims associated with existing assets. Most of all, they trade. With each other, and with other people's money.

The objective of financial engineering by investment banks and other promoters is to maximise the value of the financial claims associated with particular physical assets. This is equally rewarding whether the activity increases the value of the underlying physical assets—businesses, property or infrastructure—or whether the transaction simply represents a rearrangement of financial claims. The latter, brimful of opportunities to invoke the winner's curse by selling these claims for more than they are worth, is generally easier. The same physical assets can be sold in whatever financial form attracts the highest price.

Fee structures create misaligned incentives. Financial advice to corporations is mainly remunerated through fees and commissions on transactions. This arrangement worked tolerably well in the days when long-term relationships between banks and companies were the norm; the banker would wait patiently for the occasional (large) fee and would be unwilling to sacrifice a commercial relationship for short-term profit. But in a culture of 'I'll be gone, you'll be gone' the object of contact between bank and corporation is not to sustain informed dialogue but to urge the client to do the deal. The bias to action already in the mind of the corporate executive is reinforced.

The investment banker behind Robert Campeau's ludicrous Federated Department Stores was Bruce Wasserstein, described by *Forbes* at his death in 2009 (when he left an estate with reported value of $2.2 billion) as 'perhaps the most gifted deal maker in recent Wall Street history'.[6] Wasserstein had been characterised twenty years earlier by the same magazine as 'Bid-'em-up Bruce' for the 'psychological bullying' he was said to have employed to persuade his corporate clients to pay whatever was needed to make the transaction happen—an approach confirmed by the account of his role in the RJR Nabisco transaction in *Barbarians at the Gate*.[7]

Business and the non-financial economy as a whole would be better served if corporations sought strategic advice—to the extent that they have need for external strategic advice at all—from sources that do not have powerful incentives to promote transactions. Traditionally this role was played by boutique investment banks such as Lazard Frères, through legendary confidants of corporate executives such as André Meyer and Felix Rohatyn. But the age of financialisation established increasing pressure to trade. After President Clinton appointed Rohatyn Ambassador to France, Lazard's search for a successor alighted on none other than 'Bid-'em-up Bruce'.

The financial interest that investment banks—and the lawyers and accountants who follow on their coat tails—have in 'doing the deal' is only one, if perhaps the most egregious, of the ways in which remuneration based on fees for transactions creates a bias to action throughout the finance sector. Warren Buffett's warning against activity for its own sake is hard advice to follow, especially when facing a constantly changing screen constantly displaying 'news'.

Everyone in the finance sector feels a need to be a recipient of 'news': you see them glued to screens and tied to Blackberries. Everyone in the finance sector is under pressure from those who are paid to act, as are corporate executives. The quarterly earnings announcements of corporations are less financial statements than the outcome of a process of managing market expectations, while the monthly performance returns of asset managers have signal-to-noise ratios approaching zero. The short time horizons characteristic of actors in the investment channel today are not imposed by the needs of savers or investees—just the contrary. They have been created by the bias to action within the process of intermediation. Much assisted by the regulatory demands for transparency and liquidity. And aggravated by the use of investment consultants and the pursuit of benchmarks.

The position of the asset manager differs from that of other intermediaries in that asset managers are rewarded not for transactions but in proportion to the value of funds under their management. They have different incentives from others in the investment channel, but not necessarily ones better aligned with the interests of their clients or free of bias to action. You might increase the value of your existing funds by stellar long-term performance. But it may be easier and quicker to attract funds from other managers by stellar short-term performance. It's all about $\alpha$.

The capital asset pricing model (CAPM) has as its key parameters $\alpha$ and $\beta$ (only the dedicated need explore further letters of the Greek alphabet). $\beta$ relates to the return on 'the market', while $\alpha$ is risk-adjusted outperformance of the market benchmark. Asset managers report regularly to their investors, as they seek to beat an index defined by the average performance of all. However, to deviate much from that average is to take a risk: indeed it is common for risk managers and regulators to *define* risk as tracking error, the deviation of performance from the benchmark.

Since any substantially differentiated portfolio is bound to experience periods of underperformance, the need to avoid that possibility leads to 'closet indexation'—the construction of portfolios that are ostensibly actively managed but which are in reality close in composition to the market average. The turnover of asset managers has increased as fund managers focus on the changing expectations of their competitors rather than the underlying fortunes of companies. Just as traders are caught up in the self-referential beauty contest, more concerned to anticipate each other than to understand the properties of the securities in which they invest, asset managers are tied to each other by their shared pursuit of common benchmarks.

The pursuit of $\alpha$ is—necessarily—fruitless in aggregate. And it is fruitless in the vast majority of individual cases. On average, active fund managers underperform their benchmark, and by an amount that reflects their fees: since these managers now account for a major fraction of asset holding, this outcome is almost inevitable. Managers who charge higher fees tend to underperform managers who charge lower fees, not just on account of their charges but also because higher fees tend to be associated with higher turnover and hence transactions costs. The experience of retail investors is made still worse by their own poor timing of purchases and sales. The returns to investors in mutual funds are lower than the returns earned by the funds in which they invest, because they tend to buy fashionable, over-priced sectors and sell unfashionable, underpriced ones.

This disappointing outcome for savers is not cheap. The chain of intermediation has become too long, and that length adds to costs. Between the company and the saver are registrars, custodians, nominees, asset managers, fund-of-fund managers, investment consultants, pension fund trustees, insurance companies, platforms, independent financial advisers. And when trade occurs, a high-frequency trader, an exchange and an investment bank all take a cut. These intermediaries have their own costs, and their own business models. Their commercial objectives are not those of the ultimate users of markets—the savers whose funds are invested, and the companies whose shares are held. The strength and ethical integrity of a chain are as strong as its weakest link.

The rise of passive investment management has been a response to excessive costs and conflicting objectives in this investment chain. Vanguard—the largest asset management firm after BlackRock and Allianz—was established in 1975 by Jack Bogle, an evangelical promoter of passive investment.[8] Bogle's thesis was that, since the chances of outperforming a stock market index on a sustained basis were slight, replicating that index was a simple and inexpensive investment strategy. Passive investment has steadily grown in scale, and much of the activity of BlackRock, Vanguard and State Street is in the management of indexed funds, an activity that can now be entrusted to a computer. There are significant economies of scale in passive investment, and these large incumbents derive competitive advantage from their size.

The total costs of intermediation include management fees, administrative, custodial and regulatory costs, the costs of remunerating intermediaries, paying trading commissions and spreads between bid and offer price. If you invest directly in an indexed fund, you might be able to reduce these annual costs to 25–50 basis points (the finance sector describes one hundredth of one per cent as a 'basis point'). This figure is the minimum cost of using the investment channel. If you prefer an actively managed fund involving some kind of 'wrapper', held through a platform with the benefit of financial advice, you may experience costs of ten times that figure, and you will have a similar or worse experience if you employ the 'wealth management' services of a bank. Since the value of all shares is around $50 trillion, a single basis point is $5 billion, and so the cost of intermediation reduces individual savings pots substantially (on the one hand) and pays for limousines and private jets (on the other).

Today real rates of return on low-risk, long-term investments—such as the indexed bonds of the British, German or US government—hover around zero. The anticipated risk premium—the amount by which the return on equities exceeds the risk-free rate—is unlikely to be more than 3 to 4 per cent. After charges, many users of the investment channel are now unlikely to earn any real return on their savings at all. This is the epitome of a financial system designed for the needs of financial market participants rather than the users of finance.

This is not a book about personal investment strategy. I have written such a book, which immodesty compels me to recommend.[9] But I said there that a book which advised readers to be their own doctor or lawyer would be an irresponsible book; yet a recommendation to be one's own investment adviser (with, if necessary, the aid of a good book) is comparatively sound advice. The best and certainly least risky way to better returns is to pay less in fees and charges to the finance sector.

Neither the deposit nor the investment channel today offers any but the most confident and parsimonious saver a substantial prospect of a real return. This is an outcome that is unlikely to be either politically or economically sustainable.

## The Role of the Asset Manager

> Investment should be like watching grass grow or paint dry.
>
> **attributed to** PAUL SAMUELSON

The modern investment bank has retreated from search, the creation and discovery of new investment opportunities, into trading with other people's money for the benefit of its senior employees. Insurance companies and pension funds have withdrawn from the stewardship function of investment management and have become providers of administrative services. The positions once occupied by financial advisers are either filled by sales people or better done by computers. To describe these transitions thus is to caricature—but only a little. These various abdications from traditional roles in the investment channel have left space for the rise of the asset manager.

But to fill that space effectively, asset managers need to establish and demonstrate skills in both search and stewardship. They need to build the expertise required to fulfil the functions of the investment channel: active managers need to search out new opportunities for investment in business, property and infrastructure; passive managers must be effective stewards, supervisors of the management of the businesses, property and infrastructure in which they invest other people's money. Both types of manager will need to help households—and the state—in managing the transfer of wealth across lifetimes and between generations. Asset managers can fulfil these roles of search and stewardship effectively only if they can restore the trust relationships with savers and investees that have effectively disappeared from the financial system. There is a long distance to travel before these goals are effectively accomplished.

As I described in Chapter 5, stock markets came into being to raise capital for industry specific investments from a widely dispersed group of modest investors. But most intermediation in the investment channel takes place through large asset managers; securities markets now play a minimal role in providing funds for new investment in business. It is time to query whether the stock markets that consume so much resource and receive so much attention any longer serve an important economic function. The concentration of the asset management industry means that direct relationships between asset managers and savers, on the one hand, and companies or other users of investment funds, on the other, are not only possible but should provide a higher quality of both search and stewardship.

But the emphasis on public markets means that much of the activity of asset managers today involves neither search nor stewardship. Many fund managers have little knowledge of business or businesses and none of underlying investment opportunities in the corporate sector. Nor do these managers have time or capacity for supervision of the strategies of the businesses with whom their clients' funds are placed. The expertise of these intermediaries is in 'chasing α' by trying to anticipate each other's changing expectations rather than in understanding the character of the underlying assets.

The lack of relevant skills among asset managers is addressed to a degree by sub-contracting to managers of specialist vehicles. Many private equity firms do claim knowledge of particular sectors—principally in information technology. New specialist lenders have come into existence, such as mortgage distributors and credit card providers, but these institutions found it cheaper to finance their activities with dumb money diverted from the deposit channel than to seek funding through the investment channel.

When private equity funds are good they can be very, very good, but when they are bad they are horrid. Private equity investors can engage with companies and accept the long-term horizons necessary for much investment and appropriate to the needs of many savers. But this is not what most private equity houses do. Some readers will have shared my experience of 'the private equity hotel', whose overpriced breakfast and scuffed paintwork indicate that the priorities of the management are with current profits rather than future custom. This disappointing consumer experience is the characteristic result of a transaction in which the private equity manager buys the asset, loads it with debt, pushes up earnings temporarily and places the asset back in a public market within a relatively short period of time. The requirements of transparency and liquidity, which necessitate the promise of rapid exit, aggravate the problem, though it is one partially alleviated by the growth of a secondary market in private equity participations.

Infrastructure funds have a similarly Jekyll/Hyde character. Some have begun the process of developing genuine specialist expertise in search and stewardship of infrastructure projects. Other such funds are vehicles of financial engineering, facilitating off-balance-sheet financing by government or bemusing investors with complex transactions illustrated by glossy pictures of hospitals and roads.

In the quoted company sector there is less value in search: the businesses have already established themselves, the choice of investments is made by professional managers, and the funding for these investments

comes from the operational cash flow of the company. The key function of the investment manager of quoted equities is stewardship. The
same dichotomy between the very good and the very bad can be seen in
'activist' investment in quoted companies. At its best, activism is intervention by major shareholders when strategy is adrift or management
inadequate to the challenges the business faces.

But sometimes 'active' is only a description of high volumes of trading
activity, and 'activism' a demand for financial engineering. Businesses
are, it is claimed, worth more, or less, than the sum of their parts; shareholder value could be improved by the introduction of higher levels of
leverage. Most of this latter activity is, at best, useless, certainly from the
perspective of the economy as a whole, and often for those whose money
facilitates the transaction. The bias to action, however, remains a strong
driver of behaviour.

Constructive activism, however, is central to stewardship. And not
even the largest of asset managers can be a knowledgeable shareholder
in thousands of companies. The charge of stewardship carries with it
responsibility for ensuring effective management, but does not involve,
far less require, looking over the shoulders of the managers who take the
operational decisions required daily in any large company. Stewardship
does require securing the succession of competent managers to senior
executive roles, ensuring that business strategy is properly developed
and subjected to critical scrutiny, and—a role rendered necessary by
the effects of financialisation—preventing senior executives enriching
themselves at the expense of shareholders.

Stewardship involves rather more than the box-ticking approaches of
the proxy services that have become integral to corporate governance—
although smaller investment intermediaries, with more holdings than
they can themselves effectively monitor (itself an indicator of a problem), may need to use these agencies. Effective stewardship, however, is
integrated with investment management: there is no such thing as good
governance of a bad business.

To discharge the responsibilities of intermediaries in the investment
channel, asset managers should hold more focused, concentrated portfolios, with fewer stocks. Their activities and portfolios should be more
differentiated from each other, by style or area of expertise. Such activist stewardship would normally (but not invariably) be supportive of

current management—why else would the investment managers have chosen the stock? Engagement is currently restricted by regulatory rules and legal prohibitions, the product of the current preoccupation with liquidity and transparency. I will return to this malign effect of regulation in the next chapter.

Passive management should perhaps be defined simply as the opposite of the 'activism' represented by high levels of trading activity, rather than the mechanical replication of an index. The persuasive rationale of passive management was that most active management was not worth what it cost; the motivation of savers in seeking passive funds is to secure better value for money, not to minimise tracking error, and tracking error is a measure of risk for fund managers, not investors. A passive fund that buys and holds a well-considered selection of stocks achieves the same goal as an index fund, probably more effectively—and avoids the problem, evident on the London Stock Exchange, in which companies of doubtful reputation seek listings in order to force holders of passive funds to buy their stock.

There should be more managed intermediation. Transparency and liquidity seem at first sight a good thing, and so of course is the prevention of fraud, and certainly the regulatory provisions have been made with good intentions. But the demand for transparency is, as I have emphasised, the product of a low-trust environment. The most effective—in fact, the only effective—method of discriminating between the honest and the fraudulent is by reference to the reputation of the business and the people who run it: giving savers detailed knowledge of what these companies do, which they have neither the time nor the expertise to assimilate, is a very imperfect substitute.

And the requirements of transparency and liquidity are costly. Not just, or primarily, the administrative costs, but through the constraints they impose on engagement with companies and the composition of portfolios. The costs of transparency and liquidity are forcefully illustrated by comparisons of the returns generated by closed-end (managed) and open-ended (transparent) investment funds with identical objectives and managers, a comparison which overwhelmingly favours closed-end funds.[10] The most successful of all investment funds in history is Berkshire Hathaway, the closed-end investment vehicle of Warren Buffett, the archetypal steward of managed intermediation.

But managed intermediation requires trust. Can trust in the investment channel be restored by promoting the reputation of asset managers? Can they achieve with investors the levels of confidence which savers were once able to place in banks (and must be persuaded to do again). At present, large asset management firms such as BlackRock deal mostly with institutions, such as pension funds and insurance companies. But a significant part of their business—and a growing one—appeals directly to the public.

Different business structure may promote trust. The traditional attraction of mutuality—and one of the reasons why it once enjoyed a substantial role in the finance sector—is the elimination of conflict of interest. Organisations will be readier to recognise their obligations to other people's money if they do not have profit objectives of their own. But there is little prospect of restoring a significant mutual sector in banking or insurance, because there is no realistic means of raising sufficient capital for mutuals in these sectors to operate safely at scale. But asset management, which is not capital-intensive, is different. New organisations engaged with pensions—such as the large established schemes of Canada, Denmark and the Netherlands, and NEST in the UK—may have a wider role to play. Several of the most successful US asset managers—Capital, Fidelity, Vanguard—are not listed companies, and their executives seem particularly committed to sustaining the long-term reputation of their businesses.

Like the deposit channel, the investment channel currently fails to meet the needs of businesses and households. The deposit channel has become clogged with an excess of intra-financial sector trading. The investment channel has become too long, and too leaky. In both cases we need simplification to establish short, simple chains of intermediation. In the deposit channel that means separating the trading casino from the utility of taking deposits and lending them on. In the investment channel it requires the promotion of asset managers with skills in search and stewardship of the physical and intangible—rather than the financial—assets of the real economy. A finance sector dominated by deposit-taking narrow banks and asset managers offers the prospect of rebuilding trust in the financial sector, lowering costs and enhancing financial stability.

# PART III

# POLICY

*Few industries attract so much attention from government and the public as the finance sector. Regulation of finance fails to satisfy public demand and expectations, and is deeply resented and strongly resisted by the industry. Chapter 8 explains why financial regulation is at once extensive and intrusive and yet largely captured by industry interests and ineffective in achieving public policy goals. The multiple interactions between economic policy and finance are the subject of Chapter 9. Finance is both an instrument of economic policy and a primary influence on it, and the social and economic consequences are largely malign. The message of both chapters is that there is too much government involvement in the financial sector, not too little. The ills of financialisation are, in large part, the results of misconceived public policies. Chapter 10 sets out the elements of a programme of reform, designed both to limit state intervention and to render the intervention that is required. The objective should be to address issues of structure and incentives rather than to intensify supervision and control.*

# CHAPTER 8

# Regulation

## The Origins of Financial Regulation

> Culturally, financial service organisations were led by those whose basic assumptions were founded on money as the goal, numbers as the answers, and technology as the intermediary. The implications of replacing people with technology, judgment with money, and leadership with those skilled only in moneymaking went unrecognised.
>
> SALZ REVIEW, an independent review of
> Barclays' business practices, 3 April 2013

Financial regulation once relied on informal and often unwritten structures based on mutual respect. The men who controlled the businesses of the City of London formed a socially homogeneous group, who shared a public-school education, often followed by a spell at Oxbridge or in the army. Wall Street was mostly staffed at upper levels by WASPs with Ivy League backgrounds. In both London and New York, these 'blue blood' or 'white shoe' firms competed with businesses controlled by prominent Jewish families such as Rothschild and Lazard.

Such firms did business through agency relationships. They expected to maintain contact with their clients over many years, many transactions and many activities. These shared expectations encouraged an honest exchange of plans and information. This seeming community of interest was true at both wholesale and retail level—between the company and the investment bank, and between the individual and the retail bank or stockbroker. These relationships were fostered by an industry structure characterised by functional separation: banks, brokers and specialists performed different functions, and there was shared clarity about the nature of the relationship.

This collegiality did not preclude abuse of customers or systemic instability. Activities we would today characterise as insider dealing and market manipulation were rife: there were occasions of serial fraud and frequent exploitation of both corporate and retail customers. From time to time, important institutions failed or teetered on the brink of failure. But the practice of reciprocity, robust structures and a widely recognised sense of shared values limited malpractice, controlled risk and facilitated industry-wide co-operation to manage crises. There were few explicit rules, but there was an elaborate framework of expectations about how participants should behave.

Trust in the finance sector was always lower in the USA than in Europe and 1933 was a watershed for the industry. The Pecora hearings had demonstrated how abuse and incompetence in the financial sector had been a major cause of the Great Depression. Banks had failed; financial intermediaries had plied their clients with worthless securities. The principal objectives of the new regime were to make bank deposits safe, to ensure that future failures of individual institutions did not lead to a breakdown of the financial system as a whole, and to prevent fraud or near-fraud on investors.

Relative informality survived in Britain for another fifty years. But with financialisation, the mechanisms of enforcement of trust within and between firms were broken by the erosion of values and the emergence of financial conglomerates dominated by trading cultures. The growth of these large and powerful conglomerates would put a burden on regulators that they were not, in the event, able to shoulder.

The common-law jurisdictions of England[1] and the USA allow great freedom for parties to contract in any form they choose, in contrast to continental Europe, where more prescriptive civil law codes prevail. England and the USA are therefore preferred locations for new financial instruments and complex or idiosyncratic commercial arrangements. The global dominance of the finance industry by Britain and the USA is the result of mutually reinforcing advantages of law and language, strongly supported by London's imperial past and America's industrial hegemony.

Common commercial codes breed common commercial practices. Modern Germany embraced the social market economy in reaction against Nazi tyranny, but co-operation and collusion still come more naturally than competition to many business people in continental Europe. In these countries banking—like most other financial activities—has always been implicitly or explicitly cartelised. There have been few differences in price and limited non-price competition.

An important consequence of this difference in background and philosophy is that regulators and governments in continental Europe were more ready than their Anglo-Saxon counterparts to connive in concealing the scale of disaster that the global financial crisis represented for the banking system. Europe today has many 'zombie banks'—institutions that are essentially insolvent but which rely on central bank support as they hope, over many years, to trade their way out of difficulties. Political rhetoric in France and Germany is particularly hostile to financialisation, and indeed to market economics generally. But the corporatist flavour of policy in these countries means that reform of the financial sector, not vigorously pursued anywhere, has been imperceptible. And has created the paradox of Deutsche Bank, at once frighteningly fragile and reassuringly stable.

Traditional, national, often implicit arrangements derived from culture and history were eroded and homogenised by globalisation and meritocracy, and the rise of more individualistic and more legalistic cultures. The formal structures of the industry changed somewhat later, with the emergence from the 1980s of financial conglomerates. The combined effects changed fundamentally the nature of regulation of the industry. A curious feature of the change—most striking in the UK, but evident everywhere—was that what was commonly described as a process of deregulation led in practice to a steady increase in the scope and burden of regulation of the finance sector.

There were—and are—two main strands to financial regulation: the supervision of banks and the oversight of securities markets. I will review each of these in turn.

## The Basel Agreements

> Beneath me flows the Rhine, and, like the stream of Time, it flows amid the ruins of the Past.
>
> H.W. LONGFELLOW, *Hyperion*, 1839

The regulation of banks was a national affair, reflecting different historical developments in different jurisdictions. The banking structure of the USA was fragmented as a result of its restrictions on inter-state banking. Britain had a concentrated retail banking system and clear separation between commercial and investment banking. Universal banks prevailed in France and Germany. Since the 1980s, however, the dominant influence on banking supervision has been the attempt to reach internationally harmonised structures through the Basel agreements.

It is often claimed that the global financial crisis was caused, or exacerbated, by the weaknesses of international financial architecture. There is some truth in this view. The globalisation of capital markets restricted the capacity of any single national regulator to act. Many attempts have been made to promote co-operation between national regulators. The European Union has been one focus; other global mechanisms include the G8 and G20 economic summits and the annual meetings of the IMF and World Bank. The front cabins of planes are regularly filled with officials engaged in financial supervision travelling to international meetings in pleasant locations.

But such co-operation is longer on rhetoric than on substance, and much time is spent listening to set-piece speeches and negotiating the detail of bland communiqués. Many regulators and politicians attending these events use them as an opportunity to advance the interests of their national financial services industry, and the surrounding hotels are occupied by lobbyists who encourage them to do so. In the banking sector, where global co-ordination was most extensive, the effects of that co-ordination were harmful; international agreement imposed a model of regulatory supervision that did not merely fail to prevent the global financial crisis but actively contributed to it.

This internationalisation of regulation has origins in the resentment by American and British banks in the 1980s of competition from Japan. Japanese institutions had been aggressive lenders, and their laxity had stimulated soaring domestic stock and land prices. Judged by size of balance sheet, seven of the top ten banks in the world in 1988 were Japanese.[2] This fact was interpreted as a sign of the strength of the Japanese financial system; with hindsight, it was an indicator of weakness. Chapter 6 has explained why large balance sheets illustrate fragility not resilience. Today, four of the top eleven banks by asset size are domiciled in China, and the appropriate interpretation of this development is again ambiguous.[3]

The institution selected to deal with the imagined competitive threat from Japan was the Bank for International Settlements (BIS), based in Basel, the small historic city on the Swiss Rhine. The BIS had been established to manage German reparations after the First World War. This role had obviously ceased by 1933, and the bank's subsequent role during the Second World War in facilitating the transfer of gold stolen by the Nazis led to a decision at the Bretton Woods summit of 1944 that the bank should be abolished. But defunct public agencies are tenacious, and BIS continued a fragile existence. In the 1980s it became the chosen vehicle for international co-ordination of bank regulation. The first Basel Accord was signed in 1988.

The problem of 'unfair' Japanese competition in banking solved itself in predictable fashion, through the recognition of reality rather than the enforcement of regulation. In the early 1990s the Japanese property and securities price bubble burst and many Japanese banks became insolvent, struggling on for years through the indulgence of the Bank of Japan (in a manner that would later be imitated in Europe). But the Basel accords nevertheless became the principal determinant of banking regulation, national and global, and continue to fulfil this role. Within twenty years of their inception, the world would experience the most serious banking failures since the Great Depression—and perhaps the most serious banking failures in history.

The initial Basel accords would subsequently be elaborated into Basel II, partially operative by the time the process was overwhelmed by the 2007–8 crisis. The Basel regime has three 'pillars': capital requirements, supervision and disclosure. Disclosure reflects a belief that if sufficient relevant information is provided, the public and the markets will impose appropriate sanctions on a poorly managed bank. In reality, the financial statements of banks are opaque, and that opacity has steadily increased over the life of the Basel accords. The availability of a government back-stop further undermines the disciplining effect of disclosure.

Capital requirements and supervision are therefore key to the effectiveness of the Basel process. Supervision is a process of private discussion between the bank and the regulator. Since we have little public knowledge of the process, we can assess its quality only by results, which are not encouraging.

The basic rule on capital requirements is that a bank must have equity capital—the money that can be lost before a business is forced into insolvency—equal to 8 per cent of its assets. This figure is low by the standards applied to any other company—as pointed out in Chapter 6 a bank would be very hesitant to lend to a non-financial business whose equity represented only 8 per cent of its assets.

But in reality the effective figure is, and recently has been, much lower: the description of the balance sheet of Deutsche Bank in Chapter 7 provides some indication of the underlying reality. Banks were permitted to treat some of their debt as capital. In addition, the calculation of assets was subject to a scheme of risk-weighting. Loans to non-financial businesses were generally weighted at 100 per cent, while mortgages, deemed to be safer, carried a risk weighting of 50 per cent. Government bonds and loans to other banks were considered to carry no risk at all. Thus the actual ratio of capital to assets could be, and was, much lower than 8 per cent.

The crudity of risk weights encouraged banks to accept riskier—and higher-yielding—loans within each risk category. The risk weighting attached to a 60 per cent loan-to-value mortgage for a local physician was the same as that for the no-deposit loans to NINJAs (no income, no job, no assets) that were marketed in US cities.

The mechanics of risk weighting also stimulated regulatory arbitrage. A package of mortgages might be transferred to another bank, in which case the mortgages might be categorised as bank loans for regulatory purposes. After Basel, securitisation—the process by which financial institutions sold to each other the loans they had originated—grew very rapidly. Banks could also reduce their required capital by establishing off-balance-sheet vehicles (SIVs) which operated outside the scope of regulation.

Instruments created for purposes of regulatory arbitrage—beginning with repos and mortgage-backed securities and in time extending to credit default swaps, SIVs and other acronyms too numerous to list—were central to financialisation. Misconceived regulation created the problem it was supposedly designed to tackle—and then promoted more regulation in order to deal with the new issues that had emerged.

The mechanisms of arbitrage developed during financialisation are not restricted to methods of reducing the burden of regulation. In Chapter 4 I described four principal types: the regulatory arbitrage prompted by the Basel rules (and earlier and later mechanisms of financial regulation); accounting arbitrage, designed to flatter corporate—or government—accounts; fiscal arbitrage, intended to achieve a more favourable tax treatment; and jurisdictional arbitrage, designed to take advantage of the different regulatory, accounting or fiscal rules that are employed in different countries around the world.

All these manoeuvres have the same underlying purpose: to gain financial advantage by devising transactions with similar commercial effect but different regulatory, accounting or fiscal form. These arbitrage activities normally have negative economic value: the gain to the initiating business (and the agents who facilitate the transaction) is offset, or more than offset, by the loss to some other, generally anonymous, actor or actors—most often, the taxpaying public.

The most effective counter to arbitrage is to ensure that transactions with similar economic consequences are treated in the same way, and this is widely accepted as a regulatory objective (and a goal of accounting standards and fiscal policy). But the complexity of the modern financial world makes this ideal difficult to achieve. The idea—to which many regulators appear to cling—that arbitrage could be eliminated, or well addressed, by ever more complex rules is an illusion. In tax policy two centuries of income tax legislation designed to attack fiscal arbitrage have not abolished tax avoidance but have generated a tax code of extraordinary complexity.

Two broad lines of attack are available. One is to give regulators more discretion, so that they can implement the spirit rather than the letter of the relevant rules. The pendulum routinely swings between 'principle-based' and 'rule-based' regulation: there is often (especially in the less litigious European context) a desire to avoid the complexity of detailed prescription, but then in practice firms demand more explicit guidance as to what they are allowed to do (often with a view to pushing to the limits of what they are allowed to do), and the rulebook again adds more pages. Such discretion is least acceptable in tax policy—it is obviously undesirable to have assessments based on what inspectors think the taxpayer should pay rather than some objective rule—but even in that sphere many governments have, in the light of hard experience of fiendishly complex schemes, introduced general anti-avoidance provisions enabling them to void transactions with no genuine commercial purpose.

The alternative attack on arbitrage frames principles and rules in ways that limit the scope for such arbitrage. While few concepts admit completely unambiguous definition, sales is an easier concept to measure than income, leverage a simpler metric than risk-weighted capital. The underlying objective must necessarily always be compromised in the interests of effective administration.

Much the most serious—and a very long established—source of arbitrage in the financial system is the line between debt and equity; indeed the principle that there is a tax advantage to be gained by substituting debt for equity is so familiar to everyone in the financial world that it is regarded as a fact of commercial life rather than an instance of financial arbitrage. The variety of adverse consequences—on the costs and complexity of fiscal systems, on government's ability to collect tax revenues and on financial stability—are numerous, and widely discussed, and a variety of proposals for eliminating or reducing such distortions have been advanced.[4] The adverse effect of tax discrimination between debt and equity is, however, an issue today subsumed into the broader issue of the extensive corporate tax avoidance by multinational companies, an activity that is both a cause and an effect of financialisation, and now out of hand. In a depressingly familiar hypocritical style, politicians have simultaneously denounced these avoidance activities while introducing loopholes to attract revenue from other countries and favour the companies whose interests they espouse.

The distortions created by these inefficiencies of tax policy in relation not just to the financial sector but to the financial activities of non-financial corporations is a matter that has been exhaustively discussed elsewhere.[5] The focus of this chapter is on the regulation of banks, but the regulators of banks learned little from experience of arbitrage in other spheres. Or, as we will see below, from regulation in other sectors. The Basel process has sought to control bank activities and exposures through a prescriptive rulebook, and has responded to each instance of regulatory arbitrage—and the comprehensive failures of regulation before and during the global financial crisis—by the proliferation of more complex rules.

The best account of why this approach was bound to fail was provided by the early critics of socialism and central planning, such as von Mises[6] and Hayek.[7] The centre—the planner or the regulator—can never have sufficient local information to anticipate the needs or opportunities of the subordinate entity. In frustration, yet more rules and targets are added. The results are always more complex and rarely more effective. This was true of the Soviet Union. And of the Basel process.

## Securities Regulation

> 1984 marks the 50th anniversary of the Securities and Exchange Commission. Fifty years ago, in the depths of the depression, the nation's securities markets were demoralized. Today, they are by far the best capital markets the world has ever known—the broadest, the most active and efficient, and the fairest.
>
> JOHN S.R. SHAD, SEC chairman, annual report of the SEC, 1984

The modern framework of securities regulation finds its origins in the New Deal of the 1930s, when a comprehensive framework was introduced in response to the financial abuses that had preceded the Depression. The institutional framework and underlying philosophy developed in the USA then and elaborated in subsequent decades has influenced the thinking of securities regulators around the world. The primary objective of the Securities and Exchange Commission, established by the 1933 US legislation, was to increase the quality and quantity of information available to the public. The corollary was that trading should take place on the basis of that information alone.

The idea has superficial attractions and fundamental flaws. The framework of thought is frequently described through the sporting metaphor of 'fairness': the 'level playing field' on which all players compete on equal terms. To achieve fairness, a standard template of information should be provided to everyone, whether director of a company, investment banker or day trader with a home computer. Market participants may deal, and may only deal, on the basis of that information. No trader can have better information than any other, and success depends only on skill in interpreting it—or in anticipating the interpretations of others.

Of course, this 'level playing field' is not achievable or achieved, and would not be desirable if it were to be achieved. Yet, like the regulators of casinos, the regulators of securities markets often describe 'market integrity' as their objective; their focus is on the efficient functioning of the market, in a narrow technical sense that is concerned with process rather than outcome. The emphasis on the preoccupations of market participants rather than the interests of market users is deeply embedded in current thinking.

The mantras of regulatory dialogue on both sides of the Atlantic are liquidity, price discovery and transparency. The pursuit of liquidity often seems to mean little more than the facilitation of trading activity as an end in itself: trading is to be welcomed because it promotes trading. The term 'price discovery' has no obvious meaning at all. It derives from the self-referential world exemplified in Keynes' beauty contest. The service that the real economy needs from securities markets is 'value discovery', an estimate of the fundamental value of a security based on the underlying earnings and cash flows of the businesses whose securities are traded.

The economic purposes of securities markets are to meet the needs of companies and savers. The effectiveness of financial intermediation in promoting efficient capital allocation depends on the quality of the information available to market participants. Regulation whose primary purpose is to encourage trading by ensuring that no trader has an informational advantage actually gets in the way of efficient capital allocation, in principle and in practice. Effective information and monitoring are best achieved—perhaps only achieved—in the context of a trust relationship. Such a relationship is generally necessary, if not sufficient, for the transfer of information to be honest and directly relevant to user needs.[8]

In the mortgage market, trust relationships—between branch manager and borrower, between branch manager and head office, between the mortgage-lending company and its investors—were replaced by trading and sales activities. The outcome was a decline in the quality of information that passed across these relationships. The long-term interests of ordinary retail investors are best served by ensuring that investment decisions are made on the basis of the best information, which should not be confused with the most data. This elision leads to the emphasis on 'transparency'. While it is difficult to quarrel with an objective of transparency, the demand for transparency has led to the provision of more and more material of little or no value to users.

The answer to information asymmetry is not always the provision of more information, especially when most of this 'information' is simply noise, or boilerplate (standardised documentation bolted on to every report). Companies justifiably complain about the ever-increasing volume of data they are required to produce, while users of accounting find less and less of relevance in them. The notion that all investors have, or could have, identical access to corporate data is a fantasy, but the attempt to make it a reality generates a raft of regulation which inhibits engagement between companies and their investors and impedes the collection of substantive information that is helpful in assessing the fundamental value of securities. In the terms popularised by the American computer scientist Clifford Stoll, 'data is not information, information is not knowledge, knowledge is not understanding, understanding is not wisdom'.[9]

In one of the most bizarre cases of financial wrongdoing ever identified, Ray Dirks exposed fraud at Equity Funding, a corrupt insurance company, in the 1970s. The senior executives of the company went to prison. The SEC, which had failed to uncover or investigate the fraud, then charged Dirks with insider trading, and the case went to the highest judicial levels before the Supreme Court affirmed the obvious point that the public interest in the exposure of corporate crime was greater than the public interest in maintaining an orderly market in the worthless shares of the company. In Europe, where the law reflects the SEC position in emphasising market integrity rather than personal integrity, it is likely that Dirks would have been guilty, though unlikely that he would ever have been charged—insider trading remains a normal way of doing business in many European countries. But the focus of regulatory policy has shifted from protection of consumers to protection of markets.[10]

The effect of this regulatory approach is to undermine—ultimately, to eradicate—attempts to generate information through private activity, and to limit information to that which is mandated by regulatory prescription. But the long-term interests of ordinary retail investors, especially the vast majority who use the services of asset managers, are best served not by establishing a 'level playing field' of information between them and market professionals, but rather by ensuring that investment decisions are made on the basis of the best information.

Consumers do not buy cars, or visit their doctors, with the desire or expectation that they will be submerged in technical information. They come to obtain products or advice, and they rely on the reputation of the suppliers for assurance that their requirements will, as far as possible, be met. Financial services are different because the reputation of suppliers has deteriorated to a point at which consumers no longer have such confidence. Regulation that serves the needs of users would focus on the integrity of finance providers rather than the integrity of markets.

Rarely has the self-preoccupation of financial markets found such clear expression as in the self-congratulatory remarks of Mr Shad with which this section began. In his perception the measure of regulatory success was the morale of market participants, the means to that outcome 'activity' and 'fairness'. He might have been a cheerleader addressing a football crowd, not a regulator supervising market participants. But this was 1984 (yes!), and financialisation was only beginning.

## The Regulation Industry

If any of the great corporations of the country were to hire adventurers who make market of themselves in this way, to procure the passage of a general law with a view to the promotion of their private interests, the moral sense of every right-minded man would instinctively denounce the employer and employed as steeped in corruption and the employment as infamous. If the instances were numerous, open, and tolerated, they would be regarded as measuring the decay of the public morals and

the degeneracy of the times. No prophetic spirit would be needed to fore-
tell the consequences near at hand.

US SUPREME COURT, 88 US Trist v. Child, 1874

The complexity of regulation has encouraged the development of specialism in compliance and risk management. While superficially the del-
egation of such control was accompanied by greater professionalisation
of the function, in practice risk managers usually did not command great
respect. Risk officers were not profit-earners: most traders saw them as
people who got in the way of profits. Compliance officers, who insisted
that the administrative procedures of firms met the requirements of the
relevant rulebooks, enjoyed lower status still.

Risk management and compliance were thus separated from executive management and trading, and so financial regulation became a
business in its own right. The regulation industry comprises compliance
and risk management staff within financial services firms, the staff of
regulatory agencies, and consultants and lawyers who mediate between
them. It employs lobbyists who seek to influence the content of legislation and regulatory provisions. These people have their own language,
studded with acronyms, much of it incomprehensible even to other financial professionals.

The scale and complexity of both the industry and its regulatory regime mean that regulatory functions can be exercised only by people
with extensive experience of the sector. That experience necessarily determines their perspective. Timothy Geithner, as Federal Reserve Bank
chairman and Treasury secretary, demonstrated little understanding of
the issues that he faced or the broader context in which he worked. But
he did have considerable knowledge of the finance industry and its regulation, and of the personalities involved. It is understandable, perhaps
inevitable, that politicians should have relied on him and those like him.
It seems absurd to turn to bankers to sort out the mess that bankers have
made. But what else is to be done?

The finance sector spends more on lobbying than any other industry. In the USA its expenditures in the 2012–14 election cycle totalled
$800 million, with another $400 million spent on campaign contributions. There are about 2,000 registered finance industry lobbyists in

Washington: about four for each member of Congress.[11] This figure does not include unregistered lobbyists: former Senate majority leader Tom Daschle and House majority leader Newt Gingrich (who are now 'policy advisers' to a major law firm and to Fannie Mae respectively) are not registered as lobbyists.[12] The recruitment of once prominent politicians to these roles is itself a recent and extraordinary development; when Harry S. Truman left office 'his name was not for sale. He would take no fees for commercial endorsements, or for lobbying or writing letters or making phone calls'.[13]

Regulatory agencies are buffeted by this lobbying activity and the political pressures that result from it. Still, the top jobs in regulatory agencies—especially central banks—command prestige and public respect. Outstanding candidates have often been recruited to fill them, even though the financial rewards are almost inconsequential by the standards of the finance industry. The salary of Janet Yellen, chairman of the Federal Reserve Board, is 1 per cent of that of Jamie Dimon, chairman of J.P. Morgan Chase; but the job makes her the second most powerful woman in the world, according to *Forbes* magazine. (Angela Merkel, who is number one, earns about the same as Ms Yellen.)

But lower-level posts in regulatory agencies have fewer attractions. Their salaries, though not so disproportionately low as Ms Yellen's, are modest by the standards of the finance industry (even if they are well paid relative to other public sector employees). The status attached to such posts is low, and the work itself not particularly interesting. It is unfair to disparage individuals as 'box tickers' when box-ticking is the job they are asked to do and the job of which they are capable. In all regulated industries people who show aptitude for regulatory work are likely to receive attractive offers from firms in the industry. It is difficult for regulatory agencies to hire and retain employees of high calibre, and in the main they do not succeed in doing so.

The difficulty of attracting able staff means that the aspirations of those in charge of agencies of financial regulation—or the politicians who appoint them—are not translated into the activities of the individuals who actually perform the routine work.

A regulator cannot easily challenge the fundamental strategy of a badly run financial services business, such as Lehman or Royal Bank of Scotland. No one within the businesses themselves was willing to challenge Dick Fuld or Fred Goodwin—including the genuinely distinguished figures who sat on the RBS board (that of Lehman was decorated by friends of Fuld). Even the head of an agency may enjoy less access to the powerful than the senior executives of large corporations—if for no other reason than that the latter have considerably more largesse to dispense. Recall Gordon Brown's fulsome tribute to Fuld and Lehman (see Chapter 1), and note that Goodwin and his (then) wife enjoyed weekend hospitality at Chequers, Prime Minister Brown's official residence, even as the bank was sliding towards bankruptcy. It is not an accident that both Lehman and RBS were run by unpleasant, domineering individuals with good political connections: these characteristics are common pointers to the combination of personal success and corporate failure.

Now put yourself in the position of a junior officer in a regulatory agency who has reservations about the risk controls in these organisations. Even if you yourself feel competent to criticise, and brave enough to voice your doubts, your action may not be well regarded by people further up the agency's hierarchy, who would themselves prefer a quiet, or prospectively more rewarding, life.

Workers who are struggling with the demands of their job tend to focus on the things they can do, which may differ from the things that need to be done. It is easy to focus on minor procedural deficiencies in the management of a generally well-run financial services business: a regulatory visit will always identify some incomplete client file or lapse in record-keeping. Such identification of administrative failing will usually attract a conciliatory response—the firm concerned is embarrassed and makes proposals for remedial action. Senior managers of the regulated business, not in any way threatened, can safely blame the problem on operational lapses by subordinates. In the regulatory agency, superiors will applaud the employees' vigilance.

Carmen Segarra is pursuing a lawsuit alleging unfair dismissal by the Federal Reserve Bank of New York (the institution headed by Geithner until he became Treasury secretary). She was required to judge Goldman Sachs' policy on conflicts of interest following a series of incidents, including 'Fabulous Fab's' Abacus transaction (see Chapter 2) and the deal between El Paso and Kinder Morgan (Chapter 4). She has released tapes recording the Fed's reluctance to upset Goldman and instructions to her to tone down criticism. 'Sometimes', she claims to have been told, 'the bank examiners who are taken most seriously are the most quiet.'[14]

These issues explain, though they cannot excuse, the performance of agencies which seem to impose endless petty restrictions on legitimate business, but which are, as the SEC was, unable to recognise, far less apprehend, the fraudster Bernard Madoff despite detailed dossiers provided to it by Harry Markopolos.[15] In the face of similar inertia it was left to the zealous New York State Attorney General, Eliot Spitzer, to attempt to expose malpractice during the new economy bubble. The main forum for punishing wrongdoing on Wall Street has been the courts of New York, where District Attorney Robert Morgenthau and Judge Jed Rakoff have been staunch opponents of bank malfeasance.

The notion that regulators can, or should, second-guess the risk management strategies of Goldman Sachs is simply ludicrous. Goldman, generally believed to have the best risk management systems in the finance sector, and one of the highest-paying firms in that sector, did not have models or management structures adequate for even the early stages of market disruption (as David Viniar's flailing references to '25 standard deviation events' demonstrated). What hope is there that regulators, with far less information and resource, will do the job more effectively? In framing regulation, it is essential to be realistic about what regulation can achieve.

## What Went Wrong

[The Interstate Commerce Commission] can be made of great use to the railroads. It satisfies the popular clamor for a government supervision of the railroads, at the same time that supervision is almost entirely nominal. Further, the older such a commission gets to be, the more inclined it will be found to take the business and railroad view of things.

RICHARD OLNEY, attorney general in Grover Cleveland's administration, in a letter to Charles Perkins, president of the Burlington Railroad, 1892[16]

Suppose I went swinging off my course and came in two days late and they asked me 'where have you been all that time, Captain?' What would I say to that? Went round to dodge the bad weather I would say. Must have been dam' bad they would say. I don't know, I says, I dodged clear of it.

CAPTAIN MCWHIRR, in Joseph Conrad, *Typhoon*, 1902

Inevitably, financial services regulation and regulators have been heavily criticised since the 2007–8 crisis. Regulators were 'asleep at the wheel'. The revisionist account of the events of 2007–8 asserts that the failures and frauds in the industry were not, as the public was mistakenly led to believe, the result of managerial incompetence and individual chicanery. Business failures were the consequence of a series of errors by governments: unwise encouragement of home-ownership, loose monetary policies and weak regulation.

Although this description is essentially ridiculous, there is an element of truth in it: there were serious policy errors. The exclusion of derivatives from the ambit of US regulation in 1999 is now almost universally recognised to have been a mistake. Moreover, the changed structure of the finance industry from partnerships to limited-liability corporations effectively transferred a degree of responsibility for risk management from firms to regulators.

The Basel calculations of capital adequacy became a substitute for the prudential management of risk by banks themselves. Indeed in the revisionist account of the crisis banks blame regulators for their failure to impose more demanding requirements on them. And they have a point: bank executives were under pressure from their traders and shareholders to expand their balance sheets to the limits permissible by regulation. It is, perhaps, an exaggeration to say that the minimum standards of capital and behaviour prescribed by regulation were interpreted as maxima—but not a very great one.

But to see policy errors as the source of the problem is to fail to understand either the economics or the politics. Perhaps it was an error to eschew regulation of credit default swaps—but what is it supposed that a regulator would have done if such regulation had been in place? After all, the banks that were brought down by these instruments were themselves regulated institutions.

These failures of regulation were observed in almost every advanced country. It is implausible that so many regulators had, simultaneously and independently, fallen 'asleep at the wheel': the catalepsy had more systematic underlying causes. Among policymakers in Britain and the USA there has been little political appetite for constraints on the financial services industry, and often considerable political opposition. Even if regulators had been inclined towards pre-emptive actions, and had known which measures to implement, they would not have enjoyed political support. They had therefore little or no incentive or inclination to act. If the ship's owners will not allow the captain to move the wheel much, it hardly matters whether he is asleep at the wheel or awake on the bridge, and he might as well retire to his cabin.

Pre-emptive action by any regulator faces Captain McWhirr's dilemma. The unimaginative Scots sea captain was not 'asleep at the wheel'; he had made a considered decision that, whatever perils might lie in wait, his best course was full steam ahead. The costs and consequences of preventive action are real and measurable. But if preventive action is successful, the costs of the damaging events that have been avoided, and indeed the very nature of these events themselves, will remain hypothetical. The public applauds not the cautious captain who escapes the storm but the heroic seaman who, like McWhirr, battles successfully through.

Some regulators were essentially placemen, put there by the industry and its political cronies to represent the interests of the businesses over which they exerted nominal oversight. But others were honest and committed public servants: they were, however, constantly aware of the political influence of the industry. 'Light touch regulation' was the product not of idle regulators but of the demands of the industry transmitted through the political process. Compare the remarks of Gordon Brown (Chapters 1 and 9) with those of Theodore (Chapter 1) and Franklin (frontispiece) Roosevelt.

In northern Europe and North America there is little evidence of overt corruption in regulatory agencies, or at the senior levels of politics, finance and business. The mechanisms are more subtle. Regulators adopt the mindset of those they regulate. Regulators are dependent on the industry not just for most of the information they use but also for the frameworks within which that information is interpreted. Moreover, industry information comes from sources and lobbies that are well resourced: the public interest is, in general, poorly funded. If your job is to regulate traders, you naturally hear their concerns. And so the objectives of regulators are to stamp out market abuse and promote an efficient market in financial instruments. Life is more comfortable if one is allied with the rich and the powerful, and the regulated are always richer—and in reality more powerful—than the regulators.

Finance is a rewarding source of employment for superannuated politicians and former regulators. For people who reach the highest positions in public life, the lecture circuit alone is sufficient to secure a more than comfortable retirement. For those whose contributions are less noteworthy but influential, well-remunerated non-executive and advisory roles beckon: their contacts and inside knowledge are genuinely valuable. While a handful of politicians have built successful careers by attacking vested interests, many more have enjoyed a comfortable life by succumbing to the advances of well-funded groups.

In his film *Inside Job* Charles Ferguson interviewed many figures, including some of the economists who played significant roles in events before the global financial crisis.[17] Ferguson gives the impression of corruption—people said things they were well paid to say. Yet this description is too crude. In North America and northern Europe few people in public life can be induced to change their minds by the offer of wads of cash: nor are those who can be so swayed generally reliable allies or powerful persuaders.

The effective lobbyist approaches people who have a predilection to support the lobbyist's position; the assistance the lobby can provide reinforces that stance. Politicians who benefit from campaign support are more likely to win and, when they do win, are less inclined to take a sceptical view of the interests of their supporters. In the academic world the aid that financial interests offer both to individuals and to institutions helps to establish a professional consensus that dominates the editorial policies of journals, the grant-giving processes of research councils, the decisions of tenure committees and the education of future students.

This process may be described as 'intellectual capture', and even if they are people of scrupulous honesty, regulators, politicians and academics are vulnerable to it. Intellectual capture is evident in the shift of regulatory emphasis from a model that emphasises the legal obligations of agency to one that promotes the abstract integrity of markets.

And so it was that the professional study of financial economics came to be dominated by a set of models that provided a misleading account of what was actually taking place. As the Jackson Hole symposium revealed, those who advised policymakers were blinded by such theory to the damaging nature of reality.

There is a pressing need to focus regulation more on the interests of consumers and less on the integrity of market processes. An element in the new Dodd–Frank regulatory regime put in place in the USA after 2008 was the establishment of a new agency with consumer protection as its goal. The architect of the new agency, the feisty Elizabeth Warren, hoped to become its first head. But her appointment was vetoed by the financial services industry and its representatives in Congress. In the UK the new Financial Conduct Authority was charged with responsibility for consumer protection, but this is secondary to its statutory objective of maintaining confidence in the financial services industry. But public confidence in the industry is the outcome, not the purpose, of effective regulation.

The term 'regulatory capture' is generally associated with the Chicago Nobel laureate in economics George Stigler,[18] but the history of the phenomenon is much older. Regulation of US railroads was introduced as a result of popular agitation, particularly from farming interests, against what were believed to be excessive charges. Railroads naturally began by opposing limits on their freedom to set their own prices, and when Grover Cleveland appointed Richard Olney, a man well connected to the industry, as Attorney General, they hoped to abolish or emasculate the newly established Interstate Commerce Commission. But Olney counselled otherwise. He told the railroads to bend the commission to serve their interests. It was good advice. By the time the commission was finally abolished in 1995, it was generally perceived to be representing not the public but the firms it regulated.

Perhaps the most extensively studied case of regulatory capture is the airline industry. Regulation of airline safety is self-evidently necessary: few libertarians want to see unsafe planes flying over major cities, or have time or capacity to inspect the service records of a plane before they board. But the supervision of safety extended to control of more and more aspects of airline operation—after all, a company under financial pressure may skimp on maintenance. By the 1970s airline regulators effectively operated a cartel on behalf of incumbent carriers. The industry notoriously collaborated on the definition of a sandwich, to prevent members cheating on regulated prices by competing on food quality.

A coalition of left and right in the USA achieved the dismantling of this structure in the 1970s. One side asserted the process was a racket operated for the benefit of large corporations, the other that consumers would be better served by the operation of a free market. There was substantial truth in both claims. A regulatory historian, Alfred Kahn, was appointed chairman of the Civil Aeronautics Board, where he accomplished the unusual feat of winding up the agency he headed.

Rapid growth of low-cost carriers followed, first in the USA and then in other parts of the world. Many incumbents—such as Pan Am and TWA—failed, but some successfully adjusted to the competitive environment and new entrants came—and often went. Airline regulation today is focused narrowly on safety and related issues, and the industry has developed what is known as a 'just culture', which encourages an openness about failures and a combination of collective responsibility for integrity and competitive responsibility for service.[19] The concept of 'just culture' is now gaining traction in other areas of commercial activity of public concern, such as medicine. There are many lessons in this account for other industries—and, most of all, for financial services— but the perception of the special character of the finance sector is engrained and the degree of regulatory capture extensive.

Of course, regulatory agencies can, and should, do better. But it is inevitable that well-funded industries will use their economic power to exercise political influence. And there is no better-resourced industry than the finance sector. Although financial regulation is comprehensively captured, serving the interests of large established firms in the industry, the firms themselves see regulation as a costly burden and inhibition. It is a measure of the failure of regulation that both criticisms are justified. At once extensive and intrusive, financial regulation is nevertheless beholden to the industry it supervises and ineffective in achieving its underlying objectives.

Proposals for regulation need to be based on a recognition of the constraints under which such regulation originates, and on realistic assessments of what regulation can achieve. The weaknesses of regulation that were so clearly illustrated in 2008 will not be remedied by intensification of the policies that not only failed to prevent that crisis but which actively contributed to it.

The correct initial response to the global financial crisis was to stabilise the existing structure of the industry. But that was precisely the opposite of the required long-term response, which was to organise the orderly winding down of failed firms and destabilising activities whose immediate collapse might have imposed serious damage on the real economy. In practice, however, the objective appeared to be to prevent—at almost any cost—the commercial failure of institutions in the banking system. Geithner's memoirs leave no doubt that this was his primary goal, and European governments have generally been even more reluctant to acknowledge the scale of losses in the banking sector.

The outcome represents policy failure on almost all fronts. There has been little change in the structure or behaviour of the industry, with the result that successive crises are more or less inevitable. The huge sums of public money released into the financial system have done little to promote economic recovery since the funds provided were largely retained within the financial sector itself—or paid out in excess remuneration to senior employees.

Perhaps the long-drawn-out consequences of the global financial crisis were more damaging to the real economy than those which would have arisen from allowing the collapse in 2007–8 of major institutions, followed by a state-sponsored restructuring of the finance sector. Like Captain McWhirr, we will never know what we did not experience.

## CHAPTER 9

# Economic Policy

## Maestro

> History will judge whether Greenspan was the man who made millions
> of Americans rich—or the man who could not bear to tell them they had
> only imagined it.
>
> JOHN KAY, *The Truth about Markets*, 2003

History delivered its verdict in 2008, and the verdict did not favour Alan Greenspan. For two decades Greenspan was chairman of the Federal Reserve Board, the USA's central bank. The status he acquired during that period is epitomised in the title of a hagiographic biography, *Maestro*, by Bob Woodward (the investigative reporter who broke the Watergate story and brought down a president).[1] Rarely has public reputation experienced such a rapid reversal. In 2008 Greenspan would apologetically tell Congress, 'I found a flaw in the model that I perceived is the critical functioning structure that defines how the world works.'[2]

Greenspan was noted for that convoluted, even enigmatic, quality in his public utterances. His bumbling façade was presumed to conceal deep wisdom. In his youth he had been an acolyte of Ayn Rand, a Russian émigré who became founder and leader of an extreme individualistic cult. The hostility to state action represented by Rand's philosophy fitted uneasily with Greenspan's role as the world's chief financial regulator, but that scepticism had been an attraction for the Reagan Republicans who appointed him to the Federal Reserve post in 1986.

Greenspan's appointment coincided almost exactly with the peak of policymakers' interest in monetarism as economic doctrine. Faith in the effectiveness of Keynesian fiscal policies had faded during the troubled economic decade of the 1970s. The rightward shift of the political centre of gravity in Britain and the USA also played a role.

There is something endlessly fascinating about money. There are many schools of monetary crank: anyone who comments publicly on economic affairs will receive regular communication from them. A fetish for gold is deeply embedded in the human psyche. But few monetary economists or central bankers share this obsession with the metal (and for that reason they often arouse the ire of the cranks).

The monetary model favoured in the era of financialisation has been very different from the doctrines of the gold standard, and involves rigorous adherence to a pre-announced target. The chosen target changes according to the fashion of the time. In the 1980s money supply growth was the preferred indicator, then inflation-targeting came into vogue. The scale of indebtedness that emerged in the global financial crisis led many to favour commitment to a path of debt reduction. At the time of writing, forward guidance—a supposedly binding conditional declaration of future intentions—is coming to the end of its brief moment in the sun.

These strategies of commitment to declared goals have intellectual and ideological attractions. The political right applauds the abandonment of discretion, or at least the appearance of such abandonment, which supposedly secures economic stability with minimal political intervention. An academic defence of this theory proclaims 'policy irrelevance'—measures adopted by governments or central banks are always self-defeating because they will be offset by private-sector action. Some people really believe this.

The new emphasis on monetary policy that came with financialisation initially resulted in dramatic increases in interest rates intended to curb inflation. In 1980 short-term interest rates were at 17 per cent in Britain and at 19 per cent in the USA. These rates squeezed the budgets of home-buyers, bankrupted leveraged businesses and property developers, and depressed both asset prices and business confidence.

The assumption of full employment which had been characteristic of the 1950s and 1960s had already gone: the measures of the early 1980s broke expectations of continuing and accelerating inflation. In the two decades that followed, interest rates and inflation steadily declined, and corporate profits and asset prices increased rapidly. That was the macro-economic background against which Greenspan moved to centre-stage.

Within two months his intentions would be tested. On 'Black Monday', 19 October 1987, the major US stock indexes fell by around 20 per cent on a single day. Before trading resumed the following morning, a statement was issued that 'The Federal Reserve, consistent with its responsibilities as the nation's central bank, affirmed today its readiness to serve as a source of liquidity to support the economic and financial system.'[3] According to Greenspan, 'telephone calls placed by officials of the Federal Reserve Bank of New York to senior management of the major New York City banks helped to assure a continuing supply of credit to the clearinghouse members, which enabled those members to make the necessary margin payments.'[4] What this meant in practice was elucidated by Citigroup's John Reed: 'his bank's lending to securities firms soared to $1.4 billion on October 20, from a normal level of $200 million to $400 million, after he received a telephone call from E. Gerald Corrigan, president of the New York Federal Reserve Bank.'[5] (In 1994 Corrigan would join Goldman Sachs, where he became chairman in 2007.) Put simply, the Federal Reserve made funds available to banks to lend in support of share prices.

The measures had the desired effect, and US stocks regained pre-crash levels within a year. The readiness of the US central bank to support the US stock market would become known as 'the Greenspan put', and was exercised vigorously (if less effectively) after the new economy bubble burst in 2000. Greenspan retired from the Fed in 2006, aged seventy-nine. His timing was fortuitous. The global financial crisis began the following year.

The Fed's statement spoke of the 'responsibilities of the Nation's central bank'. But what are these responsibilities? Central banks around the world are impressive institutions: their governors or other heads are respected figures; they are staffed by many of the ablest people employed in the public sector; in many countries they are islands of integrity in a sea of corruption. The functions of a central bank include acting as cheerleader and co-ordinator for the financial sector of the country in which it operates, supervising (the traditional, and still widely used, term) or regulating the activities of its banks, and performing a role in economic policy that certainly extends to the control of inflation and may embrace wider responsibilities.

Yet there are many different kinds of central bank. The Federal Reserve System of the USA, from its inception at the beginning of the twentieth century, was conceived as a collective organisation of banks rather than a public agency. Even though the Federal Reserve Board is appointed by the president of the USA, the twelve regional banks— including the powerful Federal Reserve Bank of New York—are representative of banking interests. The Bank of England was in principle a private institution until it was nationalised in 1946, following the twenty-year governorship of the mentally unbalanced Montagu Norman. The Banque de France, on the other hand, has always been effectively an organ of the French state. The post-war Bundesbank had a different constitutional role: to act as autonomous defender of the integrity of the German currency following that country's history of hyperinflation. This conflict between French and German views of the role of a central bank feeds into different views of the role of the European Central Bank. France and the majority of Eurozone members wish to use the ECB as an instrument of European economic policy. Germany is determined to maintain the bank's independence—a provision which at Germany's insistence is enshrined in the Maastricht Treaty that established the ECB. Some central banks—such as that of Australia or, from 1998–2012, the Bank of England—are responsible for monetary policy but not banking supervision, for the Bank of Italy it is the other way round. Most central banks have a role in operating the payment system, although the details of that role vary from country to country.

A traditional function of a central bank has been to act as 'lender of last resort'. This is a nineteenth-century concept, attributed to Walter Bagehot: the 'lender of last resort' makes short-term loans on impeccable security at penal interest rates to unquestionably solvent institutions.[6] The modern interpretation differs: today's 'lender of last resort' makes medium- and long-term loans on poor security at concessionary interest rates to institutions of extremely doubtful solvency. This support began in 2007, when the European Central Bank injected funds into the

European banking system following widespread losses by European banks on CDOs based on US sub-prime mortgages: by 2009 governments would own significant equity stakes in a wide range of financial institutions and be providing loans to almost all.

Before the global financial crisis there were rarely substantial differences between the official rates of interest set by central banks and inter-bank rates—the rates at which banks would lend to each other. But the events of 2008 shattered confidence in the security of inter-bank lending. Rates at which banks could raise external finance differed radically according to perceptions of their creditworthiness. In this environment the willingness of a central bank to lend to banks—and exclusively to banks—without discrimination as to credit quality became, and is today, simply a public subsidy to favoured institutions. Central banks have lent freely to commercial banks, at nominal interest rates, on weak security. The European Central Bank is owed €12 trillion, mostly secured against collateral of uncertain quality provided by Eurozone banks. The outstanding balances within the TARGET2 system, described in Chapter 6, represent unsecured debts among Eurozone central banks. It is a fundamental principle of bad banking that it is convenient for everyone—borrower, lender, regulator—to pretend for as long as possible that doubtful loans will one day be repaid. No one thanks the person who exposes the bezzle.

Traditional monetary policy involved setting interest rates and supplying or reducing liquidity in the banking system through 'open market operations'—trading in the government's own debt. The more recent policy, known as 'quantitative easing', involves the central bank buying assets from the financial sector—not just banks, and not necessarily only government securities. Though this policy enjoyed little success in stimulating the Japanese economy when it was first tried there in the 1990s, quantitative easing has been extensively adopted since 2009 by the Federal Reserve Board and the Bank of England. The balance sheet of the Federal Reserve system totalled just under $900 billion in 2007: by 2014 this figure had risen fivefold to almost $4.5 trillion.[7] The Bank of England's balance sheet has been multiplied by ten, from £39 billion to £399 billion.[8]

As a means of stimulating business investment and household spending through easier credit, this policy of state-financed asset purchases has been like pouring public money into a leaky conduit in the hope that some will dribble through to the end. The principal consequence has been to keep asset prices high: a continuation, in effect, of the policies Greenspan instituted in 1987. How will these outstanding liabilities created by central bank actions ever be resolved? If we were talking about any other kind of institution, these would be pressing issues; but one of the merits—perhaps—of a system of central banks is that it rarely seems necessary to ask these inconvenient questions. The scale of the numbers is hard to grasp, but central banks have the power to issue money and can—perhaps—print their way out of any problem.

It is reasonable to question what the modern function of a central bank is. Perhaps even to ask whether it is necessary to have a central bank, and a monetary policy.

Is it desirable for government and its agencies—which have sensibly extricated themselves from the business of controlling most prices—to manipulate interest rates, with a view to managing not just the banking system but the economy as a whole? Electricity is an essential element in the national infrastructure, used by every household and business. It is possible to imagine a government trying to manage the economy by controlling the supply and price of electricity—restraining booms by limiting the availability of new power stations and new connections, or by raising the price of electricity, and tackling recessions with low electricity prices and plentiful power.

I suspect most people would share my instinctive reaction that this approach would be an extremely bad idea—that the outcome would be inefficiency in the supply and use of electricity, and instability in economic growth. Is the intuition that seems relevant to electricity not equally relevant to the financial sector?

I think it is. Central bank activities to raise or lower interest rates or to influence the supply of credit and liquid assets can have substantial economic effects. These tend to be focused on particular sectors—such as construction—and companies that have leveraged financial structures based on short-term debt. Interest rate rises hit recent house-buyers; interest rate falls hit pensioners dependent on income from their savings. The provision of low-cost funding to the banking system raises the profitability of banking, and increases in the supply of liquidity tend to push up asset prices, with significant distributional effects across income groups and between generations. Few of these effects are intended or desirable, and the notion that monetary policy is anonymous and impersonal is flawed.

The thought experiment—suppose electricity were like finance—is not as fanciful as it might appear. In 1996 California began a process of deregulating its electricity industry, centred round the creation of a wholesale market in electricity. The market design retained a mixture of price caps and supply constraints but encouraged the entry of traders, including some with no, or only a negligible, interest in either the generation of electricity in California or the supply of electricity to the residents of the state. In the summer of 2000 and 2001 business and social life in California was disrupted by black-outs and price hikes in electricity. Enron traders were to the fore, implementing strategies described as 'Death Star' and 'Get Shorty'.

The crisis ended in 2001, with the bankruptcy of Pacific Gas and Electric (the largest Californian electricity utility), intervention by federal energy regulators and finally the collapse, for different reasons, of Enron itself (and with it much of the apparatus of active energy trading). Critics from the political left blamed the California crisis on deregulation. Critics from the political right argued that there had not been enough deregulation. Both were in a sense right: both the old controlled and centralised system and a comprehensive free-market regime would probably have worked better than the inept mixture of complex markets, unnecessary intermediation, elaborate regulation and ingenious trading strategies which made profits but disrupted supplies. Perhaps there is a lesson here for the finance sector.

There is a pressing requirement to maintain the integrity of the payment system, and the principal vehicle for this purpose is deposit protection. The use of public money should be limited to that purpose, and the official reaction to the failure of a financial institution should be resolution, not recovery. If a financial conglomerate takes deposits, the deposit-taking functions should be financially and operationally separate from its other activities. In the event of potential inability to meet liabilities, a special administrator can take control of these functions at short notice and (as the FDIC does in the USA) manage the assets until the deposits can be transferred to a solvent institution with adequate liquidity. The remaining activities should be subject to the general processes of insolvent administration, and no public funding should in normal circumstances be involved.

Public agencies in finance have operated both to promote the interests of the national financial services sector and to regulate that sector. These roles are plainly often in conflict with each other, and the tension between them is resolved in different ways at different times. In the 1960s the Bank of England actively and successfully supported the development of London as a global financial services sector. During its life, from 1998 to 2012, Britain's Financial Services Authority was under political pressure to capture business for London from New York by imposing 'lighter-touch' regulation than the Securities and Exchange Commission.

Under Greenspan's chairmanship, there is little doubt where the emphasis of the policy of the Federal Reserve Board lay: the Fed statement of October 1987 spelled out the priorities of the reluctant regulator. To 'support the economic and financial system' it was necessary to prevent stock prices falling. The priorities of economic policy were to be dictated by the needs of financial markets. That would still be true twenty-five years later.

## Financial Markets and Economic Policy

> I used to think if there was reincarnation, I wanted to come back as the president or the Pope or 400 baseball hitter. But now I want to come back as the bond market. You can intimidate everybody.
>
> JAMES CARVILLE, Clinton policy adviser,
> *Wall Street Journal*, 25 February 1993

Carville's concern is widely shared and reiterated. Two decades later, French President Nicolas Sarkozy is said to have told his aides that his re-election depended on France maintaining its triple-A credit rating. A few weeks later the two principal agencies—Moody's and Standard & Poor's—downgraded France, and Sarkozy was duly defeated by his socialist opponent.

The political power of financial markets and financial market participants is not just derived from the efforts of their lobbyists, the impact of their money and the degree of regulatory capture—although these are central facts of modern political life. The political influence of financial market participants extends far beyond policy towards financial markets. Why?

'Smart people' is part of the answer. Investment banks have for a generation attracted a high proportion of exceptionally able graduates—especially in Britain and the USA—and it is not surprising that policymakers should look to these institutions when they want external advice. The complexity of modern finance means few outsiders are qualified to help resolve the issues that complexity poses for public policy.

But the skills and knowledge of investment bankers are confined to narrow areas. The solution to policy problems is rarely found in complex financing arrangements, although financiers display ingenuity in suggesting otherwise, promoting schemes to conceal government expenditure in public accounts, securitising foreign aid, offering bonds linked to the delivery of public services.

Some economists in investment banks—the talking heads you routinely see on CNBC—have considerable policy expertise. They form part of a global community that includes officials in finance ministries, central banks and international organisations. But any notion that traders have interesting insights into the formation of economic policy is quickly dispelled by the slightest contact with them.

Yet ministers and their economic advisers will routinely ask 'What will the markets think?' When they make policy recommendations and proposals they will pay as much attention to the reaction of 'the markets' as to the opinion polls. Policy itself comes to be dictated by market expectations of what policy should be. A central banker or finance minister will not want to disappoint 'the markets', and so is himself sucked into the self-referential world of securities trading. Why? What is the source of this influence—and does it have any rational basis? Whatever President Sarkozy may have perceived, it was the voters of France, not rating agencies in New York or bond traders in London, that turfed him out of office.

Close attention to market opinion is a corollary of the Greenspan doctrine. But the focus of the 'Greenspan put' was directed towards equity markets, where supporting consumer confidence through rising asset prices became—and remains—an objective. How did this attention to bond markets, the concern of Carville and Sarkozy, come into being?

The analysts at Moody's and Standard & Poor's who terrified the French president knew nothing that employees of national finance ministries and central banks do not know—indeed, considerably less. Rating agencies are less subject to political influence than public servants: around the time of France's downgrade there was discussion of imposing some obligations on the agencies to 'consult' the governments on which they reported, or establishing a European ratings agency that would be more 'understanding' of European concerns. But these transparent attempts to extend the influence of political spin have come to nothing.

The serious criticism of rating agencies is not that they have been insufficiently responsive to the needs of European politicians, but that they were over-attentive to the needs of investment banks. What is needed is a system in which rating agencies sell their services on the basis of their informational value to investors. This is difficult to reconcile with a market in which the issuer of the security (rather than the investor) pays for the rating, and impossible to reconcile with the official status of the agencies in the regulatory process.

In downgrading French (and subsequently US and British) bonds, the agencies examined the scale of existing fiscal obligations and prospective government income and expenditure, and general economic prospects. They acted as if the French, US and UK governments were trading organisations. But they are not businesses. The probability that the French or UK government will default on its bonds in the foreseeable future is, for practical purposes, zero. And if these governments were to default at some far distant time, the cause would be political upheaval rather than financial distress. The farcical debates over the debt ceiling in the USA created the possibility of a technical default on US Federal government debt in 2011 and 2013. But such default would have been the product of political chaos, not a deficiency of resources in the US economy.

Nevertheless, borrowing and debt targets have continued to have large, even growing, influence on economic policy, strengthened by the incorporation of such targets in the Maastricht Treaty of 1992 which formed the basis of the Eurozone. The Treaty encouraged governments to engage in regulatory arbitrage, meeting their financial objectives by adopting measures that were not technically classed as borrowing. A familiar cat-and-mouse game of accounting arbitrage between Eurostat, the pan-European statistics agency, and national governments has followed.

Without these manoeuvres Italy would not have complied with the obligations of Eurozone membership. The arrangements between Goldman Sachs and the government of Greece to assist the misrepresentation of that country's economic statistics subsequently became notorious.

It is not, however, only Club Med countries that have resorted to these devices. Indeed Britain, benefiting from its innovative financial sector, was a pioneer in the use of off-balance sheet financing to flatter government accounts. The impetus for the flagship privatisation of British Telecom in 1984 was an attempt to reconcile an extensive programme of investment in digital switching with adherence to official borrowing targets. Since then concealment of public borrowing to meet state liabilities has become a routine feature of UK public accounts, and British financial institutions have promoted these techniques around the world.

The idea that markets impose a ceiling on debt levels for countries like the UK or France, whose default is unimaginable, gained currency from the work of Reinhart and Rogoff, which observed a strong association between high levels of government indebtedness and the incidence of financial crises.[9] The claim that there is a discontinuity around debt to GDP levels of 90 per cent or above, which for a time gained widespread currency in European debate, is now largely discredited, and never had more than limited support in the Reinhart and Rogoff work.[10]

The notion of a discontinuity has some underlying plausibility: there comes a point at which confidence in a borrower (private or public) diminishes, and new debt can be raised only on onerous terms, if at all; and the inability to refinance existing debt leads inexorably to default. This can happen to you and me and Lehman, and even Greece. But the governments of Britain, France, Germany and the USA, where interest costs are no more than 2–3 per cent of national income are—to put it mildly—some distance from the threshold at which the burden of interest on government debt becomes politically or economically insupportable.

Still, the existence of a discontinuity might be powerful in the minds of financial market participants even if it has little substance in underlying reality. But such information asymmetry is a benefit rather than a problem: if the British government knows it is not going to default on debt when the bond market believes otherwise, a state that can issue as much short-term debt (money) as it likes can use the misapprehension to refinance its debt on favourable terms, buying back its own long-term debt for subsequent reissue.

The policy has been followed during quantitative easing, but at the wrong time, for the wrong reasons and with the wrong consequences. Far from being abnormally high in anticipation of a possible default, long-term interest rates in developed economies are at historically un-precedented lows. The governments of Britain, France, Germany and the USA can today borrow for decades ahead at low or negative interest rates. But instead of issuing such debt, Britain and the USA have been buying it back in exceptional quantities in order to sustain asset prices and help recapitalise the banking system.

The demand for safe long-term assets provides an opportunity to re-build the crumbling infrastructure of Britain and the USA and to invest in long-term projects in energy and elsewhere on improbably favourable terms. This opportunity has been passed by in the interests of support-ing the financial sector and satisfying the economic policy perceptions of traders in securities markets. It is time to resist the intimidation of which Carville spoke.

## Pensions and Inter-Generational Equity

> No memory of having starred
> Atones for later disregard.
>
> ROBERT FROST, *Provide Provide*, 1934

> Why should I care about posterity? What has posterity ever done for me?
>
> attributed to GROUCHO MARX, but also credited
> to various eighteenth-century English figures

The level and composition of public debt influence the distribution and transfer of wealth across the lifetime of individuals and households and between generations. Public debt is largely held domestically, so that 'we owe it to ourselves'. But, more accurately, future taxpayers owe the debt to current taxpayers—a commitment the latter have unilaterally imposed on the former.

Given the central role that debt plays in current economic policy de-liberations, it would be easy to think the management of public debt was the principal mechanism for transfers of wealth between generations. But it is not the only way, or even the most important way. The focus on the scale of public debt gives a partial and distorted picture, a picture especially distorted when, as today, public debt has been much increased by the socialisation of unmanageable private debts. The baby boomers—of whom I am one—have gained substantial advantages for themselves relative to those generations that preceded or will succeed them.

This transfer has been possible because the mechanisms by which economies make inter-lifetime and inter-generational transfers are complex and imperfectly understood. Society taken as a whole can shift consumption from one point in time to another only by investing in, or running down, the physical assets of the nation: by building houses or other property, investing in infrastructure and creating and developing businesses. Small countries can also transfer wealth to the future by building up assets overseas. A few countries—such as Norway, Singapore and Qatar—have established sovereign wealth funds, which are now a significant force in the investment channel. Still, even the largest of these—Norway's $700 billion oil fund—is much smaller than the $4 trillion of funds managed by BlackRock. The scale and distribution of this transfer between present and future are the product of collective choices about public infrastructure and private choices about business investment.

A further transfer of resources between generations is inherent in government spending. The biggest items of public expenditure in most countries are healthcare and education, which are focused on the old and the young. As family ties have become both weaker and more potentially burdensome, the people of advanced societies have come more and more to look to the state to provide financial support and practical care for the elderly. The transfer of wealth over time is the joint product of the decisions of business people and of politicians, individual choices and collective actions. But there is no coherence about the process of decision, or evaluation, far less consensus on the overall outcome.

Pension provision is the most important component of lifetime wealth transfer, and is today everywhere a partnership between the state, employers and households. Traditionally each member of this partnership took primary responsibility for one of what are often described as the three pillars of retirement security. Elderly people benefit from a basic, state-financed, retirement income (the first pillar), an earnings-related component based on employment (the second pillar) and their own voluntary savings (the third pillar). Recently, however, this neat taxonomy has become blurred.

State pensions were first introduced in Germany in the late nineteenth century, and every developed country now provides the first pillar for its citizens. A person on below-average earnings can expect to retire with a pension, funded from current taxation, which will replace between 60 per cent and 80 per cent of their net income in work. People in this income bracket can therefore rely on the state to support them in retirement, and mostly do.

Some countries have funds such as the Social Security Trust Fund of the USA or Britain's National Insurance Fund, which are designed to give retirees some assurance that their entitlements will not be diverted for other public purposes. But these funds are notional bookkeeping exercises.

There is also wide international consensus on the mechanics of state contribution to the third pillar—the treatment of voluntary private savings for old age. Fiscal concessions allow individuals to build a tax-advantaged retirement savings fund. There are normally limits on the amounts of saving that qualify for these reliefs, and restrictions on access to accumulated savings before retirement. Asset managers compete for the opportunity to invest these funds.

However, wide international divergences can be observed in the design of the second pillar—that related to earnings and employment. In Britain and the USA the common practice has been for this pillar to be provided and funded by individual employers. Even in the nineteenth century governments—national, state, municipal—commonly paid pensions to their employees after retirement. So did very large companies, such as banks and railways. Pension provision went along with a mutual expectation of lifetime employment. After the Second World War, as these company-specific pension schemes became more widespread, trust funds were established to provide that benefits promised to workers would be secure regardless of the fate of the employing companies. Some public sector schemes are funded—Calpers, the Californian public employees scheme, is the largest pension fund in the United States, with assets of $300 billion—but many are not funded, and others are inadequately funded. This under-provision poses problems where local areas decline (as in Detroit).

Today there can no longer be an assumption—once self-evident in reference to a government, a bank or a railway company—that a paternalistic employer will stay in business for ever, or that a loyal employee will remain with a single organisation throughout his working life. As *Gemeinschaft* gave way to *Gesellschaft*, the burden of formal regulation and disclosure on pension schemes has steadily increased. New accounting rules have required sponsoring companies to incorporate pension liabilities in their principal accounts, which has led company boards to take far more critical interest in the magnitude—and volatility—of these liabilities. Financialisation has forced all businesses to take a more short-term view.

There are deeper forces at work here. Throughout the era of financialisation there has been concern about the 'crisis' in social security: it is over thirty years since I was first invited to a conference to discuss this 'crisis'. It was after attending a few such meetings that I came to understand the underlying agenda. The aim of those who promoted these events was to reduce the role of the state in retirement provision and increase the participation of the finance sector. This pressure has been strongest in the USA. Although proposals under the George W. Bush administration to 'privatise' social security collapsed in the face of wide public hostility, commentators still routinely produce calculations showing unfunded liabilities of the Social Security Trust Fund running into many trillions of dollars, and proclaim imminent 'crisis'.[11] A puzzling feature of this debate is that, to the extent that deteriorating demographic fundamentals do pose a funding problem, privatisation of social security would contribute little to a solution, although it might assist politicians in disclaiming responsibility.[12]

Still, the first pillar of social security has survived attack; the second has not. Most private companies have now ceased to offer defined benefit schemes in which the employer underwrites a promise of pensions related to final salary. The second pillar is now more often a defined contribution scheme, in which both employer and employee contribute to funds administered by an asset manager. The pension entitlement of an individual depends on the performance of his or her own specific investments. Britain is in the process of making participation in such a scheme compulsory for those who do not have other second-pillar provision, and similar schemes already exist in Australia and Canada.

The substitution of defined contribution schemes for defined benefit pensions represents a major shift from managed to transparent intermediation, and a transfer of risk from employer to employee. The conferees at Jackson Hole congratulated themselves on the progress made in risk management during financialisation. But, as I emphasised in Chapter 2, the risks they were discussing were not the risks that concern ordinary people. Aside from the risks of natural disasters—such as Hurricane Katrina—the financial risks of ordinary life are associated with employment, illness, mortality and longevity. The effect of financialisation has been to transfer some of these risks that were assumed by employers—and hence collectivised—to individual households. There are arguments for such a shift—mainly around moral hazard—though also many against. In any event, this shift is probably the most important effect of financialisation on risk management on Main Street, even if the view from Wall Street, or Jackson Hole, is different.

Pensioners must now manage their own longevity risk—the possibility that they might live longer, or less long, than average. Traditionally longevity risk has been insurable: mortality tables have been used for two centuries. But as new technologies increase average lifespan, they also enhance our capacity to make personal prognoses. This potential predictability has advantages but also creates problems, as the pooling of risks, which has been at the centre of long-term savings provision through pensions and insurance, becomes more difficult to operate.

Investment risk has been transferred from employer to employee. No one knows what economic conditions will prevail in fifty years' time, and thus economic risk is uninsurable and undiversifiable. Pensioners should expect to participate in this risk—to receive, for better or worse, a share of the productive capacity of the economy when they retire. But investment returns are far more volatile than underlying economic conditions. The linking of pensions to investment returns exposes pensioners to additional uncertainty which is the product of unpredictable financial markets.

Is there any way of limiting or insuring that exposure? One proposal is the issuance of bonds on which interest and capital repayment vary with GDP, so that returns depend on overall economic performance.

These are suitable vehicles for government borrowing—liabilities will be closely related to tax receipts—and are also an appropriate investment for retirement savings.[13] Such instruments would spread economic risk across the whole population without exposing the elderly to the noisy volatility generated by financial markets. But in the absence of such financial innovation, the best individuals can do to minimise risk exposure in long-term savings is to use the indexed securities issued by all major governments (including Britain, France, Germany and the USA).

In France and Germany, in common with much of continental Europe, most risks continue to be managed collectively: the Swiss village writ large. The second pillar of retirement security is mainly provided by employer groups organised by sector, and is not funded to any substantial degree. The potential risks for pensioners posed by the absence of funding is reduced by the industry-wide nature of schemes and by state indemnity and regulation.

Most of the developed world faces a demographic challenge in the next three or four decades, as the proportion of the elderly in the population increases. Yet increased life-expectancy is accompanied by an increase in *active* life-expectancy. Customary retirement ages were fixed in times when many more workers engaged in manual labour, general health was worse and only a minority could anticipate any lengthy period of retirement.

A relatively modest increase in typical retirement age would reduce dependency ratios to more manageable proportions. Individuals may not choose individually, or societies may not choose collectively, to raise the age of retirement—in France, where *la retraite* appears to be a primary life objective for many, the very suggestion leads workers onto the streets. In that case a substantial part of future economic growth will go in financing extended and extensive retirement. This will, and should, be a reflection of these private and public choices.

Even with prolonged active lives, care costs will rise because many more people may live to an age at which their mental or physical capacity is impaired, while the need for extensive care costs is a contingency that households cannot predict. This raises a societal problem in the organisation and financing of such care, and an individual problem of managing an uncertain future.[14] Only a combination of private and social insurance is likely to be able to handle these issues.

The process of shifting consumption over lifetimes and between generations, and of managing the related risks, requires both private financial market activity and public involvement by the state. This need for effective public–private partnership is general. Voluntary agencies, neither wholly public nor wholly private, once played a major role in this activity in Britain and, within a prescriptive regulatory framework, still do in many other European countries. Risk-pooling requires elements of compulsion and group organisation to reduce problems of moral hazard and adverse selection. Financialisation, which emulates the structures of Lloyd's coffee shop rather than the Swiss village, has undermined rather than enhanced the capacity of society to pool risks and manage personal and household insecurity.

The individualistic ethos of the era of financialisation has affected wealth transfer over time in other ways. The American economist Laurence Kotlikoff created the concept of 'intergenerational accounting' to describe the government's transfer of wealth over time.[15] The journalist Tom Brokaw coined the phrase 'the greatest generation' to describe my parents and their contemporaries, who grew up during the Great Depression, fought in the Second World War and (in Europe) suffered privation in its aftermath.[16] Another author might term my generation of 'baby boomers', 'the luckiest generation' or perhaps just 'the most selfish generation'. We have not only been successful—and perhaps this is to our credit—in enjoying a time without major armed conflict or deep economic depression; we have also been effective in transferring wealth from both past and future generations to ourselves.

We reduced the debt we owed to our predecessors by rapid inflation. We promised ourselves generous state and occupational pensions, and then argued that the burden of providing them for subsequent generations could not be afforded. We sold assets that had been accumulated in the past, and would yield prospective benefits in the future, for our own current benefit, privatising state industries and monetising the goodwill in Goldman Sachs and Halifax Building Society. We let house prices and share prices rise to new highs in real terms, forcing our children to buy the nation's assets from us at prices much higher than those we had ourselves paid. To add insult to injury, we seem to have been inadequately mindful of the national infrastructure: enjoying shopping malls, to be sure, but building few houses and allowing the transport system to decay.

The John Kay of the 1980s, transported twenty-five years forward in time, would not be able to afford to buy the house I still live in, would have incurred substantial debt in higher education, would have to make greater provision for his own retirement and would look ahead to a tax burden inevitably rising to meet the costs of an increasingly adverse demography. When Jeff Skilling toasted the capitalisation of energy contracts in champagne, he was celebrating the twin benefits of the prudence of his predecessors and his own imprudence in relation to his successors. And I could join him in that toast. Lucky indeed to have lived through the era of financialisation.

## Consumer Protection

> The junk merchant doesn't sell his product to the consumer, he sells the consumer to his product.
>
> WILLIAM S. BURROUGHS,
> *Letter from a Master Addict to Dangerous Drugs*, 1956[17]

In every market a degree of consumer protection is required. Regulations not only protect us from poisonous foods but also attempt to restrict our consumption of unhealthy ones. Doctors, lawyers and many other professions are subject to control of qualifications and behaviour. The safety of pharmaceuticals and airlines is closely monitored. Mostly, these regulations work reasonably well, giving consumers the confidence they expect without depriving them of a choice of products or imposing excessive burdens on producers. But consumer protection in financial services does not score as highly. Financial regulation is burdensome to providers but is nevertheless seen as inadequate by users and commentators.

Deposit-taking banks require close regulation. They access the payment system (and should be the only financial institutions with direct access to the payments system); they hold the everyday savings of ordinary people. Since their liabilities are mostly explicitly guaranteed by government (or its agencies) and probably entirely guaranteed in practice, taxpayers also need to be protected from loss. The natural vehicles for the savings of depositors are government borrowings and good-quality housing loans (limited to, say, 80 per cent loan to value). The simplest procedure would be to require that at least 90 per cent of the assets of deposit-taking banks fall into these categories.

In many countries guarantees of deposits are provided by state-sponsored agencies funded through levies on the financial sectors. These guarantees would not be credible without government as back-stop. Iceland's compensation scheme collapsed when its banks did, and the bills reverted to the government of Iceland and to Britain and the Netherlands (where most of the depositors were located). Britain's Financial Services Compensation Scheme was bailed out by the Bank of England.

Consumer protection in finance raises particular difficulties. Many customers buy financial services from necessity, not choice. They do not enjoy the experience, and are bewildered by the technicalities of the product. It has been a repeated theme of this book that it is a mistake to believe that financial markets will work efficiently if prescribed information based on a standard template is made available, and that 'transparency' is an overrated objective. The notion that has dominated policy in Britain and the USA through the era of financialisation—that disclosure is the best means of consumer protection—is misconceived.

Finance is an especially attractive field for fraudsters and shysters. And some consumers are mugus—greedy and credulous people who naïvely conspire with those who intend to steal their money. While it is tempting to say that those who fall for such scams deserve their fate, this is not a position that it is politically possible, or perhaps desirable, to maintain.

But regulation is never the principal mechanism of consumer protection. In the main, we trust the supermarket to sell us wholesome food, the airline to seat us in a safe plane, the doctor to give us honest advice. We trust them not simply because they are well regulated, but because we think they deserve our trust. We rely on the reputation of the supermarket, the airline and the doctor, and know that they hope to attract repeat business, not just from us but also from other customers. The problem of information asymmetry, which in a modern economy extends well beyond the financial sector, is generally handled through a trust relationship between buyer and seller. Regulation for consumer protection works best when supplier reputation and state regulation reinforce each other—as they do in these other industries. Good regulation has the result that good reputations are well deserved.

In finance, however, the major conglomerates have recently come to regard restitution for mis-selling and misrepresentation as nothing more than a regular cost of doing business. The scandals have kept coming.

Reputations lost are not easily—if at all—restored. Bob Diamond was removed from the office of CEO at Barclays in 2012, and the new chairman of the bank was a City figure universally respected for his intelligence and integrity. But a few good men are insufficient to change an entire culture. To give Britain's new Financial Conduct Authority the primary objective of 'maintaining confidence in the financial services industry' is an extraordinary feat of misunderstanding. To create confidence where it is not justified, even if it were possible, would damage rather than promote the consumer interest. The appropriate objective is to create an industry that would be deserving of confidence; confidence is the result of achieving the objective, not the objective itself. Yet Britain does at least have a consumer protection agency in finance with good intentions. In the USA the power of finance industry interests means that the attempt to create such a bureau in the aftermath of the global financial crisis has stalled.

In some industries, such as pharmaceuticals, product approval, or specification of the parameters within which products must be designed, is a mechanism of consumer protection. Policy has moved towards this approach as regulators have come to specify features such as loan-to-value ratios and charges in more detail. But there is a danger that risk-averse regulators simply use these powers to delay and inhibit product innovation—and the reality of that danger is evident from other industries. So is the likelihood that such regulation is used by established firms to resist entry to the market. Regulatory capture is a constant danger.

But the most effective means to protect consumers is to address the issues of industry structure and misaligned incentives which have given rise to consumer abuse. This will be the subject of Chapter 10.

## The Economic Contribution of Finance

This is an era that history will record as the beginning of a new golden age for the City of London, and I want to thank you for what you are achieving. And I believe the lesson we learn from the success of the City has ramifications far beyond the City itself—that we are leading because we are first in putting to work exactly that set of qualities that is needed for global success.

GORDON BROWN, speech to Mansion House dinner, London, 20 June 2007 (a week before he succeeded Tony Blair as prime minister, and six weeks before the beginnings of the global financial crisis)

As for Venice and its people, merely born to bloom and drop,
Here on earth they bore their fruitage, mirth and folly were the crop,
What of soul was left, I wonder, when the kissing had to stop?

ROBERT BROWNING, *A Toccata of Galuppi's*, 1855

The finance and insurance sector employs between 3 per cent (Germany) and 5 per cent (USA) of the workforce.[18] However, most of these people are engaged in relatively mundane clerical tasks in bank branches, call centres and insurance offices. In Manhattan, around 160,000 individuals are employed in activities related to securities trading.[19] Around 400,000 people work in the City of London, the geographical area around the Bank of England which is still a partly independent municipality.[20] About one-third of these are employed in financial institutions.

Not everyone in a senior role in finance in Britain or the United States is located in the City or on Wall Street, though most are. London has a financial satellite at Canary Wharf, a self-contained area bounded by a sweeping horseshoe on the Thames. Greenwich, Connecticut, is often described as the global centre of the hedge fund industry; in London many of these new asset management businesses prefer elegant Mayfair to the mixture of nineteenth-century mausoleums and twenty-first-century skyscrapers which characterize the architecture of the City and Wall Street. And, of course, Warren Buffett operates from a modest suite in Omaha, Nebraska.

If we define 'the City' and 'Wall Street' as 'high-level financial professionals engaged in trading, deal-making and related activities' rather than as geographical places, then the headcount of those employed in each is probably less than 200,000, with much smaller numbers in other financial centres.

In addition, a good deal of high-level work in accountancy and law is related to the activities of the financial sector. Global accounting standards have been defined by US- and British-based firms. As described

Figure 11: **The growth of financial services, 1990-2010**

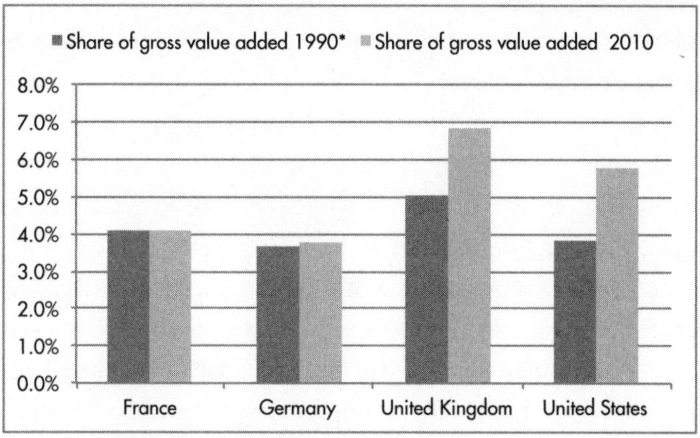

*Figure for Germany is 1991.

Source: OECD (France, Germany, US), ONS (UK)

Financial services and activities that are auxillary to finance and insurance, such as brokerage and fund management (ISIC division 64 and 66). Excludes insurance, reinsurance and pension funding.

in Chapter 8, the flexibility of English common law (and American law derived from it) contrasts with the prescriptive civil law regimes of most continental European jurisdictions, and this, together with the use of the English language and the perceived impartiality of the Courts, has been an advantage in the development of financial services. Many contracts which have little or no connection with the UK (including credit default swaps and Lehman's repo 105 transactions) are made under English law. The strength of these auxiliary services has reinforced the global financial primacy of London and New York.

The economic contribution of an activity is generally measured by its value added, or contribution to GDP. Figure 11 shows how the financial sector has grown in Britain and the United States, but not in continental Europe, during financialisation. The growth in credit intermediation and asset management activities are the main contributors to this expansion.[21] These figures tell us that the resources devoted to the finance sector, and the remuneration of those who work there, have increased sharply. But these figures do not tell us what has happened to the quality, as distinct from the quantity, of resources devoted to these activities.

And they describe the cost, rather than the value, of financial intermediation. National accounts figures relating to financial activities should be used only with considerable reservation. The impact of the global financial crisis on reported statistics should have provoked a red alert. Between 2008 and 2009, with the banking system on the point of collapse and the non-financial economy plunging into its most severe recession for more than half a century, the Bureau of Economic Analysis reported an increase of 7 per cent in the reported output of the finance and insurance sector, mainly driven by an increase in reported value added from securities trading. In the UK, the share of finance in GDP rose from 8.6 per cent in 2008 to 9.7 per cent in 2009, its highest ever level. The proportionate increases in France and Germany (from a much lower base) were even greater.[22] How could the figures be so misleading? The explanation requires some understanding of the nuts and bolts of national accounts.

The principles of national income accounting were set out around the time of the Second World War by a group of economists—notably Simon Kuznets, James Meade and Richard Stone—and these established the standard means of measuring the economic contribution of a commercial activity. We assess the car industry by its added value: the difference between the selling price of the car and the cost of the steel, rubber and other materials that went into it. By the accounting identity imposed by double entry book-keeping, that added value is the sum of the earnings of the people who built the car and the operating profit (before financing costs) of the business.

Similarly, we measure the value of a play by adding up what people pay for the tickets, and the difference between these box office receipts and the costs of operating the theatre are equal to the wages of the cast and the profits or losses of the promoters. These procedures may be crude, and mercenary, but they give a relatively objective answer, and one that is comparable across activities and countries.

But these methods don't really work for finance.[23] Few financial services are paid for in the direct way that cars and theatre tickets are paid for. The profits of financial firms come largely from varieties of trading. These businesses make money from the difference between the rates at which they buy securities or borrow money and the rates at which they sell securities or lend money. Interest costs, which are not deducted in computing the operating profits measured in national accounts, are the principal costs banks incur. Insurance companies make profits by taking premiums months or years before they pay claims, and may lose money on underwriting while being profitable overall.

The profits of the financial sector are partly a return to risk and (as with accounting for risk in financial statements more generally) the adjustments necessary to reflect a true and fair view of the profitability of risky activities are complex and unsatisfactory. Chapter 4 described the intricate nature of this problem. These cumulative difficulties mean that simple application of standard national accounts procedures gives nonsensical answers when applied to the financial sector.

From those earliest days of national accounting it has been recognised that financial services pose a special problem. Different approaches yield very different answers and the appropriate treatment has been extensively discussed among national accounts statisticians for several decades. There is now international agreement on a common approach, based around a set of concepts known as FISIM (financial services indirectly measured). But this standardisation has compounded the difficulties rather than resolving them. By unfortunate coincidence, Britain agreed to implement FISIM in 2008, just as the global financial crisis hit, and that crisis blew some of the assumptions on which FISIM was based out of the water. In 2013, the Bureau of Economic Analysis announced revisions to its calculations of commercial banks' contribution to the US GDP that reduced the reported figures by around 20 per cent.[24]

The best way to judge the value of the finance sector to the domestic economy is to start with the qualitative questions considered in the course of this book: what is the finance sector doing for households and businesses by facilitating payments, managing personal finances, allocating capital and controlling risk? However, it is very difficult to turn that qualitative assessment into the numbers needed to compare finance output with automobile output.

So a simpler approach to measuring contribution asks what finance adds to tax revenues. In 2006, US corporate income tax on finance and insurance activities yielded $68 billion, 2.8 per cent of federal tax receipts and 1.4 per cent of all US government taxes. By 2011, however, this figure had fallen to $38 billion, 0.75 per cent of total tax paid in the United States.[25] In Britain, corporation tax on the banking sector reached £7.3 billion in 2006–7, about 1.4 per cent of overall tax receipts, but in 2013–4 corporation tax on banks yielded only £1.6 billion.[26] This modest haul has been supplanted by an ad hoc 'bank levy', now imposed at a rate of 0.21 per cent of the liabilities of banks operating in the UK.

In both Britain and the United States, the major contribution to tax revenue from the financial sector comes not from banks and financial institutions themselves, but through income tax on the earnings of highly paid employees. In Britain, the banking sector alone yielded £17.6 billion in income tax in 2013–4, almost 12 per cent of total income tax revenue, and ten times the corporate tax paid by the sector. In the United States, employees in banking and finance earned $607 billion in 2011,[27] and although we do not know how much income tax they paid on this figure, it would certainly far exceed the $38 billion corporate income tax paid by their employers.

Many people in finance are paid a lot, and some are paid astronomical sums. At Barclays in 2013, 530 'code staff' (a regulatory term for those with executive responsibility) were paid an average of £1.3 million each. Yet most people employed in finance earn ordinary incomes. While 1,443 employees at Barclays earned more than £500,000 in 2013, more than half the staff earned less than £25,000. So the difference between the '1 per cent' and the rest is particularly evident within financial institutions themselves. It is likely that the best-paid 1 per cent of employees at Barclays earn 40 per cent, or perhaps even half, of the total remuneration of all the staff of the bank. While Barclays (prior to Diamond's dismissal) was extreme in the degree to which the company focused on advancing the financial interests of its most senior employees,[28] this extraordinary skewness of income is true across the finance sector.[29]

The unbalanced structure of pay raises wider policy questions. For three decades, a high proportion of the ablest graduates have been attracted by startlingly large salaries into activities of little value to business or society, activities that did little to develop their skills, knowledge or intellectual capacity except in the narrowest of areas. This is an issue of concern both for the community as a whole and for the individuals concerned.

The British dilemma is particularly stark. Britain is a global financial centre which attracts leading firms and talented individuals from all around the world. Net sales of financial services to the rest of the world in 2013 were £38 billion, more than 2 per cent of GDP and equivalent to more than 10 per cent of British exports of manufactured goods.[30] It is perhaps unnecessary to ask further questions about the value of an activity if we know that people outside the United Kingdom are willing to pay for it. But many people will find this justification insufficient. They would hesitate to be shareholders in the world's leading manufacturer of snake oil, both for ethical reasons and, perhaps, from concerns about the long-run viability of the business. And the international dimension raises a question that Robert Reich famously phrased as 'who is us?'[31]

The majority of financial business done in London is undertaken by firms that are not UK resident or that have parent companies that are not UK resident. The activities of these companies are treated in the national accounts as productive activity undertaken in the UK and included in GVA (gross value added) and GDP—or would be if they were accurately measured, which, for reasons explained above, they are not.

The profits of foreign-owned firms are not, however, included in GNI (gross national income), which is probably a better measure of the welfare UK residents derive from productive activity. GNI reports the incomes accruing to UK residents rather than the income generated in the UK (GDP). GNI therefore recognises that there is no benefit to the UK from profits earned in London by Goldman Sachs or Deutsche Bank and repatriated to the home country of these companies (or more likely to some other jurisdiction with a benign tax and regulatory regime).

What is true of firms may also be true of the people they employ. Many of those who work in the City of London are not UK citizens. Some pay full UK tax, others do not. Some go home for the weekend to Paris or New York. Others picnic in the parks or attend concerts and theatres. The presence of many highly educated foreigners has helped make London the most vibrant, cosmopolitan city in the world today—possibly the most vibrant, cosmopolitan city that has ever existed. Yet a British citizen who wanders round those parks or attends these auditoria, or who travels on a Friday evening transatlantic flight or Eurostar train, must wonder—who is us? How, if at all, should the UK value the—exceptionally high—UK earnings of foreign firms and individuals who are temporary residents of London?

There are many people in high positions in financial services who plainly relish their roles, are excited by the work they do and would want to continue such work even if they were paid much less. For Warren Buffett, happiness is 'tap dancing to work every day' and he still does it at the age of 84. But Buffett is, as so often, the exception. 'We are Wall Street' conveys no sense that its authors enjoy what they do, only a belief that the uncongenial nature of their task justifies extraordinary remuneration. Frank Partnoy provides a graphic description of a group of Morgan Stanley traders who are unable to identify a more unpleasant employment than the one they are engaged in—Wolfe's 'young men baying for money on the bond market.'[32]

If you talk to very well-paid lawyers, or doctors, or actors or sports people, you find that mostly, like Buffett, they love their work and recognise the double good fortune of a wonderful job and a massive financial reward. But less so in finance, where many people derive little intrinsic satisfaction from their employment, do not undertake it for any reason other than the money and look forward to having accumulated enough to retire from finance. Although many find that the amount they think they need to retire comfortably grows as rapidly as the amount they have accumulated. What might these individuals have done if they had not been offered the prospect of huge rewards? Built businesses? Made scientific discoveries? Written poetry?

Resentment of high-earning bankers comes up in casual conversation, a disparagement not often brought up with other high earners, such as LeBron James, Beyoncé or Bill Gates. The latter examples are people with exceptional talents and their contribution to society is obvious. In finance, however, doubts about the utility of much financial sector activity and the realisation that many are, even within their own frame of reference, not very good at their jobs stoke such resentment.

All inequality is to some degree socially corrosive, but inequality that seems unconnected to desert is particularly corrosive. The most disturbing downside of the global success of the City of London is the corrupting effects on society at large—a depreciation of ordinary morality and human values. The ethical standards associated with parts of the finance sector are deplorable.

The abuse of sex, alcohol and drugs by young people who suddenly found themselves in possession of too much money; the attractiveness of London and New York to oligarchs and corrupt foreign politicians who buy mansions with money stolen from their populations—these are not matters that society can be proud of. Yet many of the same things might have been said—were said—of ancient Athens and Rome or medieval Florence or Venice. There is a price—perhaps a high price—to be paid for being a world capital.

# CHAPTER 10

# Reform

## Principles of Reform

> Guide the people by law, subdue them by punishment; they may shun crime, but will be void of shame. Guide them by example, subdue them by courtesy; they will learn shame, and come to be good.
>
> CONFUCIUS

Since the global financial crisis there have been widespread and repeated calls for 'more regulation'. More or less without exception, what the advocates of 'more regulation' have in mind is yet more detailed rules about the everyday conduct of finance, exemplified by the multiplication of the length of the Basel rulebook.

This course of action will fail. There are already far too many rules, not too few. The origins of the problems that rightly concern the public are to be found in the structure of the industry and in the organisation, incentives and culture of financial firms. In the absence of measures to address these more fundamental issues, 'more regulation' will provide the appearance of action with little significant effect on the behaviour of the industry: the sound and fury, signifying little, that Richard Olney described to the rail bosses in the nineteenth century.

The primary objective of policymakers since the global financial crisis has been to secure the stability of the financial system. This objective has in turn been interpreted as securing the stability of existing financial institutions. The means of achieving this is to require institutions to have greater reserves of both capital and liquidity. Regulators have identified 'systemically important financial institutions' which are to be the subject of special supervision and (implicit or explicit) government support.

With crass hypocrisy, political leaders have set their public faces against future bank rescues while their operatives have reassured markets that they do not mean what they say. President Obama could assert that the passage of Dodd–Frank meant 'no tax-funded bail-outs—period', while his Treasury secretary not only upheld the 'Geithner doctrine'—no significant financial institution would be allowed to fail—but also provided an extended defence of that position in his memoirs. The European stance is essentially the same, both in its substance and in its humbug. The bail-out of the Portuguese bank Espirito Santo followed hard upon the announcement that the era of bail-outs was at an end.

Securing the stability of existing institutions was exactly the right short-term response to the global financial crisis, and exactly the wrong long-term response. The origins of the global financial crisis lay in the structure of the industry. To stabilise—indeed to ossify—that structure is not a means of avoiding future crises, but a way of making them inevitable.

Systemic instability in the financial system is the result of the interdependencies inherent in an industry that deals mainly with itself. The growth in the scale of resources devoted to financial intermediation is not to any large degree (or, in most cases, at all) the result of any change in the needs of *users* of intermediary services. The growth of financial activity has come from a massive expansion in the packaging, repackaging and trading of existing assets. The finance sector today does many things that do not need to be done, and fails to do many things that do need to be done.

Financial intermediation that meets the needs of the real economy should not be a game in which professional intermediaries compete to outwit each other. Competition between financial intermediaries is valuable and necessary, but—as with competition in other industries— success in that competition should follow from effectiveness in meeting the demands of customers. The basis of reward should be success in meeting user needs, and the rewards should be proportionate to the value of the services provided.

Parts of the finance sector today—'We are Wall Street'—demonstrate the lowest ethical standards of any legal industry. If London casinos were even accused of the malpractices to which London banks have admitted—false reporting, misleading customers and unauthorised trading—the individuals responsible would be barred from the industry and the licences of the institutions concerned revoked within hours. The finance sector has experienced actual criminality on a wide scale, from liar loans to LIBOR rate-fixing. Leading firms in the industry have come to regard the payment of billions in fines and compensation as routine. A culture has developed in which any action, no matter how close to the borders of legality, is acceptable if it is profitable for the individuals engaged in it. It is a comprehensive indictment of our system of regulation as well as our system of finance that this dismal record should be found in a sector whose primary function is to secure the financial future of businesses and households.

The guiding purpose of the legal and regulatory framework should be to impose and enforce the obligations of loyalty and prudence, personal and institutional, that go with the management of other people's money. This change in culture can only be imposed to a very limited extent by regulatory decree or management edict; change becomes effective only when the values appropriate to the handling of other people's money are internalised by market participants themselves.

Internalisation of the principles of ethical conduct is, in a sense, self-regulation, but it is not the self-regulation that allows market intermediaries to 'manage' conflicts of interest and decide for themselves what constitutes 'treating clients well': that approach has plainly failed. In an open, free, democratic society, law and regulation work—and can only work—if most of the people subjected to such law and regulation already espouse the values law and regulation promote. We refrain from murder and burglary not because we are afraid of the penalties but because murder and burglary are simply not among the courses of action we consider: and that fact makes it possible to secure resources and public cooperation to track down and punish the minority who violate these prohibitions. Speed limits and drunk-driving prohibitions are enforceable only because most people know that the rules make sense.

The tirades against regulation and regulators that I routinely hear from people in the financial sector are extremely boring, not just because they are repetitive but also because they are almost never accompanied by an account of how the legitimate public concerns that motivate financial regulation might otherwise be met. But when these complaints come, as they often do, from intelligent people with genuine concern for the public good, they illustrate a lack of respect for regulation and regulators that renders it unlikely that current styles of regulation could ever work.

Regulation based on detailed prescriptive rules has undermined rather than enhanced ethical standards, by substituting compliance for values. The fantastically detailed prescription of how the 'plumbing' of securities exchanges should operate is so far distant from the everyday needs of real businesses and ordinary households as to demonstrate a degree of disconnection from economic realities. Government has intervened in the finance sector too much, not too little. The counterproductive interactions between government and finance have been the product of mistaken ideology and the excessive influence of market participants themselves.

Finance needs a different industry structure, and altered personal and corporate incentives, so that putting clients first leads to personal reward and business profit in the long run, and both employment and customer relationships are sufficiently durable for the long run to be the relevant timescale. An end to 'I'll be gone, you'll be gone.'

The rise of the trading culture has not just led to a decline in ethical standards but has also contributed to financial instability and has enhanced the 'bias to action' that increases the costs of financial intermediation. The appropriate objective is to reduce trading volumes to the modest levels that serve the real needs of the non-financial economy. One reform suggestion that has been widely discussed is a tax on the value of all financial transactions. Levied at a low rate, such a tax would have little impact on the profitability of long-term investments but would kill the attractions of high-frequency trading, which depends on blisteringly fast arbitrage and microscopic price variations. This idea is often called the Tobin tax, after James Tobin, the American economist who proposed it in 1972,[1] and has received wide support in the European Union.

If a Tobin tax could be administered on a basis that was universal in its geographical scope and applied in non-discriminatory fashion to all forms of financial instrument, it would have considerable attractions. But if, as seems inevitable, there are some financial jurisdictions that do not impose the tax—and there is at present no possibility that even the USA would do so—and if, as also seems inevitable, there is no practical way of imposing the tax on a non-discriminatory basis between derivative transactions or other complex instruments and transactions in the underlying securities, the tax is likely to have more undesirable side-effects than benefits. Such an imperfect tax would probably be a new stimulus to regulatory arbitrage, and a further source of profit to traders, earned at the expense of the long-term investors who would actually bear the brunt of the tax. This is the thoroughly unsatisfactory experience of Stamp Duty, the established tax on equity transactions in the UK, which in practice bears *only* on long-term investors.

A preferable strategy is to 'starve the beast': to adopt measures of structural reform of the finance industry that will reduce the amount of capital available to support trading activities and eliminate cross-subsidy to these activities. What is proposed here is a radically changed regulatory approach. It is trite but true to say that what we need is not more regulation but better regulation. But this demands a different regulatory philosophy rather than better regulators. It is pointless to suggest that the solution is to appoint regulators with the foresight of Nostradamus, the detective skills of Sherlock Holmes and the political insight of Machiavelli, as well as the patience of Job and the hide of a rhinoceros. An effective regulatory structure is one that can be implemented by the kinds of people who can in the real world be recruited to work in regulatory agencies.

The following principles should underpin reform:

- Re-establish short, simple, linear chains of intermediation. Links between market participants are too numerous. Links with savers and users of capital are too few and too weak. The prioritisation of transactions among intermediaries over transactions with end-users is responsible for the excessive costs of financial intermediation, the instability of the financial system and the failure to generate the information required to achieve propriety in corporate governance and efficiency in capital allocation. These issues are, obviously, not addressed by providing more capital to support the trading activities of established financial institutions.

- Restore focused, specialist institutions with direct links to financial users of financial services, deriving competitive advantage from their skills in identifying and meeting the needs of these users. While some regulatory action to force structural reform is essential, the further proposals described below will encourage additional restructuring as a result of market forces.

- Require that anyone who handles other people's money, or who advises how their money should be handled, should demonstrate behaviour that meets standards of loyalty and prudence in client dealings and avoids conflicts of interest.

- Enforce obligations of high standards of behaviour in the management of other people's money by criminal and civil penalties, directed primarily to individuals rather than to organisations. While the culture of organisations is of central importance, culture is the product of individual behaviour, especially the individual behaviour of those with leadership responsibilities.

- Treat financial services as an industry like any other. Regulation should be targeted at specific issues—deposit protection, consumer abuse and the prevention of fraud. Public subsidies, state guarantees and other mechanisms of government support, including the increasingly ill-defined, yet extensively relied on, concept of 'lender of last resort', should be withdrawn.

- Cease using the financial sector as an instrument of economic policy, and treat the opinions on economic policy of people in the financial sector with the same (modest) regard accorded to the political opinions of other business people.

## Robust Systems and Complex Structures

> Much of the current flood plain of the ancient Euphrates now lies beyond the frontiers of cultivation, a region of empty desolation . . . Yet at one time here lay the core, the heartland, of the oldest urban, literate civilisation in the world.
>
> R. McC. ADAMS, 1981, quoted by Joseph Tainter, 1988[2]
> (The flood plain of the ancient Euphrates is today in modern Iraq and Syria.)

> What is the cause of management's fantastic faith in the machinery? . . . One reason for this may be an attempt to assure the government of NASA perfection and success in order to ensure the supply of funds. The other may be that they sincerely believed it to be true, demonstrating an almost incredible lack of communication between themselves and their working engineers. . . . For a successful technology, reality must take precedence over public relations, for nature cannot be fooled.
>
> RICHARD P. FEYNMAN, personal observations,
> Appendix F of the presidential commission on the failure of the
> *Challenger* space shuttle, 1986 (*Challenger* exploded on take-off, killing the crew of
> seven. Feynman, a Nobel Prize-winning physicist and one of the finest lecturers on
> any subject ever, was responsible for the clarity of the commission's conclusions—
> and reportedly refused to sign the report unless these comments were included.)

The complexity of modern finance has been designed, and has operated, principally to benefit financial intermediaries rather than the users of financial services. The claims of Alan Greenspan, Timothy Geithner and others, that the innovative use of new instruments made the financial system more robust, were false. Interdependencies between financial institutions have increased to a point at which the system as a whole displays fragility born of complexity.

The phrase 'too big to fail' came into wide use in the global financial crisis to describe the dilemma that policymakers faced in resolving the affairs of systemically important financial institutions.[3] The phrase provoked the justified rejoinder that 'too big to fail is too big'. But 'too big to fail' misses the key point. Financialisation has led to increases in the size of financial institutions, but the central problem is not size but complexity. Size in banking can enhance stability, at least up to a point. Britain avoided significant bank failures in the twentieth century precisely because its banks were big, in contrast to the collapse of the fragmented US banking industry in 1933. The failure of the UK banking sector in 2008 occurred, and was traumatic, not because the sector had become more concentrated, but because it had become more complex.

Lehman was not, in any ordinary sense of the phrase, a business of economic importance. If it was a *systemically* important financial institution, it was not an *important* financial institution. The business provided no services to the real economy that were not available elsewhere, and few services to the real economy at all. The company was badly run, and operated primarily for the benefit of its own staff, especially its most senior executives. But Lehman was massively interconnected. At the time of its bankruptcy the company had over 200 subsidiaries around the world, and approaching 1 million outstanding transactions, almost entirely with other financial institutions. The narrow consequence of this interdependence was that the winding down of the company's convoluted structure will employ lawyers and accountants for a decade. The broader consequence was that financial institutions with exposure to Lehman were uncertain of the value of their claims.

Because so many institutions had dealings with Lehman, uncertainty was contagious. Even businesses with little direct engagement with the failed bank were uncertain about the value of their claims against institutions with greater engagement. The collapse of confidence spread throughout the financial system, with adverse effects on the non-financial economy that persist to the present day. Lehman was not too big to fail, but it was too complex to fail.

The historian Joseph Tainter has studied collapses of civilisations—the many sophisticated societies that once thrived but exist no longer.[4] The flood plains of the Tigris and Euphrates in Mesopotamia were the site of the first urban civilisation and of the development of modern agriculture. Ancient Rome finally succumbed to the barbarians at the gate. The Mayan and Chacoan civilisations of North America were highly developed societies that we know today only as archaeological sites. The growth of complexity in social and economic interaction is the distinctive mark of civilisation, but complexity, and the inequality and specialisation that go with it, entails diminishing returns. Eventually the social and political costs of managing that complexity become overwhelming and promote internal decomposition.

Parallels between the progress of financialisation and the decline and fall of the Roman empire may seem at first sight far-fetched. Yet there are lessons. That society failed because of the ultimately counterproductive consequences of the growth of complexity, its inability to manage the scale of the organisational problems raised by its growth, its increasing attention to ritual disconnected from an external world and its incapacity to effect substantive self-criticism or self-repair. We can see all these issues in the modern financial system.

The lesson is, on the one hand, to eschew unnecessary complexity and, on the other, to pay close attention to the management of unavoidable complexity. Chapter 6 contrasted the unplanned evolution of the financial services network with the conscious design of other utility networks, such as electricity. The overriding need for system stability is embedded in the thinking of everyone engaged in electricity supply. And anyone who thinks electricity supply less complicated than the financial system knows little about the complexities of maintaining the stability of an electricity grid. Chapter 9 described the chaotic consequences of an attempt to financialise the supply of electricity. But it has not been usual to think about the financial system in the systemic way that is natural to operators of other networks. And despite recent experience of the consequences of system failure, it is still not usual to think in this way.

The organisational sociologist Charles Perrow has studied the robustness and resilience of engineering systems in different contexts, such as nuclear power stations and marine accidents.[5] Robustness and resilience require that individual components of the system are designed to high standards. Demands for higher levels of capital and liquidity are intended to strengthen the component institutions. But, as can be seen from the scale of exposures described in Chapter 6, the levels of capital and liquidity envisaged are inadequate—laughably inadequate—relative to the scale of resources required to protect financial institutions against panics such as the global financial crisis.[6] More significantly, resilience of individual components is not always necessary, and never sufficient, to achieve system stability. Failures in complex systems are inevitable, and no one can ever be confident of anticipating the full variety of inter-actions that will be involved.

Engineers responsible for interactively complex systems have learned that stability and resilience requires conscious and systematic simpli-fication; modularity, which enables failures to be contained; and re-dundancy, which allows failed elements to be by-passed. None of these features—simplification, modularity, redundancy—characterised the financial system as it had developed in 2008. On the contrary. Finan-cialisation had greatly increased complexity, interaction and interde-pendence. Redundancy—as, for example, in holding capital above the regulatory minimum—was everywhere regarded as an indicator of inef-ficiency, not of strength.

In Perrow's analysis, systems lack robustness if they are interactively complex (everything depends on everything else) and tightly coupled (the tolerance for error is low). The interactive complexity and tight coupling of a nuclear power station are an inescapable consequence of prevailing technology. Paradoxically, attempts to increase resilience by incorporating many layers of safety provision may make the system less robust by increasing its complexity. An assembly line is complex but not interactively complex—it depends on a linear sequence of events in which each step logically follows the preceding one. Such a process may be tightly or loosely coupled. The moving belt of the traditional car plant's assembly line demonstrates tight coupling, while the normally leisurely production of a book from manuscript to publication is loosely coupled: no one is surprised at the author's late delivery, nor is the pro-duction process upset.

Robust systems are typically linear. From time to time I send a parcel via UPS to my house in France. Through the company's tracking system I can follow the movements of the package. It is collected on Tuesday afternoon and shipped across the Channel to Paris during the night. On Wednesday it moves to Lyon, and during the early hours of the morning it is trucked to Nice. Its arrival there early on Thursday morning triggers a phone call at around 8 a.m. from a friendly UPS representative who arrives at lunchtime on Thursday.

The UPS delivery system, although complex, is linear rather than in-teractive in its complexity, and loosely coupled. When on one occasion a parcel failed to arrive, it was easy and quick to establish that the consignment had left Paris but not arrived in Nice and then to discover that a heavy fall of snow in central France had blocked the Autoroute du Soleil. When the drifts and stranded vehicles were cleared, the package reached Lyon two days later and agents adapted to delayed delivery. The linearity of the system permitted rapid identification and isolation of the problem; the loose coupling permitted rapid recovery. A similarly linear financial system is one in which intermediaries deal with end-users rather than each other. The basic principle should be that intermediaries in capital allocation should normally be familiar with the needs of either borrowers or lenders—or both.

The collapse of the new economy bubble in 2000 proved much less severe and enduring in its consequences than the global financial crisis of 2008. The scale of the bezzle—the imaginary wealth first created, then destroyed—was not necessarily greater in that phase of equity market mispricing than in the later episode of credit market mispricing.[7] But the rise and fall of technology stocks did not involve the complex interdependencies between financial institutions of the kind that marked the credit boom: there was little *interactive* complexity, and coupling was fairly loose.

On the other hand, the Japanese stock market and property bubble—in which Japanese banks were heavily implicated—did lasting damage to the Japanese economy, because the rise and subsequent fall of asset prices had multiple consequences for other parts of the financial sector and for the balance sheets of industrial companies. As a result of complex interactions created by the growth of high-frequency trading and the wide use of exchange-traded funds (packages of existing securities which are themselves bought and sold like other securities), it is far from certain that an equity market meltdown today could be accommodated with the same equanimity as in 2000.

Increases in interactive complexity and tighter coupling were the very innovations that the participants at Jackson Hole celebrated. Firms themselves became interactively complex. Most of the conglomerate businesses that failed in 2008 were brought down by activities peripheral to their principal business. The failure of Lehman was not the cause of the global financial crisis—that was far more deep-seated. But Lehman made no contribution to the real economy commensurate with the damage done by its failure. The public costs of its interactive complexity far exceeded any public benefits. Lehman's reliance on overnight financing, whose disappearance provoked its abrupt collapse, epitomised tight coupling.

Many aspects of the modern financial system are designed to give an impression of overwhelming urgency: the endless 'news' feeds, the constantly changing screens of traders, the office lights blazing late into the night, the young analysts who find themselves required to work thirty hours at a stretch. But very little that happens in the finance sector has genuine need for this constant appearance of excitement and activity. Only its most boring part—the payments system—is an essential utility on whose continuous functioning the modern economy depends. No terrible consequence would follow if the stock market closed for a week (as it did in the wake of 9/11)—or longer, or if a merger were delayed or large investment project postponed for a few weeks, or if an initial public offering happened next month rather than this. The millisecond improvement in data transmission between New York and Chicago has no significance whatever outside the absurd world of computers trading with each other.

The tight coupling is simply unnecessary: the perpetual flow of 'information' part of a game that traders play which has no wider relevance, the excessive hours worked by many employees a tournament in which individuals compete to display their alpha qualities in return for large prizes. The traditional bank manager's culture of long lunches and afternoons on the golf course may have yielded more useful information about business than the Bloomberg terminal.

Lehman—an ill-managed purveyor of unneeded products—represented exactly the kind of business that should fail in a well-functioning market economy. The view that it was a mistake for the US government to permit Lehman to collapse is expressed not by people who miss the services that Lehman provided but by people who regret the consequences of its failure. The lesson is not that policymakers should try to prevent such failures but that public processes should ensure that similar failures are more easily contained.

## Other People's Money

Sen. C. Levin (D-Michigan): 'When you heard that your employees in these emails and looking at these deals said "God, what a shitty deal," "God, what a piece of crap," when you hear your own employees or read about these in emails, do you feel anything?'
Mr D.A.Viniar (CFO, Goldman Sachs): 'I think that is very unfortunate to have on email.'

US SENATE, permanent subcommittee on investigations, 27 April 2010

All the money that circulates around the financial system is other people's money. Well, nearly all. In a modern institution such as Deutsche Bank around 3 per cent of the capital at risk is the bank's own: the other 97 per cent belongs to lenders and depositors. The typical insurance company has lower leverage, with shareholders' funds invested alongside those of its policyholders (Warren Buffett's Berkshire Hathaway is a cross between an insurance company and an investment fund). An asset management company, or a pension fund, deploys only other people's money.

Even the small amounts of equity in the banking system represent other people's money. Equity is provided by the shareholders: the era of the partnership, when senior management took personal financial responsibility for the funds they controlled, is gone. Some principals such as Buffett and many hedge-fund managers make significant investments alongside their investors, but these are the exception rather than the rule.

Handling other people's money was once considered an onerous responsibility. Deposits from customers were lent, selectively, to local borrowers. Or they were placed in government stock and similarly safe assets. Pension funds and life insurance companies were the main vehicles for long-term personal saving, and these intermediaries were keenly aware of obligations of prudence and loyalty in the management of other people's money.

The concept of 'eligible counterparty' is at the centre of this erosion of responsibility for other people's money. As a retail customer, you have a degree of protection when you buy financial products, though this generally falls some way short of a duty of loyalty and prudence on the part of the intermediary. But once your funds have passed into the hands of an intermediary, even these protections fall away. Your agent will certainly be a 'professional investor' with fewer rights, and perhaps an 'eligible counterparty', for whom *caveat emptor* is more or less the rule. Goldman's customers were generally 'eligible counterparties'.

Mr Sparks and Mr Viniar of Goldman Sachs showed little regard for their customers in their congressional testimony, but found—and in regulatory terms received—justification on the basis that they were not dealing with the general public. The firm's clients might be 'muppets' (a phrase that Greg Smith, writing in the *New York Times* on the day of his resignation from Goldman Sachs, claimed was frequently used to describe the firm's clients),[8] but they were financial professionals, responsible for their own follies.

But this misses the key point. The money that intermediaries were handling was the money of the general public, albeit at one, or several, removes. Obligations of loyalty and prudence in the management of other people's money should be transferred forward to intermediaries. The duty of loyalty and prudence should ultimately be transmitted to the company, government or other agency that uses the saver's funds. At that point loyalty and prudence become the obligation of the director of the company, the government or whoever is the responsible agent.

When Mr MacPherson was injured by the collapse of a defective wheel on his Buick car, Buick was held to be liable even though the company had neither sold Mr MacPherson the car nor manufactured the defective wheel.[9] The case established in US law the principle that responsibilities to the final purchaser extend along the supply chain. It is hard to see why the duties of financial intermediaries should be less onerous than those imposed on automobile manufacturers. In our everyday lives we take responsibility for other people's money very seriously, and expect even children to recognise a sharp distinction between other people's money and their own. We should not expect lower standards of behaviour from people for whom money management is an occupation. Many people in the finance sector—particularly in retail banking and asset management—would agree. The discomfort they feel about conflicts of interest is not simply, as Viniar's was, the discomfort of seeing their ethical confusion recorded on email. They would acknowledge, and practice, duties of loyalty and prudence to the other people whose money it is.

Conflicts of interest are inherent in modern financial conglomerates—conflicts plainly inconsistent with the proper management of other people's money. When Mr Sparks and Mr Viniar of Goldman Sachs described 'Fabulous Fab's' Abacus deal, they demonstrated no sense of that responsibility. Indeed Sparks and Viniar did not know—and could not have known—whose money it was. On one end of the Abacus wager were those who had directly or indirectly invested in John Paulson's hedge fund. On the other side were those who held insurance policies or placed deposits with institutions foolishly attracted by the highly rated paper created by tranching mortgage-backed securities. It is entirely possible that some individuals and pension funds were on both sides of the bet. These luckless investors would not have known, and nor would anyone else.

'Putting the client first' begins with identifying who the client is. In the case of 'Fabulous Fab's' transactions Goldman Sachs may have been acting for Paulson, who wanted to bet on widespread defaults in sub-prime mortgages. Or the firm may have been acting for the purchasers of the securities based on these mortgages. Goldman Sachs may have been trading for the benefit of the shareholders of Goldman Sachs. The business should properly have owed duties of loyalty and prudence to-wards whichever one of the three parties was its client, but could not properly have been acting for all three. The predictable outcome of this ethical confusion was that 'Fabulous Fab' was in reality acting, not for the benefit of any of these parties, but for the benefit of 'Fabulous Fab'.

Along with conflict of interest goes clash of culture. Retail bank-ing should be customer-focused, yet necessarily bureaucratic and conservative—a difficult combination to pull off, and one whose suc-cessful realisation is incompatible with the aggressive sales orientation and risk-taking of investment banks. The ethos of trading—an activ-ity that engages only a small proportion of those who work in financial services—has contaminated the finance industry as a whole.

The culture of anonymous trading is divorced from economic con-text, devalues or eliminates personal relationships and fosters the self-aggrandising self. Quite apart from its broader social implications, that ethos is not conducive to the effective delivery of financial services. Functions have become conflated and confused, undermining the need for prudence and loyalty in dealing with other people's money. Without a clear acknowledgement of these duties, people who talk of restoring trust in the finance industry are whistling in the wind.

## The Reform of Structure

> Never wear your best trousers when you go out to fight for freedom and truth.
>
> HENRIK IBSEN, *An Enemy of the People*, 1882

The progressive relaxation of restrictions on the formation of integrated financial institutions in Britain and the USA in the last two decades of the twentieth century can be seen, with hindsight, to have been a major policy error. There are some advantages to customers from a one-stop shop, where they can buy all the goods and services they need under a single roof. But such advantages are insignificant when compared with the costs that were imposed on the world economy by the global financial crisis—costs that were a direct result of interactive complexity within and between these conglomerates, and which continue to be imposed on households and businesses outside the financial system.

The effect of these emergency measures to stabilise markets in the global financial crisis was to extend still further the scope and scale of financial conglomerates. As with the emergency measures to underwrite bank liquidity and solvency, the right short-term response was just the opposite of the right long-term response. The key to a financial system that is resilient and directed to the needs of users of financial services is a return to a structure characterised by specialist institutions.

The overriding objectives of structural reform of the finance industry are to reduce complexity, lower costs, enhance stability and facilitate the flow of information between savers and borrowers. These outcomes should be achieved through a mixture of regulatory action and market forces. Regulation should be focused on structural remedies whose implementation requires only limited use of judgement—rules that can be monitored by administrators of limited capacity. The elimination of cross-subsidies across activities and of government subsidies and guarantees would allow the market to drive further reform.

The financial conglomerates that dominate finance today are, to households and businesses in the real economy, largely indistinguishable from each other. A saver who is looking to place deposits or find a home for long-term investments, a company establishing a corporate banking relationship, a personal or corporate borrower seeking funds, would be hard pressed to identify any differences between J.P. Morgan Chase, HSBC and Deutsche Bank, or to find a compelling reason for choosing one rather than the other. The similarity of business models is partly the result of over-extensive regulation which necessarily imposes a 'one-size-fits-all' framework. But the cut-throat competition between Tweedledum and Tweedledee—a competition that matters a great deal to Tweedledum and Tweedledee but hardly at all to their customers—is primarily the outcome of the finance sector's preoccupation with itself. The objective is to outstrip rivals rather than to serve the needs of users.

The proper economic role of banks is to operate the deposit channel, directing short-term balances towards borrowers—principally home-owners—and managing liquidity provision to reconcile safety of deposits with the long-term needs of users of capital. The policy objective should be to restore a linear framework of intermediation between depositors and borrowers. That simplification is key to the achievement of security for savers, economic and financial stability, effective control of the costs of intermediation, and transmission of the information needed to make good decisions on capital allocation.

The first step in implementing structural reform is to ring-fence the deposit channel to ensure that the operation of the payments system cannot be jeopardised by the failure of financial conglomerates. The subsidy to trading activities arising from the availability of the deposit base as collateral should be removed; the likelihood that the taxpayers' guarantee of routine deposits will be called will therefore be limited, if not altogether eliminated.

In the interim, financial conglomerates might become financial holding companies, as envisaged by the UK's Independent Commission on Banking[10] and the Liikanen Report commissioned by the European Union.[11] But there are disadvantages to such a half-way house. The ring-fence between deposit-taking and other financial transactions requires careful policing. And the problem of cross-contamination of cultures remains.

Still, so long as ring-fencing is effective, there will be little if any financial advantage to the conglomerates themselves from trading as holding companies. Since the management problems of combining investment and retail banking impose costs on the institutions themselves, it is likely that effective ring-fencing would lead them to choose voluntarily to spin off their deposit-taking activities.

This ring-fencing should be the first step in a process of fragmentation. If the large financial institutions of today are not permitted to take advantage of their retail deposit base, and are deprived of government funding, subsidy or guarantee, they will be unable to maintain volumes of trading on their present scale. The leverage within them would be so clearly excessive that other traders would be nervous of dealing with them. This reduction of trading volumes to more sensible levels is a further, central objective.

Further structural reform is required to restore the clear distinction between agency and trading. The attempt to manage conflicts through regulation has failed because it has spawned complex rules without achieving its underlying objective. Those who handle other people's money, or advise on the management of other people's money, are agents of those whose money it is. Financial intermediaries can act as custodians of other people's money, or they can trade with their own money, but they must not do both at the same time. The effective application of principles of loyalty and prudence towards clients, and insistence that conflicts of interest be avoided, puts an end to the current business model of the investment bank, which relies on its multiplicity of activities to provide 'the Edge'.

Some readers may think that Goldman Sachs—Goldman and Morgan Stanley are the only two large remaining standalone investment banks—has been a particular target in this book. The frequency of references to Goldman is not because Goldman executives or traders are particularly venal—perhaps the reverse: it is mainly the result of the company's success and the resulting public scrutiny. Although the reputation of the firm is today far from what it once was, in a bleak landscape the standing of Goldman Sachs remains higher than that of many others. If Goldman alumni are found in many prominent positions, it is largely because of the calibre of individuals the bank has attracted. And among these alumni are people—such as Mark Carney, former governor of the Bank of Canada and now governor of the Bank of England, and Gary Gensler, reformist chairman of the Commodity Futures Trading Commission—who have been well able to pursue the public interest even when it did not coincide with that of their former employer.

But the current investment banking model—whether applied in a standalone institution such as Goldman or in a broad financial conglomerate such as Deutsche Bank—is at the heart of the problems the finance sector poses for the real economy. Investment banks today engage in securities issuance, corporate advice and asset management; they make markets in equities and FICC, and trade in these markets on their own account. It is only necessary to list these functions to see that each of these activities conflicts with all the others. Each should be undertaken in distinct institutions. And with lower volumes of inter-bank trading, a diminished role for public equity markets and much more direct investment by asset managers the scale of most of these activities should be much reduced.

Among all the actors in the finance sector today, only the asset manager, who typically earns a fee calculated as a percentage of funds under management, is rewarded for idleness. The profits of a segregated deposit-taking bank would similarly depend primarily on the scale of the deposit base, and secondarily on its success in making good loans. Dedicated channels of capital allocation have a more appropriate incentive structure than activities focused on trading and transactions.

Whenever there is risk, there will be gamblers. The objective should not be to eliminate speculative short-term trading activity. It is hard to see how one ever would; the prohibition of gambling has failed almost everywhere it has been tried, usually with undesirable side-effects in providing a focus for criminal behaviour. And even if the objective of eliminating short-term trading were feasible, it would not be desirable to achieve it. Traders may provide capital to meet the occasional genuine needs of investors for liquidity—the ability to realise cash for investment ahead of the identification of another investor—and to help stabilise price fluctuations. The objective should be to reduce trading volumes to the modest levels that serve the real needs of the non-financial economy.

But the appropriate vehicle for such trading is the hedge fund. Hedge funds are dangerous—as is every instance of wagering with other people's money. Those who make short-term trades should be required to do so with their own money: literally their own money, or money raised specifically for that purpose (in which case there should be duties of prudence and loyalty to the subscriber of that money).

This suggestion that hedge funds have a constructive role will shock many people, for whom hedge funds are the villains of financialisation. Many people—I was certainly one—saw that the credit expansion of 2003–7 would end in tears, but thought that hedge funds would be at the centre of the storm.[12] We were wrong. Many hedge funds disappeared, but it did not much matter. The collapse became a global financial crisis because large financial conglomerates were caught in the tempest. But such activity is for people who are in close contact with those who are making the investment decisions and who are very clear about what is being done with their money. In any event, it should be entirely separate from the activity of collecting deposits in branch banks.

The retail banks that will occupy the deposit channel are intended to be rather dull institutions, in which Bailey and Banks would again feel at home. Well, perhaps I exaggerate a little. But not much. The natural vehicles for the savings of depositors are government borrowings and good-quality housing loans. It is impossible to restore the mutual structure of the thrifts and building societies that once dominated housing finance. Their capital, built up over decades, was dissipated in the windfalls paid to depositors and their unwise diversifications, and there is no source from which reserves on the scale necessary for a large mutual sector could now be obtained in sufficient quantity. New housing institutions will have to raise equity capital, and enough of it, from investors. But it should be possible to restore the local focus appropriate to lending on residential property. Such institutions should mix knowledge of the relevant property market and judgement of character with automatic credit-scoring, and manage the loans through to repayment.

Although institutions that take deposits should be limited in their choice of assets to government bonds and residential mortgages, there is no reason why other financial institutions should not also own government bonds and make housing loans. Indeed the scale of demand for government funding and higher loan-to-value mortgages requires such funding.

Asset managers should occupy the same central role in the investment channel that banks enjoy in the deposit channel. The goals are similar: good and stable returns for savers, economic and financial stability; control of costs; flows of information about physical and intangible assets and their management that promote economic efficiency for the benefit of savers, consumers, employees and taxpayers.

Managed intermediation by asset managers, which has no need of daily valuation and redemption, potentially offers greater flexibility and the opportunity for asset managers and their customers to escape the tyranny of public markets and the predation of the high-frequency trader. Asset managers can differentiate themselves by style and by expertise in the sectors to which capital is allocated, rather than the tracking errors of closet indexation. This requires specialist intermediary providers of capital for consumer credit, small business and perhaps non-residential property.

There should be greater specialisation in the needs of users. This requirement is probably most urgent in the small business sector. As described in Chapter 5, the needs of small businesses have changed. Because capital is less important and more fungible, as business is less asset-based and more knowledge-based, the requirement for capital in the SME sector is more often to fund operating losses in early stage development than to lend on the security of tangible assets. A century after J.P. Morgan told Congress that 'character' was the main factor in lending, changes in the nature of modern business have made the personality of the entrepreneur more important and the security given by the assets of the business less so: but the face-to-face interview has been replaced by the credit-scoring algorithm.

Consumers suffered even before financialisation from 'financial advisers' who were in fact sales people, although they have perhaps suffered more now that such people dominate the staff of bank branches. Commission generates a bias to action—and even without such incentive to stimulate activity it is hard to persuade people to pay much for the good advice to do nothing. Regulatory policy still clings to the illusion that it is possible to provide individually tailored financial advice to a mass market. But these levels of personal service disappeared from most areas of retailing decades ago: personalised advice of quality is simply too expensive to be provided except at the very top end of the market. The computer has two potential advantages over the financial adviser: the computer is as honest as its programmer, and the processes and conclusions of the computer can be monitored and reviewed.

A deposit channel directed by retail banks and an asset management sector populated by asset managers who can be trusted to be managed intermediaries and have a long-term horizon for investment—that is how we recreate a finance sector aimed at meeting the needs of the real economy.

## Personal Responsibility

> *Captain Renault*: I'm shocked, shocked to find that gambling is going on in here!
> [a croupier hands Renault a pile of money]
> *Croupier*: Your winnings, sir.
> *Captain Renault* [*sotto voce*]: Oh, thank you very much.
> *Captain Renault* [aloud]: Everybody out at once!
>
> *CASABLANCA,* Warner Bros, 1942

> We were all appalled and shocked when we heard about these allegations yesterday.
>
> I have to tell you that I am sickened that these events are alleged to have happened. Not just because I was editor of the *News of the World* at the time.
>
> REBEKAH BROOKS, chief executive,
> News International, in a memo to staff, 8 July 2011

After the Wall Street crash, Richard Whitney, president of the New York stock exchange, spent over three years in New York's fearsome Sing Sing maximum-security penitentiary. Even in the early 1990s Charles Keating, the most notorious fraudster in the deregulation of US thrifts, and Michael Milken, the inventor of junk bonds, went to prison.

Scapegoats for the new economy bubble were less harshly treated. The SEC devoted little energy or resource to identifying wrongdoing, and such cases were brought to light through the dogged investigations of now disgraced former New York Attorney General Eliot Spitzer. Frank Quattrone, the Crédit Suisse investment banker who expected favours from friends and clients in return for allocations of hot stocks, was prosecuted, though his conviction was overturned on appeal. Other individuals such as Henry Blodget, the Merrill Lynch analyst who was recommending 'a piece of shit' to clients, and Jack Grubman, who had traded a stock recommendation for places for his children at the sought-after 92 Street Y Kindergarten, were censured. (Grubman's up-grading of AT&T pleased that company's CEO, Michael Armstrong, whose vote on the Citigroup board was crucial to Sandy Weill's removal of joint Citigroup CEO John Reed. Citigroup donated $1 million to the school, which looked favourably on the Grubmans' applications.)

Responses to the global financial crisis suggest that the days when failed titans of finance are punished are finally over. Probably the three most culpable figures in the 2007–8 crisis were Dick Fuld, CEO of Leh-man, Joe Cassano, whose Financial Products Group was responsible for the collapse of AIG, and Angelo Mozilo, whose Countrywide Group led the sale of sub-prime mortgages. Each of these men is believed still to have wealth substantially exceeding $100 million: as noted in Chapter 5, Mozilo settled a lawsuit with the SEC for a payment of $67.5 million, but neither of the others has faced proceedings of any kind.

Only bit players in the US crisis faced criminal charges for their ac-tions. Bernard Madoff was sentenced to 150 years' imprisonment. 'Fabu-lous Fab' Tourre was fined $825,000. The most senior finance executive to have been imprisoned for his part in the 2007–8 crisis is Lee Farkas, chairman of Taylor Bean and Whitaker, a Florida-based mortgage broker.

In Britain, France and Germany there have been no prosecutions re-lated to the crisis at all. Fred Goodwin, of Royal Bank of Scotland, never sought or achieved the personal enrichment commonplace among US financial leaders, though he did appear to revel in what he regarded as appropriate perks of high office: he surrounded himself with sporting heroes who had been placed on the bank's payroll. Goodwin was, in the end, publicly humiliated, stripped of his knighthood and forced to accept a reduction in his pension from the bank. That still left him with £342,500 per year.

Smaller countries have been less forgiving. In Ireland, Sean Fitz-Patrick of Anglo-Irish Bank, perhaps the most reckless of all CEOs of financial institutions (it is a tough competition), was made bankrupt and (unsuccessfully) prosecuted. While convictions were recorded against some of his associates, the judge took the view that it would be 'incredibly unjust' to send them to prison. However, Icelandic courts did impose lengthy prison sentences on the chairman and chief executive of the failed Kaupthing bank.

To the extent that the US and UK authorities have pursued recent allegations of wrongdoing in the financial sector, their targets have been corporate rather than individual. 'Fabulous Fab' was the fall guy sacrificed by Goldman Sachs. The email trail that Tourre left was so egregious that his prosecution provided a lightning conductor for public wrath. The firm paid a $550 million fine to settle—without admission of liability—charges levelled by the SEC against the company in respect of Abacus transactions. At the same time the SEC agreed not to pursue a variety of other allegations against the firm.

Jed Rakoff, for many years Federal judge for the South District of New York, which covers Wall Street, has delivered a blistering and well-argued attack on SEC's policy of negotiating fines with corporations, of which the settlement with Goldman was an example:

> Just going after the company is also both technically and morally suspect. It is technically suspect because, under the law, you should not indict or threaten to indict a company unless you can prove beyond a reasonable doubt that some managerial agent of the company committed the alleged crime; and if you can prove that, why not indict the manager? And from a moral standpoint, punishing a company and its many innocent employees and shareholders for the crimes committed by some unprosecuted individuals seems contrary to elementary notions of moral responsibility.[13]

The *Wall Street Journal* has estimated that in 2012 and 2013 J.P. Morgan paid over $25 billion to settle charges against it—generally without admission of liability.[14] Senior executives of J.P. Morgan are willing to hand over these astonishing sums to atone for past wrongdoing because they pay with other people's money. The scale of announced fines gives the appearance of severity. But not the reality. It is telling that the reputation of J.P. Morgan—once and perhaps still the most respected of financial services firms—is now such as to be only slightly tarnished by restitution of $25 billion. Rakoff argues that 'the future deterrent value of successfully prosecuting individuals far outweighs the prophylactic benefits of imposing internal compliance measures that are often little more than window-dressing'.[15]

Regulatory agencies have chosen to follow the almost ineffectual route of imposing agreed penalties on corporations because they believe it is too hard to secure convictions against either individuals or firms.[16] Enforcement should be aimed at responsible individuals, not corporations, and convictions should be easier to secure. The UK has introduced a symbolic criminal offence of 'reckless banking'[17] and this represents a step in a new, and appropriate, direction. The objective should be strict liability which asserts the naval principle of 'on my watch'—that individuals are responsible for what happens under their supervision. Period.

Strict liability implies that it is sufficient to demonstrate that an event occurred, and not necessary to demonstrate that the person responsible caused it. It is not necessary to inquire further into motive, attribute blame or ascertain exactly what the individuals concerned knew about the wrongdoing. Strict liability ends the defence by which the person in charge expresses ignorance and horror at the actions of subordinates. The most serious of the allegations that 'appalled and shocked' Rebekah Brooks was that *News of the World* staff had hacked the voicemail of a murdered schoolgirl while Brooks was the paper's editor. Bob Diamond was 'physically ill' on learning that employees had falsified rate submissions in the setting of LIBOR.[18] The 'shocked and appalled' defence links impropriety with irresponsibility, as superior officers distance themselves from specific knowledge of what it is that those beneath them are doing. The appropriate principle should be: 'If you take the remuneration, you take the rap.'

It may seem harsh, and it is not desirable, that the chief executive of a bank should go to jail because a cashier puts his hand in the till. Strict liability should apply in relation to the actions of subordinates when they act on behalf of the financial institution in the performance of their duties. That principle of ostensible authority differentiates the thieving bank clerk from the trader who sells a customer a product that he expects to fail. And when falsification of rate submissions, or mis-selling of PPI, is common practice rather than the result of the actions of one rogue individual, then the culpability of those in charge should be automatic.

It may—and will—be argued that such measures will deter people from accepting positions of responsibility.[19] But that is precisely their purpose: to ensure that senior positions in financial institutions are taken only by people who understand and accept the burdensome obligations involved in handling other people's money. Personal liability establishes powerful incentives: it encourages responsible officers to set in place processes and procedures designed to impose effective controls on behaviour, not 'window dressing'; it reduces the temptation to make fine-sounding declarations of policy that have, and are intended to have, little influence on those who would be expected to implement them.

Personal responsibility is vital to reform. But this should not lead anyone to think that the only, or principal, issue is one of picking the rotten apples from the barrel. It is too easy to blame bad outcomes on bad people, whether by vilifying individuals or through blanket condemnation of 'bankers'. In finance, as in every walk of life, there are people with high ethical standards, and people with none; people who stand up for what they believe is right, and people who find it easier, or more rewarding, to conform to prevailing norms.

But we are social animals, and we tend to behave in the ways expected of us in the environment in which we find ourselves. Leadership, for good or bad, can influence these expectations, but only at the margin. In talking to the financial community, I have been struck by the number of people who want to do a better job, but find themselves frustrated by the system within which they work, the values and business imperatives of their employers, the unrealistic and inappropriate demands of their clients, and the regulatory framework imposed upon them. Only by addressing all these issues together can we reestablish a financial system designed for the needs of the real economy.

# CHAPTER 11

# The Future of Finance

I couldn't forgive him or like him but I saw that what he had done was, to him, entirely justified. It was all very careless and confused. They were careless people, Tom and Daisy—they smashed up things and creatures and then retreated back into their money or their vast carelessness or whatever it was that kept them together and let other people clear up the mess they had made.

NICK CARRAWAY, bond salesman,<br>in F. Scott Fitzgerald, The Great Gatsby, 1925

The ideas of economists and political philosophers, both when they are right and when they are wrong, are more powerful than is commonly understood. Indeed the world is ruled by little else. Practical men, who believe themselves exempt from any intellectual influence, are usually the slaves of some defunct economist.

J.M. KEYNES, The General Theory of Employment,<br>Interest and Money, 1936

The finance sector of modern Western economies is too large. It absorbs a disproportionate share of the ablest graduates of our colleges and universities. Its growth has not been matched by corresponding improvements in the provision of services to the non-financial economy—payments systems, capital allocation, risk mitigation and long-term financial security for individuals and households. The process of financialisation has created a structure characterised by tight coupling and interactive complexity, and the resulting instability has had damaging effects on the non-financial economy.

Volumes of trading in financial markets have reached absurd levels—levels that have impeded rather than enhanced the quality of financial intermediation, and increased rather than diversified the risks to which the global economy is exposed. The capital resources needed to reconcile these trading volumes with economic stability have not been available; nor will they be. The scale of activities undertaken by traders within a modern investment bank is not viable without the implicit and explicit support provided by retail deposits and the taxpayer.

The existing structure of the finance sector requires much more capital, not the small additional amounts required by Basel III. But equity investors will not provide financial conglomerates with fresh capital on the scale necessary. Investors no longer trust the financial statements of banks or the people who run these banks. They have little confidence in the long-term profitability of these institutions and fear that, if banks do make profits, both regulators and senior executives will have priorities other than distributions to shareholders.

The solution that has instead been adopted is that central banks lend very large amounts of money to financial conglomerates at low rates in the hope that they will make sufficient profit from trading to rebuild their balance sheets. But the taxpayer cannot reasonably be asked to subsidise banks in this way, especially when a high proportion of these profits are creamed off to reward the traders concerned and the managers who ostensibly supervise them, allowing them to achieve levels of remuneration beyond the dreams of ordinary people. At the same time bankers and their lobbyists claim that the provision of adequate equity capital for banks would drive down reported returns on equity capital to unattractive levels and inhibit the proper function of banks in lending to the real economy.

If activities cannot raise sufficient equity to ensure they are adequately capitalised, or earn satisfactory rates of returns on that equity if they are adequately capitalised, the lesson of market economics is clear: such activities should not take place; or at least the scale on which they do take place should be substantially reduced. And that is how we should view the existing banking system.

We need a finance sector to manage our payments, finance our housing stock, restore our infrastructure, fund our retirement and support new business. But very little of the expertise that exists in the finance industry today relates to the facilitation of payments, the provision of housing, the management of large construction projects, the needs of the elderly or the nurturing of small businesses. The process of financial intermediation has become an end in itself.

The expertise that is valued is understanding of the activities of other financial intermediaries. That expertise is devoted not to the creation of new assets but to the rearrangement of those that already exist. High salaries and bonuses are awarded not for fine appreciation of the needs of users of financial services but for outwitting competing market participants. In the most extreme manifestation of a sector that has lost sight of its purposes, some of the finest mathematical and scientific minds on the planet are employed to devise algorithms for computerised trading in securities that exploit the weaknesses of other algorithms for computerised trading in securities.

But finance is not, as former Treasury Secretary Larry Summers seemed to be suggesting, a mathematical puzzle. Finance exists to serve households and businesses. Individuals and companies engaged in finance should have specific knowledge of at least some of the needs of users of the financial system. We need focused financial businesses with a clear productive purpose and a management system, governance regime and capital structure appropriate to that purpose. We should aim to restore and nourish the rich variety of institutions and organisational forms that existed in the finance sector before the 1980s.

The most common criticism of this suggestion is that it would involve 'turning the clock back'. But you *should* turn the clock back if it is telling you the wrong time—and in this case it is. It is not possible, even if it were desirable, to restore a particular status quo, in the manner in which we might reconstruct a historic building. But there was wisdom in an older structure of industry and regulatory process that had evolved over decades and which was abandoned in a mixture of the ideological fervour of politicians and the personal ambition of financiers and deal-makers.

Many people struggle with the idea that the world could be more than slightly different. People I talk to in the financial world find it difficult to conceive of a future financial system in which large corporations are not active in the repo market, in which asset-backed securities are not integral to housing finance, and where there are no futures contracts or stock market indexes. Yet there was a time when none of these things existed, and there could be such a time again. We need some of the things that Citigroup and Goldman Sachs do, but we do not need Citigroup and Goldman Sachs to do them. And many of the things done by Citigroup and Goldman Sachs do not need to be done at all.

In 2008 the established finance sector was on the point of collapse. Most of the major financial institutions of the world were dependent on government support for their continued existence—as, to a large extent, they still are. During the global financial crisis governments were in a position to impose essentially any conditions they liked on the finance sector. They imposed very few.

At the meeting at which Treasury Secretary Hank Paulson explained how the $700 billion that Congress had allocated to rescue the US banking system would be distributed, John Thain, CEO of Merrill Lynch (who had already achieved notoriety by spending $1 million redecorating his office as Merrill collapsed), cut quickly to the chase. 'What kind of protections can you give us on changes in compensation policy?' he asked.[1] Thain was slapped down by his new boss, the retail banker Ken Lewis from Bank of America. Before long, both Lewis and Thain would be out of a job as a result of BoA's foolish acquisition. But in one important respect Thain would be the victor. Bonuses of $3.6 billion were paid to Merrill staff at the beginning of 2009.

It is hard to exaggerate the sense of entitlement that prevailed in the finance sector even after the global financial crisis. Within a short time Lloyd Blankfein was describing 'God's work' and Bob Diamond would proclaim that 'the time for remorse is over'.[2] Even looking beyond the vulgar nonsense of 'We are Wall Street', the complacency and self-satisfaction that by 2010 had replaced the sense of fear that had pervaded the industry in 2008 were extraordinary.

Yet the crisis was not over. New 'rogue traders' were escorted from their desks by security guards. Various rate-fixing scandals demonstrated that the origins of the crisis in fact lay deep within the culture of the finance industry. Monetary policies boosted asset prices, rewarding those who enjoyed accumulated wealth at the expense of those who derived their income from employment. The Eurozone muddle muddled on.

When the global financial crisis hit in 2008, politicians of all parties and officials were essentially at sea. 'Never allow a crisis to go to waste', said President Obama's chief of staff, Rahm Emanuel, but the crisis did go to waste.[3] Emanuel's cynical remark exemplifies the pragmatic realism characteristic of modern political life; but, as in this case, 'realism' often has no outcome because pragmatism devoid of analytic content permits no more than ineffectual tinkering. The absence of an explanatory narrative led to an incoherent response. On the political left, parties that had waited a century for capitalism to collapse under the weight of its own internal contradictions were thrown into panic by the prospect that it might actually do so. The intellectual self-confidence of the European left had been drained by the failures of socialism. Bank nationalisation, once a totemic policy, was anathema even as a temporary expedient.

For the political right, events belied the notion that markets were self-equilibrating. Neo-liberal doctrines were plainly inadequate to explain the economics or the politics of the time. It was some time before their apologists succeeded in persuading themselves, if few others, that the crisis had been caused by government interference in markets.

The failures of financialisation had barely diminished the influence of the doctrine. The belief that the profitability of an activity is a measure of its social legitimacy has not only taken root in the financial sector but has spread its poison throughout the business world. Read dispassionately, there is little to distinguish the *cri de coeur* of 'We are Wall Street' from the manifesto of a criminal gang. There has been a wide failure to distinguish profit generation from wealth creation, or to see the difference between the appropriation of resources and their production, and a willingness to license activities that border on fraud and which sometimes cross that border.

Both supporters of the market system and its critics have failed to recognise that the trading floor of the investment bank is not the epitome of the market economy but an excrescence from it. Observers on both left and right have mistakenly regarded the process of financialisation in Western economies as part of the success of these Western economies in competition with the centrally placed regimes of eastern Europe.

The absurd proposition that profit demonstrates value gave credence to its equally absurd opposite: that profit is inherently immoral. But if the contribution of an activity to society is judged by how much money the promoters make from it, it is hardly surprising if people outside finance and business form the view that such values should not be allowed near our schools and hospitals—or, for that matter, our pharmaceutical industry, our infrastructure, our supermarkets—and view bankers with contempt.

This intellectual misconception behind the thought that prosperity might be enhanced by trade in baseball cards has been associated with an economic model that misunderstands the (important) role that markets play in enabling complex modern economies to manage information. Prices act as signals, and the price mechanism is an important guide to resource allocation: that does not mean that the constantly changing price on the Bloomberg screen is a complete and comprehensive distillation of the wisdom of the ages. There are many guides to value other than price, whether we are talking about a Shakespeare play or a business organisation. Although these economic models represent at best an oversimplification, at worst a travesty, of how free markets work in reality, their rhetoric has been powerful—and convenient.

But the influence of ideologies does not depend solely on the power of their ideas. The finance sector is today the strongest of all industrial lobbies. Simon Johnson, a former chief economist at the IMF, has insightfully compared Wall Street with the oligarchies that have dominated most states throughout history.[4] Economic power is used to secure political power; political power is deployed to enhance economic power, in a self-reinforcing process.

In pre-modern European societies oligarchy was founded on the ownership of land and the ability to recruit bodies of men to serve the king or fight competing baronies. Religious oligarchies operated in parallel. Communist oligarchies were self-perpetuating cliques, resembling in many ways those religious orders of which they professed to be the antithesis. In Russia today, and in many emerging economies, oligarchy is centred on the control of infrastructure and natural resources. The attack on the robber barons was a—partly successful—attempt to prevent the emergence of oligarchy in the USA.

The influence of oligarchs has been potent for as long as governments have existed. In the USA there is not much more than money to the power of finance. The importance of campaign funding to politicians, and the readiness of the finance sector to respond, ensures that Wall Street concerns receive a sympathetic hearing on Capitol Hill. Money plays a role in European politics also, but in far smaller amounts, and its influence is less overwhelming.

Britain is a complex case. There is less corrupt trading of favours. But politicians are protective of London's success in placing itself at the centre of the global financial stage, and of the tax revenues and other economic benefits they are told it has generated. They suffer from what Adair Turner, a former chairman of the Financial Services Authority, has described as 'intellectual capture'.[5] The City of London is full of articulate, smart, wealthy people. Politicians, perhaps more articulate but often less smart and certainly less wealthy, are impressed. And if you want someone to explain a collateralised debt obligation, the pool of people you can call on is small, and does not contain many people who are critical of the innovation.

France and Germany are, among the countries with large financial sectors, the ones where anti-market rhetoric is strongest. But they are also the countries that have done the least to implement substantive financial reform since the global financial crisis. The principal reason is the instinctive corporatism of both countries, which equates the national interest in financial services with the interests of large national financial services firms. Thus the voice of Deutsche Bank is transmitted as the voice of Germany, not just in domestic German policies but also (and especially) in German positions in international financial negotiations. Germany's policy positions are also compromised by the local political links of its many regional and community banks (links that have positive as well as many negative aspects). In France the homogeneity of an elite that glides easily from boardroom to cabinet table and back reinforces the sense that its state and its national industrial champions are one. And since France and Germany are the two most influential members of the European Union, the corporate influence extends to the conference rooms of Brussels.

Little progress can be made in reforming finance unless the influence of money on politics is reduced. The situation in the USA seems beyond repair. The amounts now spent on campaigns are unconscionable, the Supreme Court ruling in *Citizens United* in 2010 that restrictions on corporate political contributions violated First Amendment rights to free speech has opened the floodgates of corporate spending. Europe generally has both legal and practical limits on campaign expenditures, but in consequence surprisingly small amounts of money can have substantial influence. The expression of opinions that people have been paid to hold is not free speech but its negation. State funding of political parties, combined with strict limits on other sources of finance, seems a cheap price to pay for (more) honest politics.

But the revolving door, which sweeps senior politicians and officials into well-rewarded positions in the private sector, continues to turn. There are real benefits to the community from exchanges of knowledge and experience between public and private sectors; but retired politicians should be elder statesmen, not multimillionaire fixers, and the expertise of former civil servants should serve the public good, not private interests. The practice of remunerating those who occupy public-sector posts at levels far below private-sector norms, in the expectation that they will later make up the difference, damages policy to a degree disproportionate to the derisory amounts of public money it saves.

Policymakers should have access to alternative sources of advice—and make use of them. I explained in Chapters 2 and 8 how and why the academic world—perhaps the most natural conduit for the expression of truth to power—has largely failed to fulfil this dispassionate role in the finance sector. The dominant intellectual paradigm was congenial to an industry that was therefore ready to promote its development and fund its adherents. Journalists, who are dependent on their sources, and inevitably influenced by the views of those they talk to daily, are easily captured. If they are not, they are likely to find themselves excluded from information in ways that drive them to ill-informed hostility.

Regulatory agencies contain many people who genuinely seek to pursue the public interest, but so long as regulatory policy is concerned with prescriptive rulebooks rather than with structure and incentives, little progress will be made. A few minutes at a meeting of regulatory professionals leave one crying out for someone who can see the wood from the trees. The global financial crisis might have been a set-back for the regulation industry, but in fact it represented a huge boost. The cry for 'more regulation' was almost universal; it was barely possible to keep up with the plethora of acronyms describing new agencies, committees and supervisory bodies. And, whatever the rhetoric, none of this activity was aimed at fundamental reform: rather, it was to make better, or at least more extensive, use of the skills and expertise that regulators and their associates already have.

Nevertheless, there are many who work or have worked in finance who are both knowledgeable and critical of the conventional wisdom: some work in asset management, others are disillusioned former employees of investment banks. But there is no organisation that collects these voices.[6] And I have come to believe that many people inside and outside the industry feel intimidated by what they perceive to be the pervasive (though publicly silent—they rarely engage in open debate) power and influence of global investment banks.

That power and influence ensure that fundamental structural reform of the financial sector is not a realistic short-term prospect. Yet it is intrinsic to oligarchy that oligarchs are a small minority, a point graphically made in the 'Occupy Wall Street' slogan of 'We are the 99 per cent'. But it is easier to identify what the 99 per cent are against than what they are for, an incoherence typical of the swell of unfocused public anger that followed the global financial crisis: anger with the finance industry and with the political failure to anticipate the crisis or respond effectively to it. Most countries ejected the governments—whether left or right—that had held office during the crisis. But that made no material difference to public policy towards the finance sector. In the absence of any intellectual framework for such policy beyond a call for 'more regulation', how could it?

Perhaps the most significant political development of our time is the populist rage of disgruntled people who are no longer confident that the country in which they live is in tune with their values, and who think they have experienced less than their share of overall prosperity. In a reaction against a democratic politics perceived as out of touch with the needs of ordinary people, fringe parties across the developed world have attracted the votes of 'left-behind' groups—the USA's Tea Party, Britain's UK Independence Party, France's Front National, Beppe Grillo's Five Star

Movement in Italy, Syriza and Golden Dawn in Greece—parties with nothing in common except a shared sense that 'they' (those in charge) fail to understand or identify with the needs and values of the protesters.

Even in the political centre there has been populist appeal in bashing bankers in the years since the global financial crisis, and campaigners across the political spectrum have won applause by indulging in it. Voters who hate bankers far outnumber bankers or even the hired 'adventurers who make market of themselves'. But most voters have other things to think about, whereas professional lobbyists for the finance industry do not. The lobbyists are always there; and when it comes to the detail of law or regulation, it is inevitably their influence that matters. Investment bankers routinely stalk the corridors of the Treasury. Timothy Geithner justly complains in his memoir that he was routinely and wrongly identified as a banker, or even an alumnus of Goldman Sachs, when in reality his career had been spent in public service. But it does not appear that he stopped to ask himself why this mistake was so frequently made.

It is possible to have a smaller, simpler financial services system that is better adapted to the needs of the non-financial economy—to achieve an efficient payment system, effective capital allocation, greater economic stability, security in planning and managing our personal finances and justified confidence in the people who advise us. We will not wake up tomorrow, or next year, and find such a reality. Is it therefore pointless to articulate that vision? I do not think so. My experience in public policy, business and the academic world has led me to believe in the truth of those remarks of Keynes with which this chapter began—the long-run power of ideas. 'Madmen in authority, who hear voices in the air, are generally distilling their frenzy from some academic scribbler of a few years back.'[7] Today, thank goodness, we have few 'madmen in authority'. The decent but undistinguished official such as Geithner is more typical but no less in need of, and perhaps more receptive to, the ideas he absorbs from the environment around him.

The measure of success in influencing public policy is that your ideas of yesterday are fed back today as the novel thoughts of someone else, and repeated tomorrow as the conventional wisdom of the time. The limits of what is politically possible have changed so much and so often in the course of my lifetime—Britain's railways have been privatised, gay couples are now allowed to marry, and a black president of the USA has been elected—that to feel constrained by what is 'politically possible' is simply a failure of imagination. The most effective counter to the misuse of power in a democratic society is the role of education in creating an informed public opinion, and this book is intended as contribution to that objective.

The proposals here are intended to represent a guide for the democratic politicians who will be confronted with the next financial crisis. And there will be another major financial crisis: the underlying determinants of the recurrent crises of financialisation are unchanged, and this book has tried to explain how and why fragility has continued to increase. The current policy trajectory is one characterised by financial crises of increasing seriousness. That does not necessarily imply that every crisis will be more serious than its predecessor: only that the trend is upward. Regulatory measures have been addressed, not very effectively, to the last crisis rather than the next.

The restructuring of the finance industry outlined in this book is intended to offer a provisional blueprint for how thoughtful policymakers might prepare for the next crisis. They might have used the control of the finance sector they achieved in the aftermath of the crisis to restructure the industry. But they did not, and that makes it certain that they will get another chance—perhaps to make similar mistakes again.

The Great Depression plunged the world into political as well as economic disaster, but skilful political leadership at that time made the domestic and international compromises that secured the future of democracy and the market economy—albeit not by a large margin. The stakes are high, but finance is not a game, and sporting metaphors are inappropriate. It is time to get back to work: the serious and responsible business of managing other people's money.

# The Emperor's Guard's New Clothes

Once upon a time there was a great emperor, who ruled over dominions far and wide. The treasure of the empire was kept in a chest, and guarded by men dressed in pinstriped suits and bowler hats, who were honest but dull and who made payments on behalf of the imperial household and received tribute from the subjects of the emperor.

But one day a newcomer appeared, wearing not the traditional pinstripe but a suit of the finest silk threaded with gold. The emperor was suspicious of fancy clothing, having a few years earlier been deceived by a pair of management consultants posing as tailors. The fraudsters had promised, but failed to deliver, a garment of transformational magnificence. So he inspected carefully. But there could be no doubt: this suit was the real Sherman McCoy.

The newcomer's clothes grew in finery, and he became known at court as The Gold Man. He acquired an extensive retinue, recruiting some of the best mathematicians from the far corners of the empire, the solvers of the differential equations. And there were the exchangers. The Gold Man's employees were not content simply to leave spare treasure in the chest. Every day the exchangers passed it round among themselves, with such speed and facility that it was barely possible to notice the slivers of gold that rubbed off along the way. Soon The Gold Man and his retainers were among the most prosperous subjects of the empire.

The Gold Man's reputation spread widely, and merchants from all across the empire travelled to seek his advice. Did not The Gold Man's exquisite raiment bear witness to his exceptional skill and sagacity? Was not the ever-increasing amount of gold on his person a measure of the prosperity his initiative was bringing to the empire? The emperor valued The Gold Man's counsel, not just in relation to the management of the imperial chest, but on all matters of state. Soon The Gold Man was the most powerful of all the emperor's advisers.

One day, there was a great scandal, when The Leh Man, one of the exchangers, suddenly collapsed. As he fell, his money chest burst open and was found to be completely empty. There was much soul-searching, and the emperor commissioned an audit of the contents of the imperial chest.

It was discovered that all the money that had paid for The Gold Man's fine clothes, and the bonuses of the exchangers, and the salaries of the solvers of the differential equations, had been taken out of the imperial chest, and the apparent increase in prosperity since The Gold Man had arrived at court was wholly illusory. The Gold Man and the exchangers were stripped of their garments and dragged through the streets, to popular cries of 'Naked they are but ordinary men!' They were dispatched to the deep dungeon in which the management consultants who had earlier deceived the emperor so cruelly with their fake clothes were still languishing. And the solvers of the differential equations returned to the task of designing rockets to extend even further the reach of the great empire.

# Acknowledgements

I have had the good fortune to have been able to combine an academic and public policy background with high-level experience of the workings of finance over two decades. I should like to thank the people who made that opportunity—unusual in Britain—possible. In particular, Mark Cornwall-Jones, Jon Foulds and the late Alan McLintock. Alan, Jon and Mark exemplified the best traditions of the City—high intelligence, complete integrity and a strong sense of the responsibilities that go with the management of other people's money.

There are still many people in finance who are like that, if perhaps fewer than there were. This book has benefited from discussion with many of them, especially in the course of the Equity Markets Review I undertook for the UK Government in 2012–3, and I am grateful to Vince Cable, Secretary of State for Business, Innovation and Skills, for inviting me to undertake that exercise, and to the team from his department that supported me.

Elizabeth Bates was a dedicated research assistant from the early stages of the project, and I am grateful to her and to Robert Metz, who succeeded her as the book neared completion. Scott Edmonds and Karen Xi provided additional support. Philip Augar, Amar Bhidé, David Bodanis, Nick Hungerford, Robert Jenkins, Mervyn King, Bronwen Maddox and Frank Partnoy made helpful comments on a draft of the manuscript. Mika Oldham supported the project from the beginning and read the proofs with dedication. And special thanks to Jo Charrington, my personal assistant now for seventeen years, without whom I would never have been able to keep the strands of my life and work together.

# Notes

Fuller notes and detail on sources can be found at www.johnkay.com

## Prologue: The Parable of the Ox

1. A version of this parable first appeared in the *Financial Times,* 25 July 2012.

2. Surowiecki, J.M., 2005, *The Wisdom of Crowds: Why the Many Are Smarter than the Few,* London, Abacus.

## Introduction: Far Too Much of a Good Thing

1. A survey is Levine, R., 2005, 'Finance and Growth: Theory and Evidence', in Aghion, P., and Durlauf, S.N. (ed.), *Handbook of Economic Growth,* Amsterdam, Elsevier, pp. 865–934.

2. The first use is widely attributed to Gerald Epstein; see Epstein, G.A. (ed.), *Financialisation and the World Economy,* Chettenham, Edward Elgar, 2005.

3. This description seems first to have come into wide use in Australia through the country's then prime minister, Kevin Rudd.

4. Summers, L.H., 1985, 'On Economics and Finance', *Journal of Finance,* XL (3), July, pp. 633–5.

## Chapter 1: History

1. Summers, L.H., 2004, 'Fourth Annual Marshall J. Seidman lecture on Health Policy', remarks at Harvard University, Boston, MA, 27 April.

2. This email was reportedly widely circulated around Wall Street in 2010 and leaflets based on it handed to 'Occupy' protesters the following year.

3. Haldane, A.G., 2010, 'Patience and Finance', Oxford China Business Forum, Beijing, 2 September.

4. Tonnies, F., 1887 *Gemeinschaft und Gesellschaft,* Leipzig, Fues; trans. M. Weber, 1978, as *Economy and Society,* Oakland, CA, University of California Press.

5. Black, F., and Scholes, M., 1973, 'The Pricing of Options and Corporate Liabilities', *Journal of Political Economy,* 81 (3), May–June, pp. 637–54.

6. This title is conferred by the SEC on about ten businesses. In practice, two—Moody's and Standard & Poor's—dominate, with Fitch a somewhat distant third.

7. Coates, J.M., and Herbert, J., 2008, 'Endogenous Steroids and Financial Risk Taking on a London Trading Floor', *Proceedings of the National Academy of Sciences*, 105 (16), pp. 6167–72.

8. Lewis, M.M, 1989, *Liar's Poker: Two Cities, True Greed*, London, Hodder & Stoughton, p. 93.

9. Salmon. F., 2009, 'Recipe for Disaster', *Wired*, 22 March.

10. Stephens, P., 1996, *Politics and the Pound: The Conservatives' Struggle with Sterling*, London, Macmillan.

11. Lack, S., 2012, *The Hedge Fund Mirage: The Illusion of Big Money and Why It's Too Good To Be True*, Hoboken, NJ, Wiley.

12. Bloomberg Billionaires, http://www.bloomberg.com/billionaires/2014-07-18/cya.

13. Bryan, L.L., 1988, *Breaking Up the Bank: Rethinking an Industry Under Siege*, Homewood, IL, Dow Jones-Irwin. Litan, R. E., 1988, 'The Future of Banking: Are "Narrow" Banks the Answer?', *Proceedings*, 219, Federal Reserve Bank of Chicago, pp. 639–45.

14. One consequence of financialisation was the development of the limited-liability partnership, following lobbying by the major accountancy firms.

15. DLJ, a much smaller institution, had converted twelve years earlier.

16. Lewis, M.M., 2011, *Boomerang: The Meltdown Tour*, London, Allen Lane.

17. Nakamoto, M., and Wighton D., 2007, 'Citigroup Chief Stays Bullish on Buy-Outs', *Financial Times*, 9 July.

18. Newton was originally reported as saying that he could 'calculate the motions of erratic bodies but not the madness of a multitude', in Francis, J., 1850, 'Chronicles and Characters of the Stock Exchange', *The Church of England Quarterly Review*, 27 (6), pp. 128–55, but the more succinct phrasing above is now in wide circulation.

19. Macmillan, H., 1957, 'Leader's Speech', remarks at Conservative Party rally, Bedford, 20 July.

20. Rieffel, A., 2003, *Restructuring Sovereign Debt: The Case for Ad Hoc Machinery*, Washington, DC, Brookings Institution Press, pp. 289–94.

21. Harris, R., 2012, *The Fear Index*, London, Arrow Books, is an amusing description of a resulting meltdown.

22. Van Agtmael, A., 2007, *The Emerging Markets Century: How a New Breed of World-Class Companies Is Overtaking the World*, London, Simon and Schuster.

23. Meeker, M., 1995, *The Internet Report*, New York, Morgan Stanley.

24. Lucas Jr, R.E., 2003, 'Macroeconomic Priorities', *The American Economic Review*, 93 (1), March, pp. 1–14.

25. Bernanke, B.S., 2004, 'The Great Moderation', Remarks by Governor Ben S. Bernanke at the meeting of the Eastern Economic Association, Washington, DC, 20 February.

26. Draghi, M., 2012, 'Speech by Mario Draghi President of the European Central Bank', remarks at Global Investment Conference, London, 26 July.

27. Tuckett, D., 2011, *Minding the Markets*, London, Palgrave Macmillan.

28. Josephson, M., 1934, *The Robber Barons: The Great American Capitalists, 1861–1901*, New York, Harcourt, Brace & Co.

29. Tarbell, I.M., 1904, *The History of the Standard Oil Company*, New York, McClure, Phillips & Co.

30. Sinclair, U., 1906, *The Jungle*, London, Werner Laurie.

31. Jensen, M.C., and Meckling, W.H., 1976, 'Theory of the Firm: Governance, Residual Claims and Organizational Forms', *Journal of Financial Economics (JFE)*, Vol. 3, No. 4. Rappaport, A., 1986, *Creating Shareholder Value: The New Standard for Business Performance*, New York, Free Press.

32. Welch, J.F., 1981, 'Growing Fast in a Slow-Growth Economy', speech to financial community representatives, Hotel Pierre, New York, 8 December.

33. Manne, H.G., 1965, 'Mergers and the Market for Corporate Control', *The Journal of Political Economy*, 73 (2), April, pp. 110–20.

34. Burrough, B., and Helyar, J., 1990, *Barbarians at the Gate: The Fall of RJR Nabisco*, London, Arrow.

35. Reader, W.J., 1970–75, *Imperial Chemical Industries: A History*, London, Oxford University Press.

36. Kay, J., 2010, *Obliquity*, London, Profile Books.

37. Langley, M., 2003, *Tearing Down the Walls*, New York, Simon & Schuster, pp. 324–5.

38. Guerrera, F., 2009, 'Welch Condemns Share Price Focus', *Financial Times*, 12 March.

39. Storrs, F., 2006, 'The 50 Wealthiest Bostonians', *Boston Magazine*, March.

40. Although as a matter of chronology, Reed (born 1939) is younger than either Welch (born 1935) or Weill (born 1933).

41. Berle, A., and Means, G., 1932, *The Modern Corporation and Private Property*, New York, Macmillan.

42. Bakija, J., Cole, A., and Heim, B.T., 2012, *Jobs and Income Growth of Top Earners and the Laws of Changing Income Inequality: Evidence from US Tax Return Data*, April.

43. US Bureau of the Census, 2013, 'Income, Poverty and Health Insurance Coverage in the US'; this figure over-dramatises the change because of the rise in single-person households, but the trend is valid and reproduced, less starkly, in the UK, where rises in benefits have partially offset it. Institute for Fiscal Studies, 2011, 'Why Did Britain's Households Get Richer? Decomposing UK Household Income Growth between 1968 and 2008–9'.

44. Taibbi, M., 2009, 'The Great American Bubble Machine', *Rolling Stone*, 9 July.

## Chapter 2: Risk

1. Rajan, R.G., 2005, 'Has Financial Development Made the World Riskier?', *Proceedings*, Federal Reserve Bank of Kansas City, August, pp. 313–69.

2. Kohn, D.L., 2005, 'Commentary: Has Financial Development Made the World Riskier?', *Proceedings*, Federal Reserve Bank of Kansas City, August, pp. 371–9.

3. Greenspan, A., 1999, 'Financial Derivatives', speech to the Futures Industry Association, Boca Raton, FL, 19 March.

4. Summers, L.H., 2005, 'General Discussion: Has Financial Development Made the World Riskier?', *Proceedings*, Federal Reserve Bank of Kansas City, August, pp. 387–97.

5. Bernanke, B.S., 2006, 'Modern Risk Management and Banking Supervision', remarks at the Stonier Graduate School of Banking, Washington, DC, 12 June.

6. Geithner, T.F., 2006, 'Risk Management Challenges in the U.S. Financial System', remarks at the Global Association of Risk Professionals 7th Annual Risk Management Convention & Exhibition, New York City, 28 February.

7. After retiring from the Fed, Kohn became a member of the Bank of England's Prudential Regulatory Authority.

8. And yet another that, with compound interest, they could now afford to buy Manhattan Island back.

9. Greenspan, A., 1999, 'Financial Derivatives', speech to the Futures Industry Association, Boca Raton, FL, 19 March

10. Albert, M., 1993, *Capitalisme contre capitalisme*, Paris, Seuil; trans. By P. Haviland as *Capitalism vs Capitalism*, London, Whurr.

11. Carlill *v.* Carbolic Smoke Ball Company, 1892, 2QB 489. The Carbolic Smoke Ball gave rise to one of the most memorable cases in English law. The Carbolic Smoke Ball supposedly provided such effective protection from flu that the manufacturers offered £100 to anyone who found it did not work. Mrs Carlill, who contracted flu after using the smoke ball, sued when the company refused to pay. One of the many specious arguments advanced for the company (by the future prime minister Herbert Asquith) was that the offer was a wager and hence unenforceable.

12. Opinion prepared for the ISDA by Robin Potts QC, Erskine Chambers, 24 June 1997, para. 5, citing Wilson *v.* Jones, (1867) 2 Exch. Div. 150; cited in Kimball-Stanley, A., 2008, 'Insurance and Credit Default Swaps: Should Like Things Be Treated Alike?', *Connecticut Insurance Law Journal*, 15 (1), p. 247.

13. Remarks of Treasury Secretary Lawrence H. Summers to the Securities Industry Association, Office of Public Affairs, 9 November 2000.

14. The fall and recovery of the Lloyd's market is described in Duguid, A., 2014, *On the Brink: How a Crisis Transformed Lloyd's of London*, Basingstoke, Palgrave Macmillan.

15. Cohan, W.D., 2011, *Money and Power: How Goldman Sachs Came to Rule the World*, New York, Random House, p. 515.

16. Ceresney, A., 2013, 'Statement on the Tourre Verdict', US Securities and Exchange Commission Public Statement, 1 August.

17. Loewenstein, G., 1987, 'Anticipation and the Value of Delayed Consumption', *Economic Journal*, 97 (387), September, pp. 666–84.

18. There are many studies of this. See, for example, Malkiel, B.G., 2012, *A Random Walk down Wall Street*, 10th edn, New York and London, W.W. Norton. pp. 177–83. Porter, G.E., and Trifts, J.W., 2014, 'The Career Paths of Mutual Fund Managers: The Role of Merit', *Financial Analysts Journal*, 70 (4), July/August, pp. 55–71. Philips, C.B., Kinniry Jr., F.M., Schlanger, T., and Hirt, J.M., 2014, 'The Case for Index-Fund Investing', Vanguard Research, April.

19. Kahneman himself is not guilty of this: Kahneman, D., 2011, *Thinking Fast and Slow*, New York, Farrar, Strauss and Giroux.

20. Rubin, R., 2004, *In an Uncertain World*, New York, Random House Trade.

21. The unknown unknowns was famously described by Donald Rumsfeld; see Taleb, N.N., 2007, *The Black Swan: The Impact of the Highly Improbable*, London, Penguin.

22. Greenspan, A., 2008, Statement to the House, Committee on Oversight and Government Reform, Hearing, 23 October (Serial 110-209).

23. Ibid.

24. Tett, G., 2013, 'An Interview with Alan Greenspan', *FT Magazine*, 25 October.

25. Ramsey, F.P., 1926, 'Truth and Probability', in Ramsey, F.P., 1931, *The Foundations of Mathematics and Other Logical Essays*, Braithwaite, R.B. (ed.), London, Kegan, Paul, Trench, Trubner & Co.

26. Buffett, W., 1988, Chairman's Letter to the Shareholders of Berkshire Hathaway Inc.

27. Fox, J., 2009, *The Myth of the Rational Market*, New York, Harper Business, pp. 86–8.

28. Isaacson, W., 2013, *Steve Jobs: The Exclusive Biography*, New York, Little Brown.

29. Hair, P.E.H., 1971, 'Deaths from Violence in Britain: A Tentative Survey', *Population Studies*, 25 (1), pp. 5–24.

30. Adams, J., 1995, *Risk: The Policy Implications of Risk Compensation and Plural Rationalities*, London, Routledge.

31. Geithner, T., 2014, *Stress Test*, New York, Crown.

32. Donne, J., 1987, *Devotions upon Emergent Occasions* (originally published 1624), Raspa, A. (ed.), New York, Oxford University Press.

33. Tuckett, D., 2011, *Minding the Markets*, London, Palgrave Macmillan, p.18.

34. Sinclair, U., 1994, *I, Candidate for Governor: And How I Got Licked* (originally published 1935), London, University of California Press, p.109.

## Chapter 3: Intermediation

1. American Legal Institute, 2006, *Restatement (Third) of the Law of Agency*.

2. George Akerlof employed the used car market as example to highlight how markets can break down when information asymmetry is present in his classic 1970 article: Akerlof, G.A., 1970, 'The Market for "Lemons": Quality Uncertainty and the Market Mechanism', *Quarterly Journal of Economics*, 84 (3), pp. 488–500.

3. Shiller, R.J., 1981, 'Do Stock Prices Move Too Much To Be Justified by Subsequent Changes in Dividends?', *The American Economic Review*, 71 (3), June, pp. 421–36.

4. Kay, J., 2012, 'The Kay Review of UK Equity Markets and Long-Term Decision Making', Final Report.

5. In the course of Enron's frauds, the company toured analysts around a new 'trading room' that was actually a sham: McLean, B., and Elkind, P., 2003, *The Smartest Guys in the Room: The Amazing Rise and Scandalous Fall of Enron*, New York, Penguin, pp. 179–80. Fannie Mae, the failed US mortgage re-insurer, produced earnings growth of such extraordinary regularity that it was eventually charged with fraud and forced to restate its accounts: Morgenson, G., and Rosner, J., 2011, *Reckles$ Endangerment*, New York, Times Books, Henry Holt & Co., pp. 118–19.

6. Galton, F., 1907, 'Vox Populi (The Wisdom of Crowds)', *Nature*, 1949 (75), pp. 450–51. This is the article with which the parable of the ox begins.

7. Keynes, J.M., 1936, *The General Theory of Employment, Interest and Money*, London, Macmillan, p. 156.

8. Lack, S., 2012, *The Hedge Fund Mirage: The Illusion of Big Money and Why It's Too Good to Be True*, Hoboken, NJ, Wiley.

9. The relationship between risk and return, and the inability of financial engineering, however sophisticated, to reduce overall risk, is emphasised by one of the most famous propositions in financial economics, usually called the Modigliani–Miller theorem. The greater the ratio of debt to equity, the greater is the risk and return of both debt and equity. Imagine a project is financed 50 per cent from debt, with a return of 5 per cent and 50 per cent from riskier equity, and an expected return of 10 per cent. Now suppose the sponsors of the project increase the share of debt from one half to two-thirds. The debt is riskier, so the yield

demanded will be higher—say 6 per cent. The equity is also riskier, so the promised return will also need to be higher—say 10½ per cent. In this example the overall cost of financing the project (x 6 per cent and at 10½ per cent) is just the same—7½ per cent—as it would have been if the original 50/50 financing method had been used. Modigliani, F., and Miller, M.H., 1958, 'The Cost of Capital, Corporation Finance and the Theory of Investment', *The American Economic Review*, 48 (3), June, pp. 261–97.

10. The problem had been effectively identified as central to trading in the financial sector by Nicolas Nassim Taleb in *Fooled by Randomness*.

11. The winner's curse was first identified in the auction of US offshore oil drilling licences in the 1970s. These licences were traditionally offered at fixed and modest prices to qualified bidders. But the rise of market fundamentalist ideology encouraged the federal government to auction them. The bidders were major oil companies. With hindsight, they paid too much. Not because they were caught up in the heat of the auction—though perhaps they were—but because the geologists working for the companies were working in conditions of considerable uncertainty. When one company came up with a higher assessment of the value of a block than any of the equally competent professionals working for the other oil companies, the usual reason was that their geologists had screwed up.

## Chapter 4: Profits

1. Buffett, W., 1988, Chairman's Letter to the Shareholders of Berkshire Hathaway Inc.

2. Goodman, A., 'Top 40 Buffett-isms: Inspiration To Become a Better Investor', *Forbes*, 25 September.

3. Zweig, J., 2011, 'Keynes: He Didn't Say Half of What He Said. Or Did He?', *The Wall Street Journal MarketBeat*, 11 February.

4. High prices will attract new entrants into the industry. This is why there are too many investment funds and estate agents. Entry into surgery is restricted by the capacity of medical schools.

5. Abrahamson, M., Jenkinson, T., and Jones, H., 2011, 'Why Don't U.S. Issuers Demand European Fees for IPOs?', *Journal of Finance*, 66 (6), December, Sabin, P., pp. 2055–82.

6. Augar, P., 2006, *The Greed Merchants: How the Investment Banks Played the Free Market Game*, London, Penguin, p. 107.

7. El Paso Corporation, Shareholder Litigation, 41 A.3d 432 (Del. Ch. 2012).

8. Goldman Sachs Code of Business Conduct and Ethics. Last accessed: 31 July 2014.

9. Cohan, W.D., 2012, *Money and Power*, London, Penguin.

10. The history is told by Gillian Tett, 2010, *Fool's Gold*, New York, Free Press.

11. Transcript of investor conference call, 9 August 2007, reported on Bloomberg.com, 25 November 2008.

12. Congressional Oversight Panel, June Oversight Report: The AIG Rescue, Its Impact on Markets, and the Government's Exit Strategy, 10 June 2010.

13. Shaxson, N., 2011, *Treasure Islands*, St Martin's Press.

14. Quoted in Ian Fraser, 2014, *Shredded: Inside RBS, the Bank That Broke Britain*, Edinburgh, Birlinn, p. 222. Royal Bank of Scotland was bailed out by the UK taxpayer four years, eight months, later.

15. Taleb, N.N., 2007, *The Black Swan: The Impact of the Highly Improbable*, London, Penguin, p. 43.

16. Edwards, J.S.S., Kay, J.A. and Mayer, C.P., 1987, *The Economic Analysis of Accounting Profitability*, Oxford, Oxford University Press.

17. Curiously, the play was a hit in London's West End but a flop on Broadway.

18. McLean, B., and Elkind, P., 2003, *The Smartest Guys in the Room: The Amazing Rise and Scandalous Fall of Enron*, New York, Penguin, p. 41.

19. Galbraith, J.K., 1955, *The Great Crash, 1929*, London, Hamish Hamilton, pp. 137–9.

20. Munger, C.T., 2000, 'Talk of Charles T. Munger to Breakfast Meeting of the Philanthropy Round Table', remarks at Philanthropy Round Table, Pasadena, CA, 10 November.

21. In a further twist, banks hold a 'trading book', to which mark-to-market accounting is applied, and a 'banking book', in which it is not. This creates obvious—and rewarding—scope to arbitrage assets between the two.

22. In a further self-referential twist, if there was no actual market you could estimate what the price would have been if there had been a market, by reference to the prices of securities for which there was a market—'mark to model'.

23. The application of mark-to-market accounting has become controversial in the European banking sector. Not—as one might naïvely expect—when credit markets were roaring between 2003 and 2007, and banks and bankers used imaginary profits from the securitisation of loans to boost profits, bonuses and balance sheets. The controversy about the accounting convention began after the crash, when many of the complex instruments that had been sold earlier at ever fancier prices became virtually unsaleable. As had always been true but was now belatedly recognised, nobody really knew or understood what was in them. The result was that these assets could only be 'marked to market' at very low prices. Banks argued—perhaps with some justice—that mark-to-market treatment understated their value.

24. Lucchetti, A., and Timiraos, N., 2010, 'After $9 Billion Loss, Trader Revives Career', *The Wall Street Journal*, 13 September.

25. Buffett, W., 1989, Chairman's Letter to the Shareholders of Berkshire Hathaway Inc.

26. Partnoy, F., 2009, *The Match King*, London, Profile Books, argues that, adjusted for inflation, Ivan Kreuger's Ponzi scheme was even larger.

27. Salz, A., 2013, *Salz Review: An Independent Review of Barclays' Business Practices*, London, April. provides an account of how this was the case at Barclays.

28. Basel Committee on Banking Supervision (BCBS), 2010, An assessment of the long-term economic impact of stronger capital and liquidity requirements, Basel, Bank for International Settlements, 21.

29. Draghi, M., 2012, 'Speech by Mario Draghi President of the European Central Bank', remarks at Global Investment Conference, London, 26 July.

30. Vickers, J.S., 2011, *Independent Commission on Banking final report: recommendations*, London, The Stationery Office.

31. Final Report: Oral and Written Evidence, 23 November 2011, HC 680 2011-12, Ev 62. House of Commons Treasury Committee, Independent Commission on Banking.

32. Haldane, A.G., 2010, 'The $100 Billion Question', remarks at the Institute of Regulation & Risk, Hong Kong, 30 March.

33. International Monetary Fund, 2014, Global Financial Stability Report: Moving from Liquidity- to Growth-Driven Markets, Washington, DC, April, p. 104.

34. *The Banker* magazine estimated total banking profits in 2013 at $920 billion, the highest ever figure, of which around one-third relates to Chinese banks.

## Chapter 5: Capital Allocation

1. Arlidge, J., 2009, "'I'm Doing God's Work.' Meet Mr. Goldman Sachs', *The Sunday Times*, 8 November. It was not only Goldman that benefited from heavenly inspiration; Jeff Skilling claimed to have been doing God's work at Enron: McLean, B., and Elkind, P., 2003, *The Smartest Guys in the Room: The Amazing Rise and Scandalous Fall of Enron*, New York, Penguin, p. xxv.

2. Putnam, R.D, 2000, *Bowling Alone*, New York, Simon and Schuster, brought the concept of social capital and the phrase into wide modern usage.

3. The data in the widely cited book by Thomas Piketty (2014) relies primarily on the first of these approaches—the assessment of physical assets—although much of his discussion would seem to concern the second.

4. The quality of these estimates is not high, especially in relation to long-lived public assets. The principal method of calculation applies the 'perpetual inventory' method, which uses a solera principle in which reported new investment is added each year and the existing stock revalued and depreciated. In the case of, for example, the London Underground it is very unclear what principles should be applied in attaching a value.

5. See, for example, Wallison, P.J., 2011, Dissenting Statement, Financial Crisis Inquiry Commission, January.

6. Useful starting-points are Lewis, M.M., 2010, *The Big Short: Inside the Doomsday Machine*, London, Allen Lane, and Mian, A., and Sufi, A., 2014, *House of Debt: How They (and You) Caused the Great Recession, and How We Can Prevent It from Happening Again*, Chicago and London, The University of Chicago Press.

7. Goldman Sachs Annual Report, 2013.

8. Lewis, M.M., 2004, *Moneyball: The Art of Winning an Unfair Game*, New York and London, W.W. Norton.

9. An excellent description of the financial aspects of this is Janeway, W.H., 2012, *Doing Capitalism in the Innovation Economy*, Cambridge, Cambridge University Press.

10. Simon, H., 1996, *Hidden Champions*, Boston, MA, Harvard Business; *Hidden Champions of the 21st Century*, London and New York, School Press, Springer Verlag, 2009.

## Chapter 6: The Deposit Channel

1. There is now an extensive—and dubious—business of brand valuation; see, for example, http://www.interbrand.com/en/BestRetailBrands/2014/best-retail-brands-methodology.aspx, for accounting for intangible assets.

2. Whittard, D., 2012, '1 The UK's External Balance Sheet—the International Investment Position (IIP)', Office for National Statistics, March.

3. Murray, A., 2009, 'Paul Volcker: Think More Boldly', *The Wall Street Journal*, 14 December.

4. Felix Martin provides the fascinating historical example of the stone fei, in Micronesia, where stones continued to be used as a unit of account even when they had fallen in the sea. Martin, F., 2013, *Money: The Unauthorised Biography*, London, Bodley Head.

5. Taleb, N.N., 2012, *Antifragile: Things That Gain from Disorder*, New York, Random House.

6. Taylor, M., 2014, 'Banks Have Failed to Exorcise Their Technical Gremlins', *Financial Times*, 30 January.

7. House of Commons Treasury Committee, The Future of Cheques, 24 August 2011, HC 1147, pp. 2010–12.

8. The research firm Hedge Fund Research puts the number of hedge funds in existence at around 10,000, of which an average of 1,000 close every year.

9. Buffett, W., 2002, Chairman's Letter to the Shareholders of Berkshire Hathaway Inc.

10. The asset in Deutsche Bank's balance sheet—that €777 billion—is the value of those outstanding derivative contracts which currently have a positive value. Under US GAAP, if one derivative contract shows a loss and another derivative contract with the same counterparty shows a profit, then you need record only the net profit or loss in trading with that counterparty. This opportunity to 'net' one contract against another applies even if one derivative is an interest rate swap and the other a forward foreign exchange contract.

11. Dodd-Frank Wall Street Reform and Consumer Protection Act, Ch. 17, 12 U.S.C., § 1851.

12. Vickers, J. S., 2011, *Independent Commission on Banking Final Report: Recommendations*, London, The Stationery Office.; Liikanen, E. (chair), 2012, *Report of the European Commission's High-level Expert Group on Bank Structural Reform*, EU Commission, October.

## Chapter 7: The Investment Channel

1. Theodore Roosevelt's trustbusters broke the original Standard Oil into many businesses, of which Standard Oil of New Jersey, subsequently Exxon, was the largest.

2. Andrews, S., 2010, 'Larry Fink's $12 Trillion Shadow', *Vanity Fair*, April.

3. 'Top Asset Management Firms', www.relbanks.com.

4. Galbraith, J.K., 1954, *The Great Crash*, Boston, MA, Houghton Mifflin.

5. McKinsey Global Institute, Mapping Global Capital Markets, 2013

6. Lenzner, R., 2009, '"Bid 'Em Up Bruce": A Winner, Hands Down', *Forbes*, 14 October.

7. And by Wasserstein's own autobiography, Wasserstein, B., *Big Deal*, New York, Warner, 1998. Burrough, B., and Helyar, J., 1990, *Barbarians at the Gate: The Fall of RJR Nabisco*, London, Arrow.

8. Bogle, J.C., 1999, *Common Sense on Mutual Funds: New Imperatives for the Intelligent Investor*, New York and Chichester, John Wiley.

9. Kay, J., 2009, *The Long and the Short of It: A Guide to Finance and Investment for Normally Intelligent People Who Aren't in the Industry*, London, The Erasmus Press.

10. See Cannacord Genuity, 2014, Annual investment trust handbook.

## Chapter 8: Regulation

1. Scotland has a different legal system.

2. Hoshi, T., 2001, 'What Happened to Japanese Banks?' *Monetary and Economic Studies*, 19 (1), February, pp. 1–29.

3. Tor, M., and Sarfraz, S., 2013, 'Largest 100 Banks in the World', *SNL Financial LC*, 23 December.

4. Mirrlees, J.A., et al., 2011, *Tax by Design*, Oxford, Oxford University Press.

5. I have written such a book, but a long time ago; Kay, J.A., and King, M.A., 1979, *The British Tax System*, Oxford, Clarendon Press, 5th edn, 1992.

6. Von Mises, L., 1927, *Liberalismus*, Jena, Gustav Fischer.

7. Hayek, F.A., 1944, *The Road to Serfdom*, London, Routledge & Kegan Paul.

8. This argument is developed powerfully in Bhidé, A., 2011, *A Call for Judgment*, New York, Oxford University Press.

9. Attributed to Clifford Stoll and Gary Schubert in Keeler, M.R., 2006, *Nothing to Hide*, Lincoln, NE, iUniverse, Inc., p.112.

10. Soble, R.L., and Dallos, R.E., 1975, *The Impossible Dream: The Equity Funding Story; The Fraud of the Century*, New York, G.P. Putnam's Sons.

11. Americans for Financial Reform, 11 December 2014.

12. Sunlight Foundation, 1 December 2009, 25 March 2013.

13. He 'would take no fees' for commercial endorsements or for lobbying or writing letters or making phone calls. He 'would accept no consulting fees'. 'Had it not been for the fact that I was able to sell some property that my brother, sister, and I inherited from our mother, I would practically be on relief, but with the sale of that property I am not financially embarrassed'. Harry Truman, 1957, reported in McCullough, D., 1992, *Truman*, New York, Simon & Schuster, p. 988.

14. ProPublica, 10 October 2013.

15. Markopolos, H., 2010, *No One Would Listen: A True Financial Thriller*, Hoboken, NJ, Wiley.

16. Cited in J.M. Smith and P.L. Murphy, 1958, *Liberty and Justice*, New York, Knopf.

17. Ferguson, C. (prod. and dir.), and Marrs, A. (prod.), 2010, *Inside Job*, United States, Sony Pictures Classics.

18. Stigler, G.J., 1971, 'The Theory of Economic Regulation', *The Bell Journal of Economics and Management Science*, 2 (1), Spring, pp. 3–21.

19. Dekker, S., 2012, *Just Culture*, Aldershot, Ashgate.

## Chapter 9: Economic Policy

1. Woodward, R.U., 2001, *Maestro: Greenspan's Fed and the American Boom*, New York and London, Simon & Schuster.

2. Greenspan, A., 2008, Statement to the House, Committee on Oversight and Government Reform, Hearing, 23 October (Serial 110-209).

3. Carlson, M.A., 2006, 'A Brief History of the 1987 Stock Market Crash with a Discussion of the Federal Reserve Response', *Finance and Economics Discussion Series 2007-13*, Divisions of Research & Statistics and Monetary Affairs Federal Reserve Board, p. 10.

4. Ibid., p. 19.

5. Ibid.

6. Bagehot, W., 1873, *Lombard Street: A Description of the Money Market*, New York, Scribner, Armstrong & Co.

7. Federal Reserve, 2014, Recent Balance Sheet Trends.

8. Bank of England, Annual Reports 2007–14, Financial Statements.

9. Reinhart, C.M., and Rogoff, K.S., 2010, 'Growth in a Time of Debt', *American Economic Review: Papers & Proceedings*, 100 (2), May, pp. 573–8.

10. Herndon, T., Ash, M., and Pollin, R., 2013, 'Does High Public Debt Consistently Stifle Economic Growth? A Critique of Reinhart and Rogoff', University of Amherst, Political Economic Research Institute Working Paper 322, has received almost as much attention as the original exercise.

11. The latest (2014) Trustees' report shows that the fund is adequate to pay current and projected benefits to 2042. The Congressional Budget Office regards this as pessimistic.

12. The 'answer' seems to be that very high rates of return would be obtained from equity investment. The confusions in this argument are too numerous to elaborate. The bread that pensioners eat is the bread that was baked today.

13. Kamstra, M.J., and Shiller, R.J., 2010, 'Trills Instead of T-Bills: It's Time to Replace Part of Government Debt with Shares in GDP', *The Economists' Voice*, 7 (3), September.

14. See the extensive discussion in Dilnot, 2011, *The Commission on Funding of Care and Support*, July.

15. Kotlikoff, L.J., 1992, *Generational Accounting: Knowing Who Pays, and When, for What We Spend*, New York, Free Press.

16. Brokaw, T., 1998, *The Greatest Generation*, New York, Random House.

17. First published in *The British Journal of Addiction*, Vol. 52, No. 2 (January 1957), p. 1, and later used as a footnote in *The Naked Lunch*.

18. International Labour Organization, 2012, Employee Distribution by Economic Activity and Occupation, OECD, 2013, Population and Employment by Main Activity.

19. New York State, Bureau of Labor Statistics, Labor Statistics for the New York City region.

20. City of London Corporation, 2013.

21. Greenwood, R., and Scharfstein, D., 2013, 'The Growth of Finance', *Journal of Economic Perspectives*, Vol. 27, 2, Spring, pp 3–28.

22. Banks, A., Hamroush, S., Taylor, C., and Hardie, M., 2014, 'An International Perspective on the UK—Gross Domestic Product', Office for National Statistics, 24 April.

23. See, in particular, Haldane, A., Brennan, S., and Madouras, V., 'What is the Contribution of the Financial Sector?' in Turner, A., et al., *The Future of Finance*, London, London School of Economics, 2010.

24. Haldane, A., Brennan, S., and Madouras, V., *What is the Contribution of the Financial Sector?* in Turner, A., et al., 2010, *The Future of Finance*, London, London School of Economics; Hood, Kyle K., 2013, 'Measuring the Services of Commercial Banks in the National Income and Products Accounts,' *Changes in Concepts and Methods in the 2013 Comprehensive Review*, Bureau of Economic Analysis.

25. IRS, Tax Statistics, by industry and in aggregate.

26. HM Revenue and Customs, 2014, Corporation Tax Statistics, Table 11.1A.

27. Bureau of Labor Statistics, Current Employment Statistics, Table B-1.

28. Salz Review, 2013, *An Independent Review of Barclays' Business Practices*, 3 April.

29. Barclays plc, 2014, *Annual Report 2013*, p. 122 (available from www.barclays.com).

30. Office for National Statistics, 2014, *The United Kingdom Balance of Payments Pink Book 2014*.

31. Reich, R.B., 1990, 'Who Is Us?', *Harvard Business Review*, January.

32. Partnoy, F., 2009, *FIASCO: Blood In the Water on Wall Street*, Profile Books, London.

## Chapter 10: Reform

1. Tobin, J., 1978, 'A Proposal for International Monetary Reform', *Eastern Economic Journal*, 4 (3–4), pp. 153–9.

2. Adams, R. McC., 1981, *Heartland of Cities*, Chicago, University of Chicago Press, p. xvii, in Tainter, J., 1988, *The Collapse of Complex Societies*, Cambridge, Cambridge University Press, p. 1.

3. Andrew Ross Sorkin's book of that title became a bestseller and even a film.

4. Tainter, J., 1988, *The Collapse of Complex Societies*, Cambridge, Cambridge University Press.

5. Perrow, C.B., 1984, *Normal Accidents: Living with High-Risk Technologies*, New York, Basic Books.

6. Admati, A.R., and Hellwig, M.F., 2013, *The Bankers' New Clothes: What's Wrong with Banking and What To Do about It*, Princeton and Oxford, Princeton University Press, pp. 176–83. Miles, D.K., Yang, J., and Marcheggiano, G., 2013, 'Optimal Bank Capital', *The Economic Journal*, 123 (567), pp. 1–37.

7. This is difficult to determine in any precise way. One indicator is the peak to trough fall in the S & P 500 index of US stocks, which was 50 per cent in 2000–2 and 54 per cent in 2008–9.

8. Smith, G., 2012, 'Why I Am Leaving Goldman Sachs', *The New York Times*, 14 March.

9. MacPherson *v.* Buick Motor Co., 217 N.Y. 382, 111 N.E. 1050 (1916).

10. Vickers, J.S., 2011, *Independent Commission on Banking Final Report: Recommendations*, London, HMSO.

11. Liikanen, E. (chair), 2012, *Report of the European Commission's High-Level Expert Group on Bank Structural Reform*, EU Commission, October.

12. See www.johnkay.com for contemporaneous assessments.

13. Rakoff, J.S., 2014, 'The Financial Crisis: Why Have No High-Level Executives Been Prosecuted?', *The New York Review of Books*, 9 January.

14. Farrell, M., 2014, 'J.P. Morgan Adds $2.6 Billion to Its $25 Billion Plus Tally of Recent Settlements', *The Wall Street Journal MoneyBeat*, 7 January.

15. Ibid.

16. The mechanism has also gained popularity because it has become a source of revenue, particularly for states. George Osborne, UK chancellor of the exchequer, gained cheap applause by donating fines to military charities.

17. Parliamentary Commission on Banking Standards, 2013, *Changing Banking for Good*, First Report of Session 2013–14, 12 June.

18. House of Commons Treasury Committee, 2012, Fixing LIBOR: Some Preliminary Findings, Vol. 2: Oral and Written Evidence, 4 July, HC 481-II 2012–13, Ev 10.

19. In October 2014 two directors of HSBC resigned, citing the new legal liabilities imposed on bank directors as the reason.

## Chapter 11: The Future of Finance

1. Sorkin, A.R., 2009, *Too Big to Fail: Inside the Battle to Save Wall Street*, London, Allen Lane, p. 525. The story is confirmed by Timothy Geithner, who was present at the meeting.

2. Goff, S., and Parker, G., 2011, 'Diamond Says Time for Remorse is Over', *Financial Times*, 11 January.

3. Zeleny, J., 2008, 'Obama Weighs Quick Undoing of Bush Policy', *The New York Times*, 9 November.

4. Johnson, S., and Kwak, J., 2010, *13 Bankers: The Wall Street Takeover and the Next Financial Meltdown*, New York, Random House.

5. Turner, A., 2009, 'How To Tame Global Finance', *Prospect*, 27 August.

6. The European Parliament imaginative funded Finance Watch to counter this lobbying, although the relative scale of its resources is minuscule. Schumann, H., 2012, 'Finance Watch: A Lobby to Break the Lobbies', *VoxEurop*, 23 February.

7. Keynes, J.M., 1936, *The General Theory of Employment, Interest and Money*, London, Macmillan, p. 383.

# Bibliography

Abrahamson, M., Jenkinson, T., and Jones, H., 2011, 'Why Don't U.S. Issuers Demand European Fees for IPOs?', *Journal of Finance*, 66 (6), December, pp. 2055–82.

Adams, J., 1995, *Risk: The Policy Implications of Risk Compensation and Plural Rationalities*, London, Routledge.

Adams, R., McC., 1981, *Heartland of Cities*, Chicago, University of Chicago Press.

Admati, A.R., and Hellwig, M.F., 2013, *The Bankers' New Clothes: What's Wrong with Banking and What To Do about It*, Princeton and Oxford, Princeton University Press.

Akerlof, G.A., 1970, 'The Market for "Lemons": Quality Uncertainty and the Market Mechanism', *Quarterly Journal of Economics*, 84 (3), pp. 488–500.

Albert, M., 1993, *Capitalisme contre capitalisme*, Paris, Seuil; trans. P. Haviland as *Capitalism vs Capitalism*, London, Whurr Publishers.

American Legal Institute, 2006, *Restatement (Third) of the Law of Agency*.

Americans for Financial Reform, 2014, 11 December, http://ourfinancialsecurity.org/#.

Andrews, S., 2010, 'Larry Fink's $12 Trillion Shadow', *Vanity Fair*, April.

ARCADIS, 2014, Global Built Asset Performance Index 2014.

Arlidge, J., 2009, '"I'm Doing God's Work": Meet Mr. Goldman Sachs', *The Sunday Times*, 8 November.

Armstrong *v.* Jackson, 1917, 2 KB 822.

Arner, D.W., 2009, 'The Competition of International Financial Centres and the Role of Law', *Economic Law as an Economic Good: Its Rule Function and Its Tool Function in the Competition of Systems*, ed. Meessen, K., Munich, Sellier, Chapter 16.

'As Goldman and Morgan Stanley Shift, a Wall St. Era Ends', 2008, *The Wall Street Journal DealBook*, 21 September.

Atkinson, A.B., and Morelli, S., 2014, *Chartbook of Economic Inequality*, ECINEQ Working Paper.

Augar, P., 2006, *The Greed Merchants: How the Investment Banks Played the Free Market Game*, London, Penguin.

Bagehot, W., 1873, *Lombard Street: A Description of the Money Market*, New York, Scribner, Armstrong & Co.

Bakija, J., Cole, A., and Heim, B.T., 2012, *Jobs and Income Growth of Top Earners and the Laws of Changing Income Inequality: Evidence from US Tax Return Data*, Office of Tax Analysis.

Bank of England, Annual Reports 2007–14, financial statements.

Banks, A., Hamroush, S., Taylor, C., and Hardie, M., 2014, 'An International Perspective on the UK—Gross Domestic Product', Office for National Statistics, 24 April.

Basel Committee on Banking Supervision (BCBS), 2010, 'An Assessment of the Long-Term Economic Impact of Stronger Capital and Liquidity Requirements', Basel, Bank for International Settlements.

Berle, A., and Means G., 1932, *The Modern Corporation and Private Property*, New York, Macmillan.

Bernanke, B.S., 2004, 'The Great Moderation', remarks by Governor Ben S. Bernanke at the meetings of the Eastern Economic Association, Washington, DC, 20 February.

Bernanke, B.S., 2006, 'Modern Risk Management and Banking Supervision', remarks at the Stonier Graduate School of Banking, Washington, DC, 12 June.

Bhidé, A., 2011, *A Call for Judgment*, New York, Oxford University Press.

BIS, 2013, *Triennial Central Bank Survey: Foreign Exchange Turnover in April 2013: Preliminary Global Results*, Basel, Bank for International Settlements.

Black, F., and Scholes, M., 1973, 'The Pricing of Options and Corporate Liabilities', *Journal of Political Economy*, 81 (3), May–June, pp. 637–54.

Bloomberg Billionaires, 2012, http://www.bloomberg.com/billionaires/2014-07-18/cya, *Bloomberg Businessweek*, 20 February.

Bogle, J.C., 1999, *Common Sense on Mutual Funds: New Imperatives for the Intelligent Investor*, New York and Chichester, John Wiley.

Brandeis, L., 1914, *Other People's Money*, New York, F.A. Stokes.

Brittan, S., 1973, *Is There an Economic Consensus?* London, Macmillan.

Brokaw, T., 1998, *The Greatest Generation*, New York, Random House.

Brumbaugh, R.D., and Carron, A.S., 1987, 'Thrift Industry Crisis: Causes and Solutions', *Brookings Papers on Economic Activity*, 18 (2), 1987, pp. 349–88.

Bryan, L.L., 1988, *Breaking Up the Bank: Rethinking an Industry under Siege*, Homewood, IL, Dow Jones-Irwin.

Buffett, W., 1988, Chairman's Letter to the Shareholders of Berkshire Hathaway Inc.

Buffett, W., 1989, Chairman's Letter to the Shareholders of Berkshire Hathaway Inc.

Buffett, W., 2002, Chairman's Letter to the Shareholders of Berkshire Hathaway Inc.

Bureau of Investigative Journalism, 2012, http://www.thebureauinvestigates.com, 9 July.

Burrough, B., and Helyar, J., 1990, *Barbarians at the Gate: The Fall of RJR Nabisco*, London, Arrow.

Burroughs, W.S., 1957, *Letter from a Master Addict to Dangerous Drugs*, first published in *The British Journal of Addiction*, Vol. 52, No. 2 (January 1957), p. 1, and later used as footnotes in *The Naked Lunch*.

Cannacord Genuity, 2014, Annual investment trust handbook.

Carlill *v.* Carbolic Smoke Ball Company, 1892, 2QB 489.

Carlson, M.A., 2006, 'A Brief History of the 1987 Stock Market Crash with a Discussion of the Federal Reserve Response', *Finance and Economics Discussion Series 2007–13*, Divisions of Research and Statistics and Monetary Affairs Federal Reserve Board, p. 10.

Cassidy, J., 2002, *Dot.con: How America Lost Its Mind and Money in the Internet Era*, New York, HarperCollins.

Ceresney, A., 2013, 'Statement on the Tourre Verdict', US Securities and Exchange Commission Public Statement, 1 August.

Chan, S., and Story, L., 2010, 'Goldman Pays $550 Million to Settle Fraud Case', *The New York Times*, 15 July.

Chernow, R., 2010, *The House of Morgan: An American Banking Dynasty and the Rise of Modern Finance*, New York, Grove Press.

Chrisafis, A., 2012, 'Nicolas Sarkozy's Worst Election Fear Realized with Loss of AAA Rating', *The Guardian*, 13 January.

Citizens United *v.* Federal Election Commission, 2010, 558 U.S. No. 08-205.

*CNNMoney*, 1999, 'End of an Era for Goldman', 3 May.

Coates, J.M., and Herbert, J., 2008, 'Endogenous Steroids and Financial Risk Taking on a London Trading Floor', *Proceedings of the National Academy of Sciences*, 105 (16), pp. 6167–72.

Cohan, W.D., 2011, *Money and Power: How Goldman Sachs Came To Rule the World*, New York, Random House.

Congressional Oversight Panel, June Oversight Report, 2010, 'The AIG Rescue, Its Impact on Markets, and the Government's Exit Strategy', 10 June.

Conrad, J., 1902, *Typhoon*, New York, Putnam.

Cookson, R., 2012, 'Here Be Dragons: Anthony Bolton', *Financial Times*, 12 May.

Crisafulli, P., 2011, *The House of Dimon: How J.P. Morgan's Jamie Dimon Rose to the Top of the Financial World*, New Jersey, John Wiley and Sons.

Dekker, S., 2012, *Just Culture*, Aldershot, Ashgate.

Dilnot, A., 2011, *The Commission on Funding of Care and Support*, July, http://webarchive. nationalarchives.gov.uk/20130221130239/http://dilnotcommission.dh.gov.uk/.

Dodd-Frank Wall Street Reform and Consumer Protection Act, Ch. 17, 12 U.S.C., § 1851.

Donne, J., 1987, *Devotions upon Emergent Occasions* (originally published 1624), ed. Raspa, A., New York, Oxford University Press.

Draghi, M., 2012, 'Speech by Mario Draghi President of the European Central Bank', remarks at Global Investment Conference, London, 26 July.

Duguid, A., 2014, *On the Brink: How a Crisis Transformed Lloyd's of London*, Basingstoke, Palgrave Macmillan.

Edwards, J.S.S., Kay, J.A., and Mayer C.P., 1987, *The Economic Analysis of Accounting Profitability*, Oxford, Oxford University Press.

El Paso Corporation, Shareholder Litigation, 2012, Del. Ch 41 A.3d 432.

Epstein, G.A. (ed.), 2005, *Financialisation and the World Economy*, Cheltenham, Edward Elgar, 2005.

Farrell, M., 2014, 'J.P. Morgan Adds $2.6 Billion to Its $25 Billion Plus Tally of Recent Settlements', *The Wall Street Journal MoneyBeat*, 7 January.

Federal Reserve, 2014, Recent Balance Sheet Trends.

Ferguson, C. (prod. and dir.), and Marrs, A. (prod.), 2010, *Inside Job*, United States, Sony Pictures Classics.

Final Report: Oral and Written Evidence, 2011, HC 680 2011–12, Ev 62, 23 November. House of Commons Treasury Committee, Independent Commission on Banking.

*Financial Times*, 2009, 'Government's Response like That of a Rowdy Drinker in a Bar Brawl', 5 July.

Fitzgerald, F.S., 1925, *The Great Gatsby*, New York, Charles Scribner's Sons.

Flyvberg, B., 2003, *Megaprojects and Risk*, Cambridge, Cambridge University Press.

Fox, J., 2009, *The Myth of the Rational Market*, New York, Harper Business.

Francis, J., 1850, 'Chronicles and Characters of the Stock Exchange', *The Church of England Quarterly Review*, 27 (6), pp. 128–55.

Fraser, I., 2014, *Shredded: Inside RBS, the Bank That Broke Britain*, Edinburgh, Birlinn.

Friedman, M., and Friedman, R.D., 1980, *Free to Choose*, San Diego, CA, Harcourt.

Galbraith, J.K., 1954, *The Great Crash*, Boston, MA, Houghton Mifflin.

Galton, F., 1907, 'Vox Populi (The Wisdom of Crowds)', *Nature*, 1949 (75), pp. 450–51.

Geithner, T., 2006, 'Risk Management Challenges in the U.S. Financial System', remarks at the Global Association of Risk Professionals 7th Annual Risk Management Convention and Exhibition, New York City, 28 February.

Geithner, T., 2014, *Stress Test*, New York, Crown.

Gilbert, R.A., 1986, 'Requiem for Regulation Q: What It Did and Why It Passed Away', *Federal Reserve Bank of St. Louis Review*, February, 68 (2), pp. 22–37.

Goff, S., and Parker, G., 2011, 'Diamond Says Time for Remorse is Over', *Financial Times*, 11 January.

Goldman Sachs Code of Business Conduct and Ethics, 2014. Last accessed: 31 July, http://www.goldmansachs.com/investor-relations/corporate-governance/corporate -governance-documents/revise-code-of-conduct.pdf.

Goodman, A., 2013, 'Top 40 Buffett-isms: Inspiration To Become a Better Investor', *Forbes*, 25 September.

Greenspan, A., 1999, 'Financial Derivatives', speech to the Futures Industry Association, Boca Raton, FL, 19 March.

Greenspan, A., 2008, Statement to the House, Committee on Oversight and Government Reform, Hearing, 23 October (Serial 110-209).

Greenwood, R., and Sharfstein, D., 2013, 'The Growth of Finance', *Journal of Economic Perspectives*, Vol. 27, No. 2, Spring.

Guerrera, F., 2009, 'Welch Condemns Share Price Focus', *Financial Times*, 12 March.

Hair, P.E.H., 1971, 'Deaths from Violence in Britain: A Tentative Survey', *Population Studies*, 25 (1), pp. 5–24.

Haldane, A., Brennan, S., and Madouras, V., 2010, 'What is the Contribution of the Financial Sector?', in *The Future of Finance*, ed. Turner, A., et al., London, London School of Economics.

Haldane, A.G., 2010, 'Patience and Finance', Oxford China Business Forum, Beijing, 2 September.

Haldane, A.G., 2010, 'The $100 Billion Question', remarks at the Institute of Regulation and Risk, Hong Kong, 30 March.

Harris, R., 2012, *The Fear Index*, London, Arrow Books.

Hayek, F.A., 1944, *The Road to Serfdom*, London, Routledge & Kegan Paul.

Henderson, P.D., 1977, 'Two British Errors: Their Probable Size and Some Possible Lessons', *Oxford Economic Papers*, Vol. 29, No. 2, July, pp. 159–205.

Herndon, T., Ash, M., and Pollin, R., 2013, 'Does High Public Debt Consistently Stifle Economic Growth? A Critique of Reinhart and Rogoff', University of Amherst, Political Economic Research Institute Working Paper 322.

Hoshi, T., 2001, 'What Happened to Japanese Banks?' *Monetary and Economic Studies*, 19 (1), February.

House of Commons Treasury Committee, 2012, Fixing LIBOR: Some Preliminary Findings, Vol. 2: Oral and Written Evidence, 4 July, HC 481-II 2012–13, Ev 10.

House of Commons Treasury Committee, 2011, The Future of Cheques, 24 August, HC 1147 pp. 2010–12.

Institute for Fiscal Studies, 2011, 'Why Did Britain's Households Get Richer?', London.

International Labour Organization, 2012, 'Employee Distribution by Economic Activity and Occupation', Geneva.

International Monetary Fund, 2014, Global Financial Stability Report, https://www.imf.org/external/pubs/ft/gfsr/2014/02/pdf/text.pdf.

Isaacson, W., 2013, Steve Jobs: The Exclusive Biography, New York, Little Brown.

Janeway, W.H., 2012, Doing Capitalism in the Innovation Economy, Cambridge, Cambridge University Press.

Jensen, M.C., and Meckling, W.H., 1976 'Theory of the Firm: Governance, Residual Claims and Organizational Forms', Journal of Financial Economics (JFE), Vol. 3, No. 4.

Johnson, S., and Kwak, J., 2010, 13 Bankers: The Wall Street Takeover and the Next Financial Meltdown, New York, Random House.

Josephson, M., 1934, The Robber Barons: The Great American Capitalists, 1861–1901, New York, Harcourt, Brace & Co.

Kahneman, D., 2002, 'Mapping Bounded Rationality: A Perspective on Intuitive Judgment and Choice', Nobel Lecture, Stockholm, Sweden, 8 December.

Kahneman, D., 2011, Thinking Fast and Slow, New York, Farrar, Straus and Giroux.

Kamstra, M.J., and Shiller, R.J., 2010, 'Trills Instead of T-Bills: It's Time to Replace Part of Government Debt with Shares in GDP', The Economists' Voice, 7 (3), September.

Kay, J., 2003, The Truth about Markets, London, Allen, Lane.

Kay, J., 2009, The Long and the Short of It: A Guide to Finance and Investment for Normally Intelligent People Who Aren't in the Industry, London, The Erasmus Press.

Kay, J., 2010, Obliquity, London, Profile Books.

Kay, J., 2012, 'The Kay Review of UK Equity Markets and Long-Term Decision Making', Final Report, https://www.gov.uk/government/uploads/system/uploads/attachment_data/file/253454/bis-12-917-kay-review-of-equity-markets-final-report.pdf.

Kay, J.A., and King, M.A., 1979, 5th edn 1992, The British Tax System, Oxford, Clarendon Press.

Keeler, M.R., 2006, Nothing to Hide, Lincoln, NE, iUniverse, Inc.

Keynes, J.M., 1936, The General Theory of Employment, Interest and Money, London, Macmillan.

Kindleberger, C.P., 1978, Manias, Panics, and Crashes: A History of Financial Crises, London, Macmillan.

King, A., and Crewe, I., 2013, The Blunders of Our Governments, London, Oneworld.

Kohn, D.L., 2005, 'Commentary: Has Financial Development Made the World Riskier?', Proceedings, Federal Reserve Bank of Kansas City, August, pp. 371–9.

Kotlikoff, L.J., 1992, Generational Accounting: Knowing Who Pays, and When, for What We Spend, New York, Free Press.

Kynaston, D., 2011, City of London: The History: 1815–2000, London, Chatto and Windus.

Lack, S., 2012, The Hedge Fund Mirage: The Illusion of Big Money and Why It's Too Good To Be True, Hoboken, NJ, Wiley.

Langley, M., 2003, *Tearing Down the Walls*, New York, Simon & Schuster.

Lenzner, R., 2009, "'Bid 'Em Up Bruce": A Winner, Hands Down', *Forbes*, 14 October.

Levine, R., 2005, 'Finance and Growth: Theory and Evidence', in, *Handbook of Economic Growth*, ed. Aghion, P., and Durlauf, S.N., Amsterdam, Elsevier, pp. 865–934.

Lewis, M.M., 1989, *Liar's Poker: Two Cities, True Greed*, London, Hodder and Stoughton.

Lewis, M.M., 2004, *Moneyball: The Art of Winning an Unfair Game*, New York and London, W.W. Norton.

Lewis, M.M., 2010, *The Big Short: Inside the Doomsday Machine*, London, Allen Lane.

Lewis, M.M., 2011, *Boomerang: The Meltdown Tour*, London, Allen Lane.

Liikanen, E. (chair), 2012, *Report of the European Commission's High-Level Expert Group on Bank Structural Reform*, EU Commission, October.

Litan, R.E., 1988, 'The Future of Banking: Are "Narrow" Banks the Answer?', *Proceedings*, Federal Reserve Bank of Chicago, pp. 639–45.

Loewenstein, G., 1987, 'Anticipation and the Value of Delayed Consumption', *Economic Journal*, 97 (387), September.

Lucas Jr, R.E., 2003, 'Macroeconomic Priorities', *The American Economic Review*, 93 (1), March, pp. 1–14.

Lucchetti, A., and Timiraos, N., 2010, 'After $9 Billion Loss, Trader Revives Career', *The Wall Street Journal*, 13 September.

Macmillan, H., 1957, 'Leader's Speech', remarks at Conservative Party rally, Bedford, 20 July.

Malkiel, B.G., 2012, *A Random Walk down Wall Street*, 10th edn, New York and London, W.W. Norton.

Manne, H.G., 1965, 'Mergers and the Market for Corporate Control', *The Journal of Political Economy*, 73 (2), April, pp. 110–20.

Markopolos, H., 2010, *No One Would Listen: A True Financial Thriller*, Hoboken, NJ, Wiley.

Martin, F., 2013, *Money: The Unauthorised Biography*, London, Bodley Head.

McArdle, M., 2009, 'Why Goldman Always Wins', *The Atlantic*, 1 October.

McCardie, J., 1917, Armstrong *v.* Jackson, 2KB 822.

McCullough, D., 1992, *Truman*, New York, Simon & Schuster.

McLean, B., and Elkind, P., 2003, *The Smartest Guys in the Room: The Amazing Rise and Scandalous Fall of Enron*, New York, Penguin.

Meeker, M., 1995, *The Internet Report*, New York, Morgan Stanley.

Megginson, W.L., and Netter, J.M., 2001, 'From State to Market: A Survey of Empirical Studies on Privatization', *Journal of Economic Literature*, 39 (2), June, pp. 321–89.

Mian, A., and Sufi, A., 2014, *House of Debt: How They (and You) Caused the Great Recession, and How We Can Prevent It from Happening Again*, Chicago and London, The University of Chicago Press.

Miles, D.K., Yang, J., and Marcheggiano, G., 2013, 'Optimal Bank Capital', *The Economic Journal*, 123 (567), pp.1–37.

Mirrlees J.A., et al., 2011, *Tax by Design*, Oxford, Oxford University Press.

Modigliani, F., and Miller, M.H., 1958, 'The Cost of Capital, Corporation Finance and the Theory of Investment', *The American Economic Review*, 48 (3), June, pp. 261–97.

Morgenson, G., and Rosner, J., 2011, *Reckles$ Endangerment*, New York, Times Books, Henry Holt & Co.

Munger, C.T., 2000, 'Talk of Charles T. Munger to Breakfast Meeting of the Philanthropy Round Table', remarks at Philanthropy Round Table, Pasadena, CA, 10 November.

Murphy, A.E., 1978, 'Money in an Economy without Banks: The Case of Ireland', *The Manchester School*, 46 (1), March, pp. 41–50.

Murray, A., 2009, 'Paul Volcker: Think More Boldly', *The Wall Street Journal*, 14 December.

Nakamoto, M., and Wighton, D., 2007, 'Citigroup Chief Stays Bullish on Buy-Outs', *Financial Times*, 9 July.

Neal, L., 1990, *The Rise of Financial Capitalism: International Capital Markets in the Age of Reason*, New York, Cambridge University Press.

OECD, 2011, Life Expectancy and Healthy Life Expectancy at Age 65, http://www.oecd-ilibrary.org/.

ONS, 2013, Business Register and Employment Survey, http://www.ons.gov.uk/ons/rel/bus-register/business-register-employment-survey/2013-provisional/index.html.

Parliamentary Commission on Banking Standards, 2013, *Changing Banking for Good*, First Report of Session 2013–14, 12 June.

Partnoy, F., 2009, *The Match King*, London, Profile Books.

Partnoy, F., 2009, *FIASCO: Blood In the Water on Wall Street*, London, Profile Books.

Pecora, F., 1939, *Wall Street under Oath: The Story of Our Modern Money-Changers*, New York, Simon and Schuster.

Perrow, C.B., 1984, *Normal Accidents: Living with High-Risk Technologies*, New York, Basic Books.

Philippon, T., and Reshef, A., 2012, 'Wages and Human Capital in the US Financial Industry, 1909–2006', Quarterly Journal of Economics, 127 (4): 1551–1609.

Philips, C.B., Kinniry Jr, F.M., Schlanger, T., and Hirt, J.M., 2014, 'The Case for Index-Fund Investing', Vanguard Research, April, https://advisors.vanguard.com/VGApp/iip/site/advisor/researchcommentary/article/IWE_InvComCase4Index.

Piketty, T., 2014, *Capital in the Twenty-First Century*, Cambridge, MA, The Belknap Press of Harvard University Press.

Porter, G.E., and Trifts, J.W., 2014, 'The Career Paths of Mutual Fund Managers: The Role of Merit', *Financial Analysts Journal*, 70 (4), July/August, pp. 55–71.

Potts QC, R., Erskine Chambers, 24 June 1997, para. 5, citing Wilson *v.* Jones, (1867) 2 Exch. Div. 150; cited in Kimball-Stanley A., 2008, 'Insurance and Credit Default Swaps: Should Like Things Be Treated Alike?', *Connecticut Insurance Law Journal*, 15 (1), p. 247.

ProPublica, 2013, 10 October, http://www.propublica.org/article/ny-fed-fired-examiner-who-took-on-goldman.

Putnam, R.D, 2000, *Bowling Alone*, New York, Simon and Schuster.

Rajan, R.G., 2005, 'Has Financial Development Made the World Riskier?', *Proceedings*, Federal Reserve Bank of Kansas City, August, pp. 313–69.

Rakoff, J.S., 2014, 'The Financial Crisis: Why Have No High-Level Executives Been Prosecuted?', *The New York Review of Books*, 9 January.

Ramsey, F.P., 1926, 'Truth and Probability', in Ramsey, F.P., 1931, *The Foundations of Mathematics and other Logical Essays*, ed. Braithwaite, R.B., London, Kegan, Paul, Trench, Trubner & Co.

Rappaport, A., 1986. *Creating Shareholder Value: The New Standard for Business Performance*. New York, Free Press.

Rawnsley, J.H., 1995, *Going for Broke: Nick Leeson and the Collapse of Barings Bank*, London, HarperCollins.

Reader, W.J., 1970–75, *Imperial Chemical Industries: A History*, London, Oxford University Press.

Reich, R.B., 1990, 'Who Is Us?', *Harvard Business Review*, January.

Reinhart, C.M., and Rogoff, K.S., 2010, 'Growth in a Time of Debt', *American Economic Review: Papers & Proceedings*, 100 (2), May, pp. 573–8.

Rieffel, A., 2003, *Restructuring Sovereign Debt: The Case for Ad Hoc Machinery*, Washington, DC, Brookings Institution Press, pp. 289–94.

Roosevelt, T., 1975, *The Autobiography, Condensed from the Original Edition, Supplemented by Letters, Speeches, and Other Writings*, ed. Andrews, W., New York, Charles Scribner's Sons.

Rubin, R., 2004, *In an Uncertain World*, New York, Random House.

Salmon, F., 2009, 'Recipe for Disaster', *Wired*, 22 March.

Salz, A., 2013, *Salz Review: An Independent Review of Barclays' Business Practices*, London, April.

Schumann, H., 2012 'Finance Watch: A Lobby to Break the Lobbies', *VoxEurop*, 23 February.

Sedgwick, R., 1970, *The House of Commons 1715–1754*, New York, Oxford University Press.

Senor, D., and Singer, S., 2009, *Start-Up Nation: The Story of Israel's Economic Miracle*, London, Little, Brown.

Shaxson, N., 2011, *Treasure Islands*, New York, St Martin's Press.

Shiller, R.J., 1981, 'Do Stock Prices Move Too Much To Be Justified by Subsequent Changes in Dividends?', *The American Economic Review*, 71 (3), June, pp. 421–36.

Simon, H., 1996, *Hidden Champions*, Boston, MA, Harvard Business School, HBS Press.

Simon, H., 2009, *Hidden Champions of the 21st Century*, London and New York, Springer Verlag.

Sinclair, U., 1906, *The Jungle*, London, Werner Laurie.

Sinclair, U., 1994, *I, Candidate for Governor: And How I Got Licked*, orig. pub. 1935, London, University of California Press.

Smith, A., 1776, *An Inquiry into the Nature and Causes of the Wealth of Nations*, 5th edn, 1904, ed. Edwin Cannan, London, Methuen.

Smith, G., 2012, 'Why I Am Leaving Goldman Sachs', *The New York Times*, 14 March.

Smith, J.M., and Murphy, P.L., 1958, *Liberty and Justice*, New York, Knoff.

Soble, R.L., and Dallos, R.E., 1975, *The Impossible Dream: The Equity Funding Story, The Fraud of the Century*, New York, G.P. Putnam's Sons.

Sorkin, A.R., 2009, *Too Big To Fail: Inside the Battle To Save Wall Street*, London, Allen Lane.

Stafford, P., 2010, 'Spread Networks Unveils Managed Services', *Financial Times*, 22 November.

Stephens, P., 1996, *Politics and the Pound: The Conservatives' Struggle with Sterling*, London, Macmillan.

Stigler, G.J., 1971, 'The Theory of Economic Regulation', *The Bell Journal of Economics and Management Science*, 2 (1), Spring, pp. 3–21.

Storrs, F., 2006, 'The 50 Wealthiest Bostonians', *Boston Magazine*, March.

Summers, L.H., 1985, 'On Economics and Finance', *Journal of Finance*, XL (3), July, pp. 633–5.

Summers, L.H., 2000, Remarks of Treasury Secretary Lawrence H. Summers to the Securities Industry Association, Office of Public Affairs, 9 November.

Summers, L.H., 2004, 'Fourth Annual Marshall J. Seidman Lecture on Health Policy', remarks at Harvard University, Boston, MA, 27 April.

Summers, L.H., 2005, 'General Discussion: Has Financial Development Made the World Riskier?', *Proceedings*, Federal Reserve Bank of Kansas City, August, pp. 387–97.

Sunlight Foundation, 1 December 2009, 25 March 2013, http://sunlightfoundation.com.

Surowiecki, J.M., 2005, *The Wisdom of Crowds: Why the Many Are Smarter than the Few*, London, Abacus.

Taibbi, M., 2009, 'The Great American Bubble Machine', *Rolling Stone*, 9 July.

Tainter, J., 1988, *The Collapse of Complex Societies*, Cambridge, Cambridge University Press.

Taleb, N.N., 2001, *Fooled by Randomness: The Hidden Role of Chance in the Markets and in Life*, London and New York, Texere.

Taleb, N.N., 2007, *The Black Swan: The Impact of the Highly Improbable*, London, Penguin.

Taleb, N.N., 2012, *Antifragile: Things That Gain from Disorder*, New York, Random House.

Tarbell, I.M., 1904, *The History of the Standard Oil Company*, New York, McClure, Phillips & Co.

Taylor, M., 2014, 'Banks Have Failed To Exorcise Their Technical Gremlins', *Financial Times*, 30 January.

Tett, G., 2010. *Fool's Gold*, New York, Free Press.

Tett, G., 2013, 'An Interview with Alan Greenspan', *FT Magazine*, 25 October.

Tobin, J., 1978, 'A Proposal for International Monetary Reform', *Eastern Economic Journal*, 4 (3–4), pp.153–9.

Tolstoy, L.N., 1886, *Anna Karenina,* trans. N. Haskell Dole, New York, Thomas Y. Crowell & Co.

Tonnies, F., 1887, *Gemeinschaft und Gesellschaft*, Leipzig, Fues; trans. M. Weber, 1978, as *Economy and Society,* Oakland, CA, University of California Press.

Tor, M., and Sarfraz, S., 2013, 'Largest 100 Banks in the World', *SNL Financial LC*, 23 December.

Tuckett, D., 2011, *Minding the Markets*, London, Palgrave Macmillan.

Turner, A., 2009, 'How To Tame Global Finance', *Prospect*, 27 August.

US Bureau of the Census, 2013, 'Income, Poverty and Health Insurance Coverage in the US', http://www.census.gov/prod/2013pubs/p60-245.pdf.

Van Agtmael, A., 2007, *The Emerging Markets Century: How a New Breed of World-Class Companies Is Overtaking the World,* London, Simon and Schuster.

Vickers, J.S., 2011, *Independent Commission on Banking Final Report: Recommendations*, London, HMSO.

Voigtländer, M., 2009, 'Why Is the German Homeownership Rate So Low?', *Housing Studies*, 24 (3), pp. 355–72.

Von Mises, L., 1927, *Liberalismus*, Jena, Gustav Fischer.

Wallison, P.J., 2011, Dissenting Statement, Financial Crisis Inquiry Commission, January.

Wasserstein, B., 1998, *Big Deal,* New York, Warner.

Welch, J.F., 1981, 'Growing Fast in a Slow-Growth Economy', Speech to financial community representatives, Hotel Pierre, New York, 8 December.

Whittard, D., 2012, 'The UK's External Balance Sheet: The International Investment Position (IIP)', Office for National Statistics, March, http://www.ons.gov.uk/ons/rel/bop/the-international-investment-position/2010/art-uk-s-iip.html.

Wolf, M., 2008, *Fixing Global Finance*, Baltimore, MD, The Johns Hopkins University Press.

Wolfe, H., 1930, *The Uncelestial City*, London, Gollancz.

Wolfe, T. 1987, *The Bonfire of the Vanities*, New York, Farrar, Straus and Giroux.

Woodward, R.U., 2001, *Maestro: Greenspan's Fed and the American Boom*, New York and London, Simon and Schuster.

Zeleny, J., 2008, 'Obama Weighs Quick Undoing of Bush Policy', *The New York Times*, 9 November.

Ziegler, P.S., 1988, *The Sixth Great Power: Barings, 1765–1929*, London, Collins.

Zuckerman, G., 2010, *The Greatest Trade Ever: How John Paulson Bet against the Markets and Made $20 Billion*, London, Viking.

Zweig, J., 2011, 'Keynes: He Didn't Say Half of What He Said. Or Did He?', *The Wall Street Journal MarketBeat*, 11 February.

# Index

**JOHN KAY** is a visiting professor at the London School of Economics and a fellow of St John's College, Oxford University. He is a director of several public companies and contributes a weekly column to the *Financial Times*. Kay is the author of nine previously published books and the coauthor of *The British Tax System* with Mervyn King. He lives in London. Follow him at @JohnKayFT and www.johnkay.com.

PublicAffairs is a publishing house founded in 1997. It is a tribute to the standards, values, and flair of three persons who have served as mentors to countless reporters, writers, editors, and book people of all kinds, including me.

I. F. STONE, proprietor of *I. F. Stone's Weekly*, combined a commitment to the First Amendment with entrepreneurial zeal and reporting skill and became one of the great independent journalists in American history. At the age of eighty, Izzy published *The Trial of Socrates*, which was a national bestseller. He wrote the book after he taught himself ancient Greek.

BENJAMIN C. BRADLEE was for nearly thirty years the charismatic editorial leader of *The Washington Post*. It was Ben who gave the *Post* the range and courage to pursue such historic issues as Watergate. He supported his reporters with a tenacity that made them fearless and it is no accident that so many became authors of influential, best-selling books.

ROBERT L. BERNSTEIN, the chief executive of Random House for more than a quarter century, guided one of the nation's premier publishing houses. Bob was personally responsible for many books of political dissent and argument that challenged tyranny around the globe. He is also the founder and longtime chair of Human Rights Watch, one of the most respected human rights organizations in the world.

·　·　·

For fifty years, the banner of Public Affairs Press was carried by its owner Morris B. Schnapper, who published Gandhi, Nasser, Toynbee, Truman, and about 1,500 other authors. In 1983, Schnapper was described by *The Washington Post* as "a redoubtable gadfly." His legacy will endure in the books to come.

Peter Osnos, *Founder and Editor-at-Large*